WORKING-CLASS CHILDHOOD

By the same author

WORKING-CLASS CHILDHOOD

by

JEREMY SEABROOK

LONDON
VICTOR GOLLANCZ LTD
1982

© Jeremy Seabrook 1982

British Library Cataloguing in Publication Data
Seabrook, Jeremy
  Working-class childhood.
  1. Children – 19th century – Social conditions
  2. Labor and laboring class – 19th century
  – Social conditions
  I. Title
  305.2'3 (expanded)   HQ780

  ISBN 0-575-03147-6
  ISBN 0-575-03198-0 Pbk

Printed in Great Britain at
The Camelot Press Ltd, Southampton

*For my dearest Aunt Em,
a child in Edwardian England.*

CONTENTS

Samoa knows but one way of life and teaches it to her children. Will we, who have the knowledge of many ways, leave our children free to choose among them?

Margaret Mead, *Coming of Age in Samoa*

FOREWORD

IN THE WAKE of the increase in violence and disturbance among the young, I have tried in this book to look at some of the long-term processes which have led to these things. It is a partial and sketchy account; vast areas of experience remain untouched. But I have tried to give some hint of what may help to explain why a generation which has been given the best of everything, nevertheless too often feels cheated, purposeless and confused.

LONDON   J.S.
October 1981

ACKNOWLEDGEMENTS

I SHOULD LIKE to thank all those people who shared their experience with me over the past three years or so, not only those whose story is fairly comprehensively represented here, but the many more of whose memories I have been able to use only a brief passage.

A version of the Introduction and the last chapter have already appeared in the *Guardian*; parts of Chapters 6 and 12 have been published in *New Society*, and I acknowledge permission to republish here.

INTRODUCTION

CHILDHOOD IS A comparatively recent discovery in Western society. In *Centuries of Childhood*, Philippe Aries traces how in the iconography of the Middle Ages, children were rarely depicted, and when they did appear, it was as adults on a smaller scale. In the medieval world, an undifferentiated humanity grew, and much of it perished on the way to maturity. Even in the sixteenth century Montaigne could write that he had lost two or three children, 'not without regret, but without great sorrow'. Until the seventeenth century, what Aries calls 'the density of society' left little room for the family. The family emerged as an aristocratic institution, which only in the last two centuries has imposed its disciplines on the rest of society. 'Starting in the eighteenth century, it spread to all classes and imposed itself tyrannically on people's consciousness.' He describes the emergence of childhood as a recognition that the child needs to be specially prepared for life, as 'a kind of quarantine before he was allowed to join the adults'. The acceptance of child labour in the early years of the Industrial Revolution was in part a survival of the earlier attitude, and echoes of it are to be found in the testimony of some of the older working-class people in this book.

The family gradually took over the functions of a wider sociability, says Aries. 'The history of modern manners can be reduced in part to this long effort to break away from others, to escape from a society whose pressure had become intolerable. The family has advanced in proportion as sociability has retreated. It is as if the modern family had sought to take the place of the old social relationships . . . in order to preserve mankind from an unbearable moral solitude.' The working class was the last group to be reached by this process; and it is the impact of this upon that group that has caused so much of the dislocation and bewilderment among working people in our own generation.

From his – historically – recent recognition, the child has

progressed rapidly until he/she occupies a central position in contemporary Western culture – a complete reversal of his/her non-existence, or rather social effacement, in the medieval world. As the survival of children has become more assured (also a recent development – within living memory working-class people can be found who echo Montaigne), and with growing control over their conception, and the relative scarcity of children as a result, they have become the focus of our preoccupations. They are now objects of caring and giving, the recipients of all that is best in our lives. Nothing is too good for them. Childhood has become a major source of industry in the twentieth century. A vast edifice of economic activity has been constructed like a kind of baroque shrine around their alleged innocence and vulnerability. An enormous body of professional knowledge has grown, which, for the most part, does not reach into the lives of parents, enriching their understanding, but is owned by experts, in a kind of landlordism of knowledge which has to be bought. Childhood has become to the twentieth century a little what coal was to the nineteenth: a raw material which gives employment to scores of thousands, a source of immense energy and profit.

But the most significant function of children in the West is ideological. If childhood gradually became a quarantine, it has become a kind of holiday from life: another place, a resort, a beneficent exile, a man-made Garden of Eden and innocence. This hastens the detachment of the young from older surviving forms of upbringing, which are made to appear barbaric and oppressive by contrast.

In Western society children have come to represent a last frontier: the politics of hope reside in them. This is a quite separate process from the traditional function of children as guarantors of continuity and renewal. They are the last resting place of dreams and visions that have been lodged, tested and failed with all the other social groups who, at one time or another, have been made the repository of future hopes. Children can remain perpetually unblemished, because always untried. They have the advantage of being constantly replenished, in a way that is not true of all the other vehicles for the ideology of hope – whether the peasantry, the working class, the poor, blacks, even women. These have shown a tendency to

display all too human characteristics, and to dash the dreams
that have been cherished on their behalf by the societies they
were to have transformed. But a society can believe in its
children and their incorruptibility; and it can defer indefinitely
the consequences of its belief by transferring it to the next
generation.

That this is so emerges from almost any discussion with
parents about their children. There is a recurrence of religious
imagery in the way children are evoked, an intensity that has
faded from almost every other area of experience. The children
embody something holy and exalted, which goes beyond
traditional feelings of kinship, pride in the lives one has created,
a sense of the continuity of the generations. 'I worship that
child'; 'I idolize him/her'; 'he/she is the apple of my eye'; 'my
child is more to me than life itself'; 'I adore my children';
'children should be revered'; 'children have a wisdom adults
can't understand'. Expressions like these occur naturally when
people speak of their young; and they show where some of the
decayed spiritual sense of the culture has gone. But the very
intensity of them bears within it inevitable disappointment. It
is an emanation of ideology, a distortion of human love. Human
relationships are not like that, as we all know. Feeling cannot be
maintained at that pitch through time without abatement or
loss. And what is true at the personal level is also true of the
social purpose assigned to children – that of redeemers. 'Our
children's children', 'future generations' are always being
invoked in tones of reverence. But it is also an evasion. It is
above all a measure of the defection of adults who, instead of
being able to furnish their children with meaning and purpose,
demand that their children should provide these things for
them. That such a role should be attributed to the most
vulnerable and dependent group in society is as cruel as it is
perverse. In this way, the ostentatious caring and altruism of
parents also contains their opposite, selfishness. When I was a
social worker, I can remember many parents who felt very
insecure and inadequate as parents, and who would whip
themselves into a frenzy about imaginary assaults on their
children. 'I'd swing for anybody who touched my kids'; 'If
anybody laid a finger on any kid of mine I'd slit him from his
crotch to his throat' were extreme versions of this reaction.
The fear of children being molested in some way has such

resonance because it is not only a real fear, but also a metaphor for parents' sense of their own dwindling control. The obsessive caring is also accompanied by more violence by parents against children, more disturbance and destructiveness among children themselves. Parents cannot actually live up to the imposed ideology. And then they say they don't know what to do, they've lost confidence. 'I can't cope' is the most frequent despairing cry. At the same time children are given over increasingly to the care of professionals – not only pediatricians and child psychologists, experts and educators – but especially to the influence of all the manufacturers of possessions, toys and stimulants and pacifiers for children. The market-place has usurped many parental functions; has obscured the identity of the working class, and is a counterpart of the kind of de-skilling that has been taking place in recent decades among working people. As the historical function of the working class decays, so this is reflected within the domestic sphere, within families, within child-raising practice. The revolution in knowledge comes from the fact that so much of it has been taken away from people and sold back to them. 'We used to be each other's psychiatrists,' said an old lady in Bolton, talking about the losses she felt her family had incurred in the long journey from subsistence to material ease.

The guilt which these processes set up in parents – the uncertainty, the sense of not knowing what to do or how to behave with their children – expresses itself above all through material provision: the one single thing that seems to stand out as being unconditionally good and desirable. Providing for the children 'a better life'; even though it is set against no defined good. All the children's rooms I have been shown over the past two or three years are essentially shrines; and all the offerings, rewards and prizes with which they are filled are a votive tribute, a homage – the tangible sacrifices parents have made.

In recent years there has been what appears to be a happy conjunction between the anxiety of parents to give their children the best of everything, and the vast providing apparatus that seems expressly designed to help them do it – the great engines of production of the Western world, which alone can create all that children need if they are to fulfil their destiny, the exalted hopes parents cherish on their behalf. The values which stem from this beneficent process must be good.

And parents expend themselves tirelessly in striving to get the money which will give their children access to the fullness and abundance which flash before their senses from the moment they are born. It is impossible that there could be anything wrong with it. So many working-class parents grew up starved of basic material things; this, surely, must be the way to fulfilment. Here lies the vindication they seek, through this their guilt may be assuaged.

But at the same time, the coincidence of parental caring and the cascade of desirable things that serves it, turns out to have hidden disadvantages; hidden, because they are not always discernible at the point of giving. The heaping of material things on children, this best possible start in life, has other consequences, not foreseen at the moment of bestowing. It is only when they come towards maturity that some of the concealed drawbacks begin to appear. For one thing, the giving has encouraged the growth of only limited aspects of children. Appetites have developed, needs expanded, expectations dilated. They have achieved satisfaction of their needs without effort or struggle. No skills have been called forth, no abilities tested. They have remained passive recipients as the rewards and offerings have accumulated. No creative response has been required. The sense of achievement remains undeveloped, energies are extinguished. Instead, there comes a growing dependency on the flow of things. The sweetness of all that has been fed them is addictive.

Their growing appetites ensure that the dynamic of the capitalist economy will be sustained – the clamour for more, the impetus for growth and expansion. The market-place is the instrument whereby this dependency is created; and in this way, the mechanism through which the better life was to be assured imposes its own disciplines and compulsions. All the advantages which the children have been given turn out to serve other purposes: the systematic under-use of their real powers and possibilities, the suppression of their energies and abilities, the passivity and subordination in the face of all that can be bought for money has helped them to accept the vast unemployment – and what is perhaps even more significant, the underemployment of their skills and intelligence – all over the Western world. They do not even know the price they have paid, because they have never been aware of any alternative.

And as the children grow into young adults, the absence of purpose in their lives, the eroded sense of identity, the lack of function and definition, the boredom and the dearth of skills, and yet the unappeasable hunger, simply reflect to the concerned adults their own evasions. Across gulfs of guilt and anxiety, the parents have thrown their children to the market-place and hoped for the best; and when it is too late, they see they might as well have thrown them to the wolves. The promises have all been used up, the future has been consumed in advance, leaving nothing of worth or value, only discontinuity, restlessness, dissatisfaction.

The children have been left to find a sense of purpose where they may, to seek an identity dislocated from any sense of social function, of any definition except that provided by the market-place. Their culture is a kind of by-product of the process of selling things to people. Human development (at least the social part of it) is simply an aspect of commerce. This is one of the cruellest impositions of Western society upon its children. Even the most well-adjusted organism as defined by the abstract perfection of child-rearing manuals, is not equipped to invent its own meaning, to conjure a purpose out of its own existence. Of course most of us survive; and this is reflected in the testimony of many individuals in this book, even though they often do so at great cost. Those who do not survive are those who contribute to much of the increase in violence among the young, drug – and solvent – abuse, alcoholism, self-damage and destructiveness, nihilism and mental illness – all the things which concern us so much, but which we dare not look at in their social context: the cause goes too deep and is too disturbing. It is even said sometimes that these terrible things are the price, the necessary price for the freedom given to children.

It is said that they are 'more free' than they have ever been. Rather, it would be true to say that a part of our children – the part that used to be crushed by the disciplines of poverty and work – has been set free; while other, and equally important, parts of the human whole have been repressed. It is true that the aspect of individuals that was inhibited by primary poverty – the appetites – is no longer discouraged. But other aspects are; and we are so dazzled by the one area of liberation that we haven't noticed the limits and repressions elsewhere. A world which offers children no other challenge than a vast display of finished products to compete for has nothing to do with a very profound sense of freedom. What is sad is the constricted idea of freedom offered to people who have traditionally suffered the unfreedom of poverty and hardship. It is true that poverty – an absence of basic necessities – is an unfreedom. But its opposite is not vested in the freedoms of the market-place. 'Free choices' funnelled through the market-place are simply consolations for all those other areas of human experience that have been crushed – that is everything that cannot be bought or sold; and it includes some of those of the greatest worth of all.

Our lives are free only in the sense that to live is to be free for a time from oblivion and insentience. To bring up children to the values and beliefs of any society is like cutting figures from blocks of stone – most of the material will be pared away, all the other possibilities that might have been realized in other societies, at other times. It is not the freedoms we give our children now, but the pitiful restrictions on them which should be our concern; restrictions which, unlike those of our inheritance, our repeat of patterns of living and feeling woven into us by our parents, the burden of all the previous lives that help to shape and limit our own, are arbitrary and alterable. It is the way that children are deformed to support a particular social and economic system which serves money and not humanity, that makes of them all miniature Atlases, supporting a whole world on their shoulders.

In view of this, it is perhaps not surprising that so many people remain unaware of their childhood and its influence on their lives. There are even those who deny the importance of their childhood experience to the concerns of adult life. 'Childhood', said one man in his 40s who had come from a particularly poor home, 'is something you grow out of'; and he was quite unaware of the ambiguity of his declaration. And yet, so much is *known* and written about childhood. Although that knowledge is in theory available to everybody, much that is known to be of vital importance fails to penetrate the prevailing ideology, and does not reach those who most need it. Thirty years ago, John Bowlby wrote, denouncing the fatalism towards 'the twin problems of neglectful parents and deprived children [which] are viewed as inevitable and left to reproduce themselves'. Bowlby saw three main reasons for the lack of concern – the fact that most such children were believed to be orphans, the persistence of poverty, and the lack of understanding of psychiatric factors in such cases. But since then, the orphaning influence of the war has worked itself out, the standard of living has risen significantly, and there has been a vast expansion of the social work profession. If these developments have also been accompanied by an increase in violence and disturbance and instability among the young, clearly other factors are involved. These have to do with the evolving capitalist processes, the decay of traditional productive work in the West, and with it, the decay of the old working-class function and identity; and the substitution for these of definitions and identities provided by the market-place. If these things disconcert those raised to discipline and work, they damage the young, who have not felt social purpose and cohesion other than the fantasies and vapours of the market-place. Care for the upbringing of children, and the circumstances of each individual child is the proper concern of us all; but if the wider context in which they grow is damaged and unhealthy, then all our work and goodwill is undermined. The myths and the ideology which envelop childhood cannot be dispelled by professional knowledge: they grow out of the very social and economic structures in which we live. To be effective, the understanding has to be part of the common store of shared experience by which we live.

Most of the people in this book have achieved some insight. Many of those willing to talk about their childhood have a sense of something unfinished or unresolved. In them, there is nearly always an absence, an ache, an injustice, a lack of love. In that sense, there is nothing representative about the people who offered to share their experience with me. For one thing, women tend to speak with greater readiness than men; this is no doubt a result of the society's belief that being in touch with feelings is a more fitting activity for women (and the contempt it is thought proper for men to have for such things). But if the book comprises in the main the stories of people who have a sense of something negative or incomplete about their childhood, this may perhaps shed some oblique light on what stability and contentment might mean for a child – an absence of such incapacitating experiences. Certainly the testimony of people here makes no concessions to the ideology of the childhood idyll. It does not feed those myths that are at the core of much alterable human misery, of which many of them feel they have been the victims.

THE CHANGING CONTEXT

IF WE CONSIDER all the possible ways of raising children as practised across the globe, it is obvious that any society will cause certain human traits to be given value and prominence, and others to be discouraged or suppressed. If we look at children in Western society at the end of the twentieth century and assume that these children have the best possible life that any society could give them, we make the same error that those colonialists and missionaries made when they went across the world in the eighteenth and nineteenth centuries, and, mistaking the *power* of the culture they represented for truth, thought fit to impose it on other societies, other ways, other values. What these people did formerly in other cultures, we now also do through time. Because of the great gains that have been made in health and medical care as well as in the capacity for material production, we assume that these of themselves ensure children the best of all possible lives; no matter on what terms these gains are imposed, no matter what tribute is exacted in return for them. We assume that the perfection of technology calls forth a corresponding perfection in the human experience that is shaped by it. We take for granted that values are built into it and determined by it, relieving human beings of the painful and difficult task of having to determine what kind of a society they want, what kind of standards are the good ones to live by. Because technology promises further unlimited refinements, we have come to expect the future to yield up all the desirable things that have eluded us in the past – abundance, fulfilment, even happiness. One important consequence of this has been the neglect of past experience, especially of that embodied in those who are old. It is no longer simply the traditional impatience of the young with received wisdom. It goes further than that. Our own past has been expunged, and the experience of the old – rooted in a poverty we shall never see again – has no relevance for our lives. When they try to tell us of the extent to which things of great worth have been extinguished in those who are young today, beneath the obvious – too obvious – benefits that have been showered upon them, we cry sour grapes, and assume that it is envy that prompts them to speak in that way.

The whole cliché of the 'generation gap' – which is the idea of children as representatives of a future that must be better because of the accelerating rate of technological progress, in contrast with the superseded knowledge of the old, with their function-burdened, place-bound anchorage in the past – speaks of a cruel discontinuity in human experience. It exalts technology above human purposes, and with one careless gesture throws away precious irreplaceable freedoms.

In this century, we have lived through a profound reversal of the role of children; not, of course, so profound that it alters the foundations on which this society is constructed, but far-reaching enough to convince most people that some kind of advance has been made. From the experience of childhood as an apprenticeship to discipline and labour, it appears to have evolved into an opportunity for self-determination, the chance for self-expression, increasing leisure accompanying a dying sense of function, the development of needs and appetites in place of a feeling of purpose. This means that we have two very different kinds of human being still living within the same culture, who speak a language unintelligible to each other; and of course between the two extremes, a whole range of people who represent completely neither the one nor the other type. The existential gains – prolonged and healthier life – only conceal from us the social forfeits – the loss of function, the growing sense of nihilism, the acquisitiveness which becomes exaggerated in the absence of any other object in life, and which becomes also a symbolic gesture towards redeeming some of the intangible things that have been taken away from them.

We are talking about deep changes in what it means to be a child, so deep that they look almost like a complete reversal of what the experience was within the space of no more than two or three generations. But they are changes that have occurred within an even deeper stasis, that is, the exaltation of money above humanity; and in the stories people tell in this book, it is the children who continue to pay, even though the tribute exacted of them now is in a different coin.

An impression of the mirror-image effect of change can be

gained from the juxtaposition of some characteristic passages from the over-70s and some representative responses of the under-16s; childhoods separated by well over half a century.

'When I was a child of three, there were 13 of us sat round our table. Ten years later that number had been reduced to seven. The oldest was married, and four of them had died, three of them within ten days of one another.' Woman, 87.

'You never sat down to have your meals till you were earning. I was 14 before I was allowed to sit with me Mam and Dad. I never drank tea – only water – until I was 14. I can remember the first time I was given a cup of tea. You felt proud. You knew you were growing up.' Woman, 60s, Liverpool.

'When my sister was four, she fell ill, and they diagnosed peritonitis. That was very serious those days. The doctor came and said she'd have to have an operation. It was very primitive. The washstand in the bedroom had to be thoroughly scrubbed down, a marble washstand; and she was operated on on this washstand in front of the window. Anybody who was going by could see what was going on. All the curtains had to come down, mother had to take the carpet up. Afterwards, they hung a sheet over the door, and there was a big bowl of carbolic, to disinfect the room.' Woman, 90, Lincolnshire.

'My grandmother used to tie me to a chair of a Sunday afternoon, so I should learn to sit up straight. I had the Bible to read. I didn't think there was anything unusual in it. I just accepted it. It wasn't done in a spirit of cruelty. She just wanted me to grow up straight-limbed.' Woman, 75, Birmingham.

'They always kept a dog-whip over the door' (Man, 80) . . . 'a bamboo cane along the picture rail' (Woman, 78) . . . 'a stair-rod in the corner' (Woman, 76) . . . 'Father's razor-strap hanging on a nail on the kitchen shelf' (Man, 70) . . . 'A carpet-beater in the corner. Mother didn't have to use it. If we were being naughty, we just followed her eyes to the corner, and that was enough for us' (Man, 74).

'When I started work, I was nearly 14. I worked in a pawnbroker's shop. I got five shillings a week, and my hours were from eight o'clock in the morning until eleven o'clock some nights. The pawn-broker had partitions in his shop, booths, like they have today in Social Security offices. There were racks of boots and shoes for sale, clothes, jewellery, unredeemed pledges. A police list came round every week with all the stolen goods you had to watch out for. I used to be upstairs in the attic above the shop, where all the pledges were kept. The pawn-broker would shout up to me the number of the bundle he wanted. "Hurry up, boy." There was no gas or electricity in this room, just a hurricane lamp to work by, day or night. The counter was concave and all shiny, where the bundle had been passed to and fro for so many years.' Man, 80, Northampton.

'We would all sit and watch our father eat a lamb chop; and we would wait, all five of us, to be allowed to dip our bread in the fat he left on his plate. That's how we knew whether he was in a good mood or not. If he was feeling generous, he'd leave the fat, if not, he'd mop up the last drop himself.' Man, 71, Southwark.

'My mother and father died within six months of each other when I was just turned 13. There were four children younger than me: the youngest wasn't quite 5. I didn't want the family to split up. I went round all the factories until I got a job. I don't know why they didn't stop me leaving school, but they didn't. I was only a little dot of a thing. They had to stand me on an orange box to reach the machine, and it was a rickety old box, it could easily have given way and made me fall in the machine. I got eight shillings a week. Somehow we managed. Nobody ever interfered with us, we just got on with it. We were a family and I was the head of the house at 13. The neighbours were good to us, kept an eye on us. Somehow we got through. Many a time there wasn't enough to feed us all. If I made dumplings, I'd see all their eyes fixed on this saucepan, and I knew there wouldn't be enough to go round. I had to pretend I didn't want any, I wasn't hungry. Many a time I've left the house at seven in the morning faint with hunger. I've burnt crumbs of toast and then poured boiling water on it to make out it was tea.' Woman, 85, Birmingham.

'I used to walk three miles a day with a pudding basin with our Dad's dinner in it to the place where he worked. We lived in a village when I was little, and he worked as a labourer on the farm; but he gave that up because he could get more money in the factory. I had an hour off from school at dinner-time, so I had to walk these three miles there and three back in my dinner-hour. And if I spilt so much as a drop of it, I got a clout round the head. I used to walk careful going, but I had to run all the way back over the fields to be in time for afternoon school.' Woman, 79, Rushden, Northamptonshire.

'Oh he did used to knock her around. When he hadn't been drinking, he was all right. He could be charming. But when he got home, Saturday night, Sunday dinner-time, we were all waiting there in fear and trembling. He'd come in Sunday, pick up whatever was on his plate, and if he didn't like the look of it, throw it at the wall. He did terrorize us kids. As a rule, Sunday afternoon we went to Sunday School, and were glad to go to get out of it. But if it was wet, and we couldn't go out for some reason, we had to sit still as mice. You didn't hardly dare breathe for fear of waking him. You couldn't read a book, you couldn't play with anything. It was more than your life was worth to talk. Even our mother just sat there for two hours. She wasn't allowed to poke the fire or even make a cup of tea. I've often wondered since what she thought about those long dreary afternoons, with her hands just lying in her lap. Poor old gal, it was probably the only rest she had all week.' Man, 70s, Nottingham.

'When I was nine, our Billy died. He had what I suppose must have been diphtheria. And he was laid on the sofa in our living room for three days and nights. Our Mam sat with him. She hardly slept herself. She said you had to wait for the crisis; and we all tiptoed round the house. He was the favourite, Billy. He was the youngest, only five. I had an old peg doll, and I remember giving it to him. It was the only toy I had, but I thought if I gave him this doll, the sacrifice would make God see how good I was, and He'd help Billy get better. But he never recovered. I felt angry and hurt by God. The morning Billy died, I sat with my mother, and I said "Is he going to get better Mum?" and she put her arm round me and said "He's better now, he's with Grandma and Auntie Hetty"; and he was dead. She never got over losing him. Her life, well it had been one long story of loss, you'd've thought she'd got used to it. But she mourned that child for the rest of her life.' Woman, 70s, Northampton.

'My brother joined up in 1914. He had to lie about his age to get in the Army. We heard nothing from him for months, and then a telegram came, saying he was in hospital and not expected to live. My mother – and she'd never been out of Wolverhampton all her life – took me with her, and we went to France to see him. I can't remember much about the journey, except she was so anxious and petrified with fear at travelling to such a strange place. It was September; I remember the sea was smooth as glass. The hospital, I can still smell it, the men there, crying and moaning, all wrapped in bandages like rows and rows of ghosts. They've haunted me to this day. They held out their hands to my mother, some of them asked her to kiss them. I was ten. I don't know how my mother managed to do it.' Woman, 75, Rochdale.

'One day I shocked my grandma, because I asked for jam on my bread and butter. "If you have jam," she said, "you don't have butter; and if you have butter, you don't have jam." The way she said it, it was as if I'd committed some terrible crime. I didn't accept what she said. I screamed and screamed. I went to my father and complained. His remedy was that I should go without tea for a week.' Woman, 80, Shropshire.

'I was never allowed to stay off school. Illness was regarded as weakness. My mother was very tough, hard. I suppose she had to be. She didn't believe in illness: it was an expression of moral feebleness. I had a grumbling appendix for years, but my mother pooh-poohed it. When it did flare up, I was 14. She gave me senna for my bowels. When I had to have an emergency operation, she said "You should be thankful you're not losing your leg, like your Uncle Joe did." ' Man, 80s, Hackney.

When the old working class talk of childhood, they speak of the circumstances that tended towards the effacement of children's needs: the violence, not only of industrial life, but of war, disease and early death, that expressed itself in the way children were brought up within the family; and yet, these testimonies of the old are not full of resentment against their parents. On the contrary, they brim over with love and tenderness as they remember. It is as if they recognize the harsh conjuncture of the family discipline and the world beyond which shaped it. They knew their parents had no choice.

But if the old were influenced by the often oppressive circumstances of their lives, the young don't talk with gratitude about the absence of those cruel conditions. They don't speak thankfully of the survival of their brothers and sisters, the capacity of their parents to provide for them; they don't celebrate their health and the sufficiency of food. Why should they? They have never known anything else. On the contrary, what they talk about is not an appreciation of all the good things they have been given, but, following the altered material circumstances of their lives, it is the unfulfilled needs they stress, the unmet wants; and material longings stand as metaphors for all the intangibles that their lives lack, and the absences obscurely felt in the midst of the abundance in which they have grown. And the cruelty of the lives of their grandparents and great-grandparents hasn't been eliminated; but finds an echo, not in the circumstances of the lives of the young, but in their fantasies. In the same way, the fantasies of the old were dreams of the kind of future the young now enjoy – a time of sufficiency, an absence of drudgery, a release from the old disciplines. Over the period of living memory, it is as though reality and fantasy had changed places. All the cruel influences from which the young have been protected hold a powerful fascination for them: the lack of experience of physical suffering, the removal of hunger and want as a daily insistent reality, the unfamiliarity with death, except as something that happens to shadows on the TV screen, the unawareness of the consequences of conflict and war, all give rise to an increasing preoccupation with images of struggle and violence which, in the end, cannot of course be contained within fantasy. Instead of feeling that they have been shielded from something ugly and damaging, their sense is of having been excluded from something significant.

Many old working people remember their childhood as a time when they were constantly cold and hungry. They knew even then that they were destined for mill, factory, service or the army; and to prepare them for this inescapable necessity, their personal needs and wants were repressed, their personality often crushed and stunted. As they grew up, many of them vowed that their children and grandchildren should be protected from the privations they had known. A happy conjunction of what had always been parents' deepest wishes for their children and a change in material circumstances seemed to ensure that this vow to do better for their children could now be realized. During the middle years of the twentieth century, the whole working class bettered itself (or was it bettered?); and as a result of this, a generation of children has grown up with a quite different sense of its destiny. Because the social changes seemed to represent what everybody most fervently wanted – improved material circumstances – parents were quite happy to take credit for the changes that had occurred. They believed they had brought them about; it was some kind of reward; it was their own personal victory over circumstances. And in this way, economic shifts, the coming of the postwar miracle, the advent of the consumer society looked like what they had dreamed and worked for for so long. It appeared to be a release and a liberation for them. That it could be anything but benign didn't occur to them. And in good faith, they fed their children to the market-place, throwing them to the future; quite unaware that a price would have to be paid by their children; in another coin certainly, than that in which they had paid with their labour, but still in a way that would maintain power and wealth intact; and if this disturbed them, they could thrust it back into the dark places of the mind. And although the children had been liberated from the ancient scourges of hunger and want and pain, these things were not banished; and they continue to recur like an insistent nightmare in the daily discourse of the young. The taboos only excite their curiosity.

'My mate was coming out of this disco, and he was stabbed by a gang of Teds in the stomach. He couldn't feel it because he had been drinking, and he'd had some dope as well, he was high as a kite. He went on down the street, and he felt something wet on his coat; and it was blood. He tried to stop all these cars going past, only none of them would stop. In the end, he had to jump on the bonnet of one of them; and he pointed to his guts that were all coming out; and the driver took him to hospital.' Boy, 15, South London.

'What I want to do is fight. It's the only thing I'm any good at, and I want to have a go. I shan't be happy till the last coon in this country has gone. I don't care what I have to do to get rid of 'em. I don't care if everything burns. It won't make any difference to me. I get £7 a week when I've paid my board, so poverty don't scare me. I've got nothing to lose and everything to gain. I'm in the November 9th Group; that was the date when they announced officially that Hitler was dead . . . It's got to come. Civil war. It might not make any difference. I don't care. The fight for something you believe in, that's the main thing.' Boy, 17, Nottingham.

'I was with my Dad in the car, and this E-type came round the corner at about 80, and it couldn't take the corner, and it went smack into this tree, telescoped, like a bit of old tin . . . and the bloke who was driving went clean through the windscreen; and the metal cut his head clean off. It landed on the grass . . . and it went on talking for five minutes after it happened . . . There was his body in the car, and this head that went on talking . . . It just gabbled on. I don't know what it said; but it didn't know it had come off the body.' Boy, 14, South London.

'I read in the paper about these people in an aircrash up in the mountains in South America, and they ate their own father's body. They were stranded there, and there was no way they were going to be rescued. There was no food, and they drew lots to see who was going to be sacrificed. And the one who went first was this bloke; and he'd got two kids with him. And they knew if they didn't eat his flesh, they'd starve to death.'

'So what did they do?'

'They ate it.' Boy, 12, Ramsgate.

'In our flats, the kids ride up and down on top of the lifts. You can force the door, and then you jump on the roof of the lift; then somebody sends for the other lift, and you can jump across from one to the other. There's one place near where we live, and one kid missed when he was jumping from the top of one lift to the other, and he fell down the shaft between the two lifts. Nobody knew what had happened to him. The other kids just thought he'd gone home. His Mum and Dad thought he'd run away, because he'd done it before. So they thought he might have gone to his Auntie's. But then, in a few days' time, there was this terrible smell in the lifts, and nobody knew what it was. They tried shifting it with disinfectant, but it still came back. And it was his body, all smashed and decomposed at the bottom of the shaft.' Boy, 15, East Ham.

'I saw this film on TV, it was fantastic. There was this virus that had been let loose in an American town; they'd been experimenting with bacteriology warfare. And what this virus did to people, it made them go berserk and start murdering anybody in sight. People started killing everybody: this man murdered his children and his wife, and this old woman started stabbing people with her knitting needles. They had to stop it spreading, so they cordoned the town and had to destroy everybody in it.' Girl, 15, East Ham.

A woman in her 50s, on a new estate on the fringe of a Midland town. Her son, 17, comes home from school: a cheerful boy with a friendly smile. 'Where's my dinner?' he asks banteringly. His mother responds with good humour: 'Well it's not ready. You can get your own for once.' I ask him what he is studying. He is doing 'A' level Biology and Chemistry at the nearby Comprehensive School. His mother says, 'The trouble with him is that he's more interested in the side of science that can blow up the world, rather than the side that helps people.' Graham is scornful of his mother's concern for the underprivileged, and her work as an auxiliary in the Social Services department. 'She takes it too much to heart.' His is a more brutal view. 'I think the last war did more good than harm. It helped keep the population down, and it helped a lot of scientific development which wouldn't have occurred otherwise – television, space travel, nuclear research. A lot of advances were made that we wouldn't have had but for the war.' He looks at his mother as he speaks, because he knows it distresses her. She always rises to it, and says passionately that what happened in the last war must never happen again. 'If you excuse the killing of a single human being,' she says sternly, 'it won't be long before it's your turn, somebody will come up with a foolproof reason for killing you because you've got red hair or wear glasses.' Graham says, 'I think a war is necessary every so often. What interests me is science fact, not science fiction. I mean, we have a duty to develop interplanetary travel, because if we don't, how shall we survive if we make this planet uninhabitable?'

'I don't think dying matters . . . I think you come back to life in other forms; and each time you go one stage higher. You have so many lifetimes to progress in . . . I might come back next time as a bird or a butterfly.' Frances, 16. 'You're a bloody butterfly this time,' says her mother, pausing over the ironing board.

'Me and my mates, we want to survive. We're training so that we're ready for it. We're excavating a shelter in the woods, and getting a store of stuff, so as soon as they drop the bomb, we can go and hide out; we're collecting things a bit at a time. By the time it happens, we'll be ready to endure anything. We practise being in a cramped space for hours at a time. We've got an old tea chest, and we take turns going in it. Make sure your nerve doesn't crack. Nobody knows where our hideout is; we keep it covered up, it's where nobody ever goes, and even if they did, they wouldn't find it. We shall be able to stay in there for months if we have to; and then we'll come out and look around, see who's survived. Go hunting for whatever we need. It'll be great; there'll be nobody left. We'll have to get guns, in case there's anybody else.' 'Yeh, it'll be great, we'll be able to rule the world.' Mark and Ian, 13, Leicestershire.

When children talk in this way, they are, for the most part, talking in metaphors. They are trying to say something to the adult world in the only way that they can. They don't articulate it directly; and their preoccupation with the very things which they have been so carefully protected from says something very significant about what has happened to them.

First, in contrast to the world of poverty and scarcity of their grandparents, they have come into a society in which material things have been brought close to perfection. All that is desirable and beautiful already exists: toys, possessions, goods, things. And there is nothing for the children to do but to desire them, to struggle competitively for all the good things that are held out to them from the moment they are born. It is as though the starting point in their life were the rewards at the end of a fairy-tale; and they have no other purpose than to aspire to the ownership of as many of them as possible. In this way, the young very soon develop a sense of the absurdity of wanting to change the world; and one of the ancient, traditional purposes of the young is usurped from the start. The world so obviously doesn't need changing. It seems to them that everything has been achieved, everything accomplished before they arrived. They have been born too late to have any part in the production of the magnificent display of things around them – and this is where there is direct continuity with the processes that have made so many working-class people redundant from their work in recent years: the redundancy of someone brought up to a lifetime of work for only modest rewards is one thing, but to grow up to an extinguished sense of purpose is something quite different.

Of course the children can see nothing wrong with the perfection of the material world, through which their parents strive to express their love and concern for them. But when you look at the children's rooms, filled with games and books and toys and possessions, so many of them discarded, used up, disregarded, the grottoes of fantasy which have already ceased to stimulate seven- and eight-year-olds, it quite obviously isn't enough. But it isn't an insufficiency of material things they suffer from, even though that is the principal way it is expressed. It is an insufficiency of something else – it is the absences, the suppressed needs, everything which cannot be expressed in material tokens – the extinct sense of purpose, the life of the spirit, morality beyond getting and having, the need to contribute something that tests them, that evokes their slumbering powers.

That is why they flee into fantasy. They need to escape from the best of everything which they have been given. From the earliest years, they are fascinated by dinosaurs, monsters, creatures from elsewhere in time and space: the friezes round their room will be of prehistoric landscapes on one side, and panoramas of outer space on the other. Already, they are beating against the limits of time and space in search of an identity; but none of this tells them who they are. Then there is the longing for something darker, vampires and werewolves, demons, devils, Dracula, Frankenstein. But all these things, even the terrors of childhood, the nameless shadows in the corner, the coming of night and the foreshadowing of death, have all been given concrete form through the extended market-place in which they have grown up. In the same way that all that children could possibly desire has been realized through the products so tantalizingly held out to them, so the fears and even the nightmares have been sold back to them for money; the four- and five-year-olds walk with their mothers round the supermarkets, wearing masks – a monster, a distorted ape-face, a giant with an eye gouged out; the comics they carry are full of skeletons and death's heads and the undead. Even their spiritual longings, the awe at the mystery of existence, the sense of wonder at the universe belong to the great corporations of the entertainment industry. The world that produces all that is good and desirable for children, also creates its own sense of evil; and this shapes a closed universe, in which there is no possibility of change. The escape routes themselves are owned by the existing structures. Static, unalterable, it denies its children even the possibility of triumph over circumstances which their grandparents achieved. This is why, in the end, the young people become fascinated by the apocalypse, the holocaust, cosmic cataclysm.

If their grandparents were brought up to the crippling constraints of work and want, they beat in vain against the disabling licence of their own experience. They can imagine no other change than total destruction. If they have recourse to violence, rioting, destruction for its own sake, these things are a measure of the curious kind of captivity in which they have grown.

They can have no sympathy with their grandparents' triumphs over poverty and hunger. To their world these things are futile and irrelevant. And the sense of continuity is broken between the generations; even between members of the same family. The system is what survives; the same system which formerly denied and crushed its children with poverty and work, and now divides them from the next generation by turning today's young into diminished shrunken dependants of the market-place. The old, for all their poverty and suffering, could at least still work for change. There was for them some imaginable alternative. This has been perhaps the greatest loss of all to the children whose eyes and ears and senses have been so flooded with the spectacle of what is, that the visions of a different and better way of life have been washed away.

The cruel conditions in which the old working class lived made people turn to each other for consolation. Of course there are stories of cruelty and indifference, many of them recorded in this book, but the common stream of memory talks of closeness and solidarity between people. And although there is a strong tendency for the old to idealize their long-dead parents, the old man in Sheffield who said, 'When I was young the children ran around barefoot; now it's their hearts that are bare' wasn't speaking idly. Even if it was necessity that compelled people to stay close, no matter what the cause of it, that kind of human solidarity is our greatest strength. The idea that it is simply a function of poverty, and something for individuals to buy their way out of is a poor and doomed substitute.

'My father never had any tuition at all. He never went to school. He used to roam around the farms for jobs; but he taught himself to play the violin. And he finished up playing in some of the big houses, like the Pytchley Hunt Ball. He was in the town band of the little place where he lived. He was a bespoke bootmaker by trade, and he made boots for royalty. He made shoes that were on exhibition in London, and he knew how to make this special dye that gave a unique colour and sheen. He mixed it according to a formula that existed only in his mind. And it died with him. A boot and shoe manufacturer once came to the house to ask him to sell the secret. It wasn't that he wouldn't; he just couldn't describe it or explain it properly. It was just something he knew. He could show them, as he tried to show my brother; but my brother went into a different trade, and it was lost.' Woman, 79, Long Buckby, Northamptonshire.

'We spent our summers out on the common, among the beech trees there, wooding for the winter. When we were kids, we could make anything. We made a canoe out of an old tree, we could make whistles from wood. We made bows and arrows, trolleys, trucks, sledges. We never had any money, but there was nothing we needed that we wouldn't have a go at making for ourselves. We knew where the wild raspberries grew, the wild strawberries, very tiny but sweet. We went nutting in the autumn. My father knew a tree near Bedford that was a witch's tree. On a particular night of the year, he said, the tree used to shake by magic, and all the nuts would fall down. If you happened to be there, you'd see it . . . We never did, of course. But we believed him. At cherry-ripe time, we used to help ourselves to cherries. There was a row of cherry trees, they never seemed to belong to anybody. And then the hedges weren't cut, so you could get sloes and crabapples.' Man, 70, Aylesbury.

'My mother promised me a bonnet for the Sunday School feast. That was in August, and she started putting money by right from the Christmas. We never had much money, but every time there was a halfpenny, or even a farthing, it went straight towards this bonnet. And when it got to summer, I went with her to buy it. It cost half a crown. It seemed a fortune. But I can't tell you how proud I was of our mother, the day we walked into that shop, and came out with the hat I'd been promised. You'd've thought she shopped for bonnets every day. And that hat, I loved it. I cherished it. I was still wearing it when I was courting, ten years later. It meant sacrifice, and it meant my mother's love. I've still got the ribbon off it to this day, and I still shed a few tears over it, even after all these years.' Woman, 78, Manchester.

'My mother was very harassed by life. She was a very

frightened woman. My father drank; he had an accident and lost his leg. In the end, she broke down completely. She couldn't take any more, six kids, the poverty. I can remember the day she broke down, when the illness came on her. I remember she just sat in the chair, rocking to and fro, looking vacant, moaning to herself. I got home from school, and I was the only one in the house with her. And I didn't know what to do. So I sat and sang to her. I was in the choir at church, I had a good voice. I loved singing. I sat and I took hold of her hand, and I just sang, hymns, songs, anything I could remember. I sat beside her for hours it seemed. At the finish, they took her away. She went to the asylum. I never sang again after that. I never used my voice again. I was eleven.' Man, 70s, Berkhamsted.

'My father was killed by a dray when my mother was expecting me. And after that she was an invalid. She lived till I was ten. But my sister Maud, my mother more or less told her to take her place as the mother of the family when she died. And we did, we all stayed together. Our uncles and aunties used to bring in a rabbit or a bit of anything they'd got left over. My brother did an allotment, and that only cost the bit of ground rent. I used to collect bottles, ginger beer bottles, anything that had money back on them. We picked bunches of primroses and sold them; we made lavender bags. We all contributed. And all five of us, we stuck close. Maud was only 14; but we've all stayed close ever since. We all see one another every week. My sister went to live on a new estate, but she felt lonely and said she wanted to come home. She lives in the street next to mine now. We've always lived in walking distance of each other, all five of us, even though we all married and had our own families. We struggled together and stayed together.' Man, 73, Blackburn.

'Every Sunday I had to recite to my mother a chapter of one of the Books of the Bible. I had to learn it during the course of the week, and Sunday evening, all of us, we had to say what we'd learnt without making a mistake. I can still remember much of the Old Testament, I still have it by heart. It was no penance to me. My mother knew what she was doing. She helped train my memory. It kept me alert as a child, and I believe I still benefit from that today. I look at some of the youngsters now, they can't keep anything in their heads for five minutes. I don't blame them; it's the conditions of your life, you see.' Man, 84, Stoke-on-Trent.

'My mother used to talk about her grandmother and the stories she had told her; and all the members of the family who had died before I was born, they were real to me. They were still part of the family, they lived on in the memories and the stories. You loved them too: they helped to anchor you in time, you were grateful to them, they had bequeathed their love to you.' Woman, 80s, Northampton.

2

LEEDS, JANUARY 1981

A SHOPPING PRECINCT, imposed on a neighbourhood of abandoned redbrick terraces, wasteland rustling with the dead weeds of last summer, dumps of rusting and decaying household debris. Where the ground has been cleared, some new long blocks of flats are under construction. All around are the shells of mills, factories, warehouses, symbols of the vanished function of the young. The shopping mall, with its marble and potted plants and piped music is what draws them, source of consolation for the obliterated sense of purpose.

A day of heavy snow, dingy where it has been trodden, but still white on the tops of the neglected houses. Work has stopped on the building site because of the weather. The redbrick is damp with melting snow and seems to bleed into the misty afternoon.

Four boys, 15 or 16. None of them wears an overcoat or gloves; they exude health and strength; only the absence of any energizing activity in their lives persists like a physical pain. They have decided not to go back to school this afternoon. The idea of half a day in the snow appealed to them; but they soon exhaust the possibilities of pelting the passengers at the bus-stop with snowballs, rolling each other in it, and stuffing it in handfuls down each other's neck. They roll a huge snowball into the shopping centre, through the front entrance of Tesco's and leave it to melt there.

By mid-afternoon they are wet through and chilled. They light a fire in one of the half-demolished houses. One of them has some glue and some plastic food bags; another has some potatoes which he has taken from a market stall, which he intends to roast in the fire. Their jeans steam in the heat, the soles of their shoes crack. There is something eerie in the firelight, the darkening indigo sky visible through the lattice of the rafters, the shadows on the floral pattern of the wallpaper, the smell of plaster and earth; almost a sense of survivors of some terrible catastrophe.

But the excitement and anticipation of their youth, which are touching and contagious, have already been annexed to the market-place; their imagination has been deeply penetrated by the images of capitalist production, and these have become primary influences on their lives. They know what they want; but they know also that these are not all they want. Once they have expressed the banal obligatory fantasies – the Jensen Interceptor, the Norton 850, the mansion guarded by dogs and guns, the recording studio, they start to express the suppressed forbidden needs that find no outlet in the culture that has formed them. When they evoke violence and destruction, these are the only metaphors they know to convey their sense of being caged. The fantasies dilate, but their real possibilities become more and more circumscribed: the dole, sleep, wanking, drink and glue.

'I'm bored. What is there for us? You sit and talk, you might talk about women, what you'd like to do to them . . . I know some lads, they got this girl, and they raped her under the garages. She was so shocked like by it, it drove her mad. She's in the bin now.'

As they talk, their conversation merges into a kind of collective monologue. There is little differentiation in what each one says about his hopes and ambitions, and even his fantasies. And yet, they are all immovably centred in their own individual experience. Each sees his life as a picaresque adventure, and is unaware of its resemblance to the life, not only of his friends, but of teenagers everywhere.

'You think "Oh yeh, everything'd be all right if I had some money." So you might do a bit of thieving. You take a car, drive it round, then take it to some waste ground, strip it of everything, radio, speakers, lamps, wheels. Soon you've got a couple of hundred quid between you, and you feel like a god. Life is great for a little while.'

'I wouldn't thieve from old women. You've got to have a lot of bottle to do that. I couldn't touch defenceless people. The kids who do that are a bit sick. But you might go and re-arrange the neighbourhood a bit if you're feeling choked off; put your boot through a window, go and get some chips from the Paki take-away without paying. They're too scared to run after you.'

'Your parents give you most things you want. I don't care about working, as long as I get enough money. I'm all right as long as my old man's in work. You have to know your parents, work round them a bit. Your parents are like fruit machines: you play them all the while, but they only pay out every so often. That's life.'

'They like to be left alone. Me Mam likes a bit of fun, her Valium and her Bingo and she's happy.'

'I sometimes see my old man with a woman in a pub round town. They daren't get too heavy with me. I've got too much on them.'

'My Mam is a fucking old slag. I don't give that for her (V-sign). I went down to see her last summer, first time since she pissed off when I was 11. She said "Oh what do you want?" I said "I thought you might want to see me." She says "What for?" I says "You are me Mam." She says "Thanks for reminding me. Now piss off." She didn't want to know. The bloke she was living with is about the same age as my brother.'

'My old man says he don't care what I do as long as I don't bring any trouble home. He says if I get in any bother I'm on my own.'

'The only thing I can't stand is staying in. I can't stand being there with them. My Dad calls me the lodger. I don't stay out all night without telling them . . . I did stay in for a week last year. I got into a bit of a rough house like, and we left this kid laying on the path. We'd kicked him about a bit after he pulled a knife on my mate, and somebody said we'd fucking killed him. We hadn't though; he was back at school after a couple of days. But I was scared shitless for a couple of days; you don't want to wind up on a murder rap just for having a bit of a laugh . . . No excuse for that, that's just being careless . . . That was the longest week in my fucking life.'

'My old lady slags me off sometimes. When my old man goes and stays away for a few nights, she takes it out on me. She tries to tell me he's working; she says he's driving long distance. If he is, it's not on sodding wheels.'

'My Mam never mentioned sex to me. They just expect you to know it all. Kids know about everything from about the age of seven or eight, but you don't do anything till you're 12 or 13, you don't go all the way . . . I was 13. This girl in our flats, we used to go there in the afternoons. Her Mam and Dad were at work, couple of cans of lager, and she'd sit there with her legs open, and if there's a few of you, you muck about, and you start

to get horny, and she more or less shows you what to do . . .
Then somebody on the estate told her old woman, and we had
to pack it in.'

'We don't look for trouble, but if somebody starts pushing
you around, that's it. If people think you're a bottle job, you get
a reputation for being really hard, they'll come from all over to
try you out. There's one lad I know, he's had more stitches in
his body than a darned sock; his skin, he's like a bit of walking
embroidery.'

'The big fight will come. It'll have to. Definitely. Black and
white. Things have got to be sorted out, all the coons, they've
got too cheeky. There's only one thing could stop it – you hate
the Bill more than you hate the blacks. If it's not against the
blacks, it'll be against the Bill.'

'You can't do anything in this town without getting stopped
by them. They've always got my description. I say to them,
"That's not my description, that could be any one of ten
thousand lads . . ." They come up to you, something's been
nicked, some old woman of 92's been raped, where were you
last Saturday. They only pick on you when you're on your
own . . . I've been done over down the cells, a dozen times. It's
just one of the risks of being young.'

'It's only natural you'll hit back if you get the chance. That's
why the kids are learning, go round together, if there's a load of
you, people respect you.'

'I hate living here.'

'I want to get out of Leeds.'

'I want to get out of this country.'

'I want to leave this planet. That's my ambition. I don't like
it here; people are greedy and stupid. If beings did come from
another planet, we'd just blast them out of the sky, even if they
came in friendship. I believe there are creatures in the universe,
much more advanced than we are, but they'll never land here,
not till we've learnt to be not so greedy and violent. They could
land. It stands to reason – look at all the UFOs that have been
seen all over the world. They must be more advanced than we
are, because they've come from further than we've ever been.
But they won't land, give us the knowledge they have, because
we don't deserve it.'

'That's my fantasy, escape the world. I don't like it. It's all
been spoiled here. There's too many people. If we got rid of

about three-quarters of the population, we'd be all right. Other people have got all the good things. I'd like to start afresh somewhere else. There's other planets to colonize; I think that's what'll save mankind in the finish. You could live on a space-station, somewhere where you could grow your own food, self-sufficient, in orbit for ever. If they do poison the earth, if they drop the bomb, that'll be the only hope for the future. People here have got too selfish.'

And yet, those who remember the rickety tubercular children of the slums, the death of infants as a weekly occurrence in the streets and tenements of the industrial cities, all the afflictions, scars and injuries of work and poverty, find it hard to believe that there can be much wrong with a world in which children are as healthy and beautiful as they are now. Millions of parents, pursued by long memories of hunger and cold, have resolved that their children will grow up free from care of that kind. But do they really believe it is their doing? Do they imagine that their own parents wouldn't have shielded them with something more than love and duty, if the means to do so had been there? But because parents have identified themselves with the changed circumstances of recent decades, they have been pleased to take credit for the changes, which they see as wholly beneficent. They see no need to interpose themselves between their children and the conditions which shape them. And through time, the parents find their hold over their children gently, subtly loosened. Almost it is as if they are transferring their children to a higher authority. They say, defensively, 'I want to give my kids all the things I never had', 'I want the best for them', 'Nothing is too good for my children.' But somewhere in these assertions lies a troubled sense of loss, a disturbed, half-guilty consciousness that they have no control over the processes that have been set in train; and that once their children have gone their own ways, there will be no calling them back; perhaps because it is not their own way at all, but a way determined by the same system that gave their parents and grandparents no choice either, in their lives circumscribed by poverty and want.

The children are aware of it too. Ray Gosling, in *Personal Copy*, describes his guilt at not following his parents, when he talks of the Americans in his provincial town in the 1940s.

'They were the great temptation, the thing to be aware of. And I fell for this first temptation, head over heels in love with their freedom and their dollar. I don't understand this, looking back, but I mean looking back from now, I see my parents' way of life as something absolutely admirable and full of goodness and strengths I should have followed and built upon. I can't rationally understand why I didn't . . . They were the first attraction that made me want to rebel – and then came rock 'n' roll. That sent me hell-bent to smash to smithereens everything my parents' generation had built. And I don't know why. If we had known what we were doing, I don't think we'd have done it. But we didn't know what we were doing. That was the attraction – an adventure into the unknown through the jukebox, loud music, sultry music, American music . . . And this was a very superficial kind of life. Whereas my parents lived a deep life, I threw up the deep life for the superficial.'

When we look back on the youth culture of the past 30 years, what appeared in the 1950s as an exciting and liberating experience – the emergence of teenagers, the rise of pop music, the development of styles which young people chose as symbols of a kind of elective identity – it now seems a less benign phenomenon than it did then. Of course, even at that time, newsreel pictures of cinema seats torn up wherever 'Rock Around the Clock' was playing, the screaming girls with tears running down their anguished faces, evoked fears of anarchy, warnings of social breakdown. But there was a moment of extraordinary excitement: the sight of indigenous working-class singers on stage, the discovery by the working class that they too were beautiful, that life could be enjoyed, that youth no longer had to be an apprenticeship to drudgery – it felt like a liberation. The social and economic forces that had permitted this change were felt to be good and positive: spoilsport authoritarian figures were mocked in the popular press, fuddy-duddy bishops, retired colonels in Cheltenham. Life as carnival seemed to be taking the place of life as toil. It looked as if the young were beginning to throw off the old disciplines associated with poverty and work. The old were shocked. Richard Hoggart, in *The Uses of Literacy*, cautiously warned that 'it is easier to kill the old roots than to replace them with anything comparable'; that 'the strongest objection to the more trivial popular entertainments is not that they prevent their readers from becoming highbrow, but they make it harder for people without an intellectual bent to become wise in their own way'. But he felt that 'the considerable moral resources of working-class people' would help them to overcome the worst effects of the changes he had monitored.

Through the 1960s the process expanded and accelerated. A new generation appeared to enjoy even more ample space in which to express themselves. Even then though, there were warning signs. The young began to wonder who they were: this was no longer defined for them by what they did or where they lived. But these were the years of sexual liberation, and that overwhelmed every other consideration. Ironically, it is the children of those who were young in 'Swinging Britain' – emancipated from the old repressions and Puritanism, who are now in their teens. Born into an atmosphere of obsessive expectancy and hope, the future seemed to dilate before them.

But the time of excitement and freedom didn't last. It was immobilized somehow; became rigid and constricting. Of course, it was really all about selling things to the previously poor. What happened was that the working class were delivered to the market-place, not as labour, but as consumers. And it did seem like a deliverance at the time: the market seemed the perfect mechanism for supplying the needs of those with money to spend for the first time. It made the brief socialist alternative of the postwar years look drab, and was, indeed, a substitute for it. And if we had any doubts, we had only to look at the impoverishment and greyness of Eastern Europe. It all seemed so straightforward. Everybody welcomed the gains.

To be young was like a holiday from life. It was assumed that they would grow out of it. They would enjoy a few easy years between leaving school and settling down, and then be absorbed into the old networks, the traditional patterns of work and living. And that did seem to be what was happening. For the first time, even young working-class people could spend a year or two bumming around, taking casual work, going abroad; and then they did get married, started a family, began to take life seriously. You did sometimes see the elderly Teddy-boy in his 30s, but he was felt to be a bit bizarre, with his crêpe soles and drainpipe trousers; and more often than not he was pushing a pram. Even though there was an increase in crime and delinquency, more broken families, more violence, this was felt to be the necessary price that had to be paid for more open attitudes. The smugness and hypocrisy had gone. This was how people really were; there was no use trying to pretend otherwise.

During the 1960s it became increasingly unfashionable to ask young people what they did (meaning work), but rather what their tastes were, which music they preferred, what kind of life-style they chose. Not their work-role, but who they thought they were became the main determinant of identity. In other words, the flight into fantasy had begun.

The market-place, following steady increases in real income, seemed to influence wider and deeper areas of human experience. Most of this was presented as the opportunity to buy release from unnecessary work – it was the time of supermarkets and convenience foods, the boom in consumer products, the vast spread of the entertainment industry, the preoccupation with status as an escape from class, which meant that things, rather than function, increasingly determined the way people thought about themselves. This process speeded up even more in the 1970s. The market could be seen to invade even non-material areas of life. Children were the first to be affected: they found themselves in a world of expanding fantasy and escape, even before they had become aware of what they were escaping from. The child's bedroom – where the old working class had huddled six or eight to a room – became a gilded cell: giant posters of fantasy figures, pop stars and footballers took the place of real people as significant influences. As they reached out for definition and identity, which were no longer going to be anchored in any work function. The market-place filled the vacuum with its manufactured excitements – horror films, epics of journeys to distant galaxies, effortless travels through time; and this was as close as many children came to spiritual or religious experience. It is not simply by chance that all this occurred as the economy was undergoing a great shift from its base in primary production, from the hard tangibility of mines, mills and factories, towards nonproductive, immaterial and service industries. The detachment of the working-class young from traditional purposes and patterns of work is, of course, a continuing and evolving process. It is a long-term change, which continues into the present. It isn't something that has simply happened like an event.

In theory, the market-place, as a reflection of free choices freely made, would be all right, if it were possible to start afresh from an ideal beginning with each generation as it made its free choices. But of course there are no generations, there is only continuity. And that is how the market-place ceases to be a neutral phenomenon: it becomes a primary determinant on the lives of the young, imposing its imperatives of getting and having. They are born with exhortations to buy ringing in their ears. Its elaborate displays of merchandise leave them no purpose but a sustained longing to possess and enjoy. When this is allied to a diminished role in the production of it, it is a narrowing and not enhancing influence. Its promise of fulfil-ment drowns out any sense of what is missing in their lives – the lost intangibles, the human resources that have long ago been exchanged for perishable and rapidly used-up commodities. The cry of rewards, free offers, prizes, gifts that have issued from the market-place for 30 years has served to conceal the opposite of these things – the draining away, the emptying, the distraints on the working class. Just what these losses add up to we can now see in the former working-class areas, the sad and robbed humanity in the inner city areas: not only the loss of the sense of worth from necessary work, but the loss of any other morality in those poor and proud, stoical working communities than the shrill imperatives to buy. There has been a loss of the human comforts of the formerly poor; above all, the surrender of that sense of a shared situation that united people in the face of pain, suffering and death. All this has been usurped by the power of money and the promise of what it can buy.

These children of the poor have been brought up to the kindling of their appetites, and the suppression of their unwanted redundant abilities; and then many of them have been denied access to all the things they have grown to depend on. This new, modernized version of poverty – where people learn to depend on the market-place and are then denied the money to fulfil that dependency – offers a sharp contrast with the testimonies of that older poverty, where people united against cruel material privations, and discovered the possibili-ties of the human consolations they could offer each other. This is not, of course, to argue for that older poverty. That would be absurd: looking at the great shopping malls and precincts, who can doubt that there is enough for everyone to be properly clothed and shod, sheltered, warmed and nourished? Looting, rioting, 'gratuitous' violence make an ugly kind of sense in this context. The images of looting in the inner city areas in the summer of 1981 are disturbing, not because people are getting something for nothing, but because they have the doomed dreamlike quality of individuals reaching out vainly for something they feel has been denied them or taken away from them; only they no longer even remember what it is. Looting has a symbolic dimension – a gesture of despair, a blow, however unwitting, against the causes of the unacknowledged captivity in which they have grown.

The destructive power of the market-place lies in this, that it can rob even the poorest, those who appear to own nothing, but who have still managed to mitigate the wretchedness of their poverty with the humanity of their response to it. This is as true also of the migrants from Jamaica or Pakistan, who had developed skills to deal with the poverty of their society that were not so different from the skills of the old working class. But we have all been lured by hopes and promises of something better – and rightly so; but we have been induced to set aside those abilities and that knowledge, which seem irrelevant in the changed context. But, of course, human skills and responses can never be superseded; and if we behave as though they could, we work towards our own injury, we collude with forces that will damage and impoverish our children whatever material advantages seem to be gained in doing so. All the children of the poor have been given over, in good faith, to the influence of the market-place. We are just beginning to live through the consequences of this, not only in terms of the violence, of rioting, of increased crime, destructiveness, nihilism and racism; but in the psychological damage too, the lonely, apparently 'private' tragedies – the disturbance and maladjustment, the sense of worthlessness and mental illness. The promised freedoms fail to appear; only a new kind of subordination.

It isn't that childhood is a worse experience now than it was for the very old; only that it should be so much better than it is. Having had the opportunity to eliminate poverty, we have failed to take it, but have substituted another kind of poverty for it: the poverty of the market-place, which means the growth of dependency in children on the goods and services and artefacts of capitalism, accompanied by the withering, and not an expansion, of their own powers. The changes that were to have rid us of that old poverty have exacted a terrible tribute, and it is the young who pay, in terms of the suppressed abilities, unwanted skills, atrophied development. In the end, it is the static nature of the society that stares us in the face, in spite of all the upheavals. All the talk of change turns out to be changing people so that they fit the modified needs of cold economic processes; and the only revolution turns out to be the revolution of the fixed wheel.

3

MR BAINES, 94

THE CHILDHOOD OF the very old is like myth, beyond corroboration or denial. Most of the generation are dead; the slowness and confusion of old age blur more recent memories. But the intensity of feeling is not impaired, and their power of evocation is a reminder of the use of human memory, in their time, as a means of transmitting experience. In their childhood they learned, above all, to remember.

Those who grew up poor remember most vividly the way living conditions bore upon them. Personal conflict with parents is usually subordinated to a sense of joint venture against circumstances. The parents tend to be idealized, and individual relationships with them are seldom the subject of elaborate reminiscence. Love for parents is often expressed through a lasting regard for 'what my mother and father taught me about life', values, principles; and the struggle of parents against adversity for the sake of their children is seen as self-evidently loving. The expression of needs and preferences of individuals was not the purpose of children's lives; on the contrary, childhood was a time for stifling them in preparation for a life of work and probable hardship. And although this now appears harsh and crushing, it did produce some astonishing strengths and powers; just as the easier life of our children involves some terrible losses.

Mr Baines was born in Northampton in 1887, more than 50 years before I was. At that time, the town was still in the process of being built in the shape it would largely retain for the next half century. The landmarks which I always took for granted – the great church, called by the sceptical boot and shoe workers 'Phipps's fire-escape', after the brewing family who built it, was still a construction site – and the speculative builders were still adding houses, in twos and threes, to the redbrick terraces which, by the time I was a child, seemed to have been there for ever.

Mr Baines's father had much to teach him. It was expected that poverty – or at the least, frugality, the need for an austere life – would continue; and because of their certainty of continuity, his parents could give him, not only the means of understanding the world, but also the knowledge that would help him to live in it. His experience would confirm theirs, and he grew, avid to learn from them. When Mr Baines talks of his father now, you feel his father's presence in him. As he reports conversations, his eyes water with the feeling rekindled by memory; the old man lives through his son, exists again and merges with him. The tenderness and reverence speak of a dependency more than personal; and human identity is seen for a moment as the compound it is, of self and others, often many others.

The father came from the Northamptonshire countryside; and there was more of this world to be passed on to his son than there was to be forgotten. And this was so, in spite of the fact that the father, a shoemaker, wanted his son to work on the railways, because they seemed to belong to a secure future; even though it broke the tradition that had been in the family for many generations. And it had been the father who had made the seven-mile migration from his village, where he made shoes in his own home, to Northampton, where he worked for the first time in a factory, as the outwork gradually ceased. What they did must have seemed radically and frighteningly new to them; but what stands after all the years, is the sense of continuity, the feeling for all that they preserved of their past.

Mr Baines's father was born in 1857; and some of the first stories he told his son belonged to his own childhood, and to the powerful grandmother who had helped to bring him up. She, in her turn, had spoken of her young life, in the early years of the nineteenth century. And as Mr Baines talks, he evokes again the world of his great-grandmother, and time is momentarily bridged – almost two centuries – by the profound and affecting power of love through time. It is clear that he feels he knows her, this strong and spirited woman he never met. She is to him a more real acquaintance than many of the people in the old people's home where he now lives. There is a magical power in the ability of human beings to live on through their words that reverberate in others long after their death. In recent years this power has been broken. Mr Baines's grandchildren and great-grandchildren still collect his stories; but they do so with a tape-recorder, and not for the practical wisdom they embody. What they are doing is recording the extinction of this means of binding people to us through time.

But for Mr Baines, it still lives; and in his dark eyes there is a glint of the child he was, as he listened with hungry delight to his father. He recounts the stories with great accuracy as he was told them, not departing by a detail from the information so carefully transmitted. The old man speaks with the slight rasp of the old country accent; but as he reports his father's speech, the dialect intensifies; and as he calls forth his great-grand-mother, the country burr thickens even more.

'Well, in the early years of the last century, there used to be a gospel tent in Northampton, where the Mission building stands now. It was an open piece of ground there. And there was a Methodist preacher, a man who couldn't read or write, but who held the people spellbound with his voice. He would stand up and say, "As I am lying on my bed at night, I can feel myself being swept through the pearly gates, and I am being washed in the blood of the Redeemer, and my sins are washed away, and His blood leaves me whiter than snow." And everyone would be carried away by his eloquence, and the whole assembly of people would be singing and moaning with him. Well, my great-grandmother was a young woman at the time; and she and her friends used to walk from Ecton of a Sunday night, six or seven miles, to hear this preacher in his tent. One Sunday night they'd been to hear him, I don't know which year, it was before 1820; and it was a fair night, half moonlight, a bit cold, and as they walked home after the meeting, they were so full of the spirit of this preacher that they went singing hymns at the top of their voice. When they got to Ecton, they had to turn off the main road by the World's End pub, down a lane that led to the village. They were still singing as they went down the street, and they separated one by one as they reached their homes. Grandma Baines lived right down the bottom end of the village, in a courtyard, where there were a few cottages and some stables. So she was the last one to reach her house, and she had to cross a dark bit of the street before she got there. Well, as she was coming down the street, the ostler was going round the stables to make sure the horses were all right for the night, and he heard her coming. He'd been up at the World's End that evening, and he was full of a different sort of spirit from those who'd been to the gospel tent. When he heard Grandma Baines, he thought he'd play a trick on her. He took the saddle cloth off one of these hunters; and when she turned in the gate to the yard, he let out such a groan it would curdle the blood. Of course Grandma Baines, being full of the fighting spirit of the Lord and His works, when she saw this thing in the corner of the yard, she had only one thought – it must be the Devil come to challenge her. So she stood her ground, and instead of running away, she went at him, and she set about this ostler, and gave him a really good pasting. He yelled out to her to stop, and at the finish, he'd had enough; he got out from under this cloth and ran away over the fields. The next day of course, the story came out, what had happened. But Grandma Baines wouldn't have it. Ever afterwards, as long as she lived, she insisted that she, single-handed, had taken on and fought the Devil. And not only had she fought him, but she'd won.

'Her son was my grandfather. He married the daughter of an Irish serving maid who worked at Ecton Hall. They had six sons. My grandfather was a shoemaker who worked at home. He would walk to Northampton, to the shop where the work was issued to him, leather to make so many pairs of boots; and then he'd bring it home, and when he'd finished, take the completed work back, to have it passed.

'My father was the third son. He was 11 when the family left to live in the town; that was 1868. Before that, he was working in the fields. One of his jobs was to lead the horses in the harvest field. They used to cut the corn and bind it and gather the sheaves into a stook – that was 15 sheaves; and they were left in rows, ready to be picked up after six or seven days' drying. Picking up the harvest was a skilful and orderly occupation. There would be a farm cart and two horses; three or four men on the ground, and a man in the cart who had to sort out the sheaves as they were thrown up to him, so that they would ride steady. The cart had to be drawn down the line of stooks in a straight line; and my father led the horse by taking the bridle. At ten, he could just reach it if he stood on tiptoe, and the cart had to be made to come to a halt beside each stook. The men would say 'Owdjer', and the horse would lean in the collar with its foot poised, till it felt the weight of the stook, and then the foot would come up, and off they'd go. The horse knew more than he did; but he had to make sure they proceeded in a straight line. Those harvest fields are as clear to me as if I'd been there. I can see the harvest rabbits and the corn poppies with my mind's eye. I was a listener as a child. I listened to everything my parents said. I learned more from them than from anyone else.

'One field where he worked, half of it was planted with barley, and part of it grassed off. Between the two parts, there was a footpath. One year, just before the harvest, the farmer had put two sows on the grass, each with a litter of piglets, to feed off the summer grass. Dad was given a waggoner's long whip, and was told to see that neither sow led her litter of pigs to the corn to eat it; that would, of course, have been death for the piglets, because if they ate it, it would swell up in their bellies and they'd die. Well, the two sows got separated. One was at one end of the grass, and the second was at the other end. As one crossed the path into the corn, Dad would rush up the field and drive it back. By then, the first one would have strayed back into the corn; and so it went on. While he was at one end of the field, the old sow sidled in, got hold of a sheaf of corn, gave it a shake, and the piglets were at it. In the end, they beat him. He simply sat down and began to cry. As he sat crying, the old blacksmith passed by, old Tom Bradshaw, a man as never picked up a jar of ale if it had less than a pint in it. "Well b'oy, what are you crying about?" Dad explained. "I'll soon put that right." He took off his blacksmith's apron, and started waving it in the air. He shouted and waved this apron, and the sows both turned and ran, and they ran till they got to the corner of the field. Tom said, "There y'ar b'oy. Just keep 'em up the corner agen the hedge, keep 'em together and you won't have no more trouble." '

The family narrative was slowly assimilated by the child, an essential part of learning. The achievements of the dead, as well as their shame and suffering, were still talked of, because they deeply concerned the living. Each new generation gained stature from their long extinguished joys and lost something through their faded, but not forgotten wrongs.

Mr Baines absorbed the past as part of his identity; the passing on to him of his parents' experience was an expression of their love. Because social change in recent years has detached children from the social experience of their parents, we sometimes behave as though the forms and patterns of human relationships of the past have also been outgrown; as though the sharing of lives, the transmission of values between people who love each other could be supplanted by something better; as though human beings had something more valuable to seek than what issues from their own lives and experience. We do those who lived before us a grievous wrong, and ourselves irreparable injury, if we imagine that, bound as they were by place and circumstances, their lives were necessarily impoverished. There was often a sense of great richness and diversity accumulated through time, however wretched their lives may have been in other ways.

'My father would tell me the story of the village slut and the cowman. The village slut, oh that's going back to my father's young days, the sixties. She was what you might call public property, anybody used her sort of thing, but nobody wanted her, nobody would take responsibility for her. Well this cowman, he lived alone in his little old cottage in the fields, and it was very lonesome for him. He just went about his work, then went home; hardly spoke to anybody all day long. But one day he astonished the whole village by announcing that he was going to marry the village slut. They didn't think he meant it. They thought he'd never go through with such an outrageous plan. But the day fixed for the wedding came, and he married her. He took her to live with him in his lonely little house. Now being a cowman, he had to get up at five-thirty of a morning and milk the cows; no time for a honeymoon. So the first morning, he woke up, it was still dark. He went downstairs for his breakfast, but it wasn't ready. His wife was still snoring away in bed upstairs. So he gets a ladder and lights a lantern, and goes and hangs this lantern outside the bedroom window. Then he goes to his wife and says, "Look love, the sun's shining, it's a lovely morning. I've got to go to work, and I want my breakfast." So she gets up and makes him his breakfast. The next day, five-thirty, it's the same thing. She's still in bed, snoring away. He goes and lights the lantern, and does the same thing as the day before. "Look love, the sun's shining. It's a lovely day. I've got to go to work and I want my breakfast." She gets up and makes his breakfast, and he thinks, "Oh I won't have to tell her again." The next morning, she's still in bed snoring when it's time for him to go to work. So he goes and fills a bucket with water. She opens an eye and says, "Is the sun shining love?" He says, "No love, it's a terrible morning. It's raining cats and dogs, but I've still got to go to work and I want my breakfast." And he chucks the bucket of water all over her. But he doesn't have to tell her again.

'My first memory as a child is from 1890. One Sunday we were out for a walk. We'd gone to look at St Matthew's church. The roads were muddy, and my younger brother was being pushed in the mail-cart. Half the spire of the church was built, and I leaned back to look at the crane lifting a great stone; but I leaned too far and fell over in the mud. My Dad picked me up and turned me over his knee for it.'

Mr Baines's own direct experience merges with that of his father and grandfather; a strange kind of mobility through time, as though he could enter and leave the lives of others at will; and it contrasts sharply with the kind of mobility his grandchildren understand – the restless movement from place to place tends to obliterate the traces of that older more subtle movement.

'My grandfather came to Northampton when my Dad was ten and a half. At that time, they were getting the men together to work in factories for the first time. The Northampton cobblers were an independent lot and they didn't like it. They were used to getting their money on a Friday, and they wouldn't be ready to start work again until the next Tuesday or Wednesday; and then they'd work like Sam Scratch to get it done by the Friday. And you couldn't do that in a factory.

'By the time my father was ten, he'd be working in the farmer's fields – if he was a good boy. If he was naughty, he was sent to school. After the ploughing, they'd give the boys a bucket, and they'd walk over the fields picking the stones and carting them away. When I heard my father talk about these things, I always thought how lucky I was.

'On a holiday, we'd always walk out in the country; my father never lost his love for it, and he passed it on to us. He'd teach us to make a whistle out of an ash stick. He'd cut a good length of green ash, loosen the bark with his knife gently, and with the sap all wet, you could pull the bark off. Then he'd split the wood, cut a bit out of it, and you had a whistle. You could get all sorts of notes out of it. I taught my boys to do it when they were children. I don't know if they taught theirs.

'We moved to a new house when I was five. There were seven of us. Father had to be at work at seven-thirty, so we were all up at half past six. He always lit the fire until we were a bit older and then we could be trusted to do it. After breakfast he'd push his chair back, go down the cellar and get half a bottle of beer. He used to have a niner of beer delivered by the brewery dray. Sometimes I'd go and get his beer for him; you had to feel your way down the cellar steps – there was no light. The lights in the house were just raw gas jets.

'But you felt it was a privilege to do things for your parents. You never had to be asked twice. My father worked in the tapping shop in the factory; and he got to be foreman. He worked on a bench at the top end of the room, and he dished the work out to the operatives, and they had to bring it back, and he'd tell them if it was good enough. "You've stuck this heel awk'ard", "this'll have to be done agen".

'One day our father came home and said he'd been put on the staff. You've no idea what that meant to us. It meant he'd get paid for his two weeks' holiday, and a regular 30 shillings a week. My mother, she clapped her hands and she cried, "We'll never be poor again."

'Mother made most of our clothes. She made breeches, no fly, just a flap and a hole. If you wanted to do a diddle, you just fished it out and peed down the drain. The privy was only a straight hole down into the drain; you always had to take a bucket of water with you. The mothers always used to tell their children, "Don't you stand over those drains, you'll catch the fever."

'Life was very well regulated. It had to be. We always sat down to meals, always in the same place round the table. And we all had our own jobs in the house. I used to peel the potatoes. Peeling potatoes is a science. I had an old potato peeling coat, so I could rest the potato against it, three strokes top to bottom each side. On Friday nights I used to go and get the groceries. Mother would never let me write down the shopping list. We had to remember everything. There would be so many items, and you had to commit them to memory, 16 or 17 items. Then I'd go down to the shop – there were only men at shop-counters then, the mid-nineties. I can still recite those shopping lists.

"Half a stone of best flour" – you took your own bag with you, and they'd scoop the flour out of a drawer; "six pounds of white sugar, two pounds of demerara, one and a half pound of roll bacon" – the rashers were cut with a knife of course; "one and a half pound of Golden Meadow butter, a packet of Hudson's strong soap" – that was soap powder; "two squares of blue, two pounds of soda, a tin of blacking for boots, a pound of rice . . ." Then I'd count up the items to see if I'd got them all. You had to use certain skills, and your mother knew what she was doing by not letting you write it all down – she wanted to help us to get on. I can remember things I've only heard once. We were trained to listen, and we valued it. There was a poem my sister learned when she started school; I can remember her standing on the kitchen table and reciting it. She was four and a half. She said, "I've learned a new poem", and we all gathered round to hear what she had to say. It was quite an event when somebody had something new. I'd forgotten the poem until my own children were little, and we were all gathered round trying to amuse them one Christmas. I only heard this poem two or three times, but there it was, still there. It's called "The Idle Bee".

> What in the world would children say
> If I told you about a bee at play?
> Would you believe that this idle fellow
> Refused to brush his coat of yellow,
> Declined to polish up his sting
> Or shake the dust from either wing?
> Not, so to speak, for love or money
> Would he go out to gather honey.
> And so they built a narrow cell
> With door that fitted close and well,
> And in much less than half a minute
> They plastered that idle bee up in it.
> He's in there still; and I much doubt
> That they will *ever* let him out.

'My mother never shouted. She just spoke in an ordinary voice. You simply did what she said. The worst thing that could happen to you would be that you'd get the cane. It only happened to me once. I was playing about with a holly stick, and she told me not to; but I carried on, and by accident, I poked my brother in the eye with it. "Get upstairs." "Yes

Mum." It was the only time I was physically punished at home. And only once at school; that was old Mother Dunham. She had a strip of leather, about four inches wide, with a handle and half a dozen thinner strips at the end.

'My mother's father was a hedgecutter. He lived at Brington and rented under the Squire. My mother's sisters all went out to service. My mother came as a maid of all work to a maiden lady in Northampton when she was 13. She stayed there until the old lady died, and then she went to a mental asylum near Shrewsbury, where one of her sisters worked; she was married to an attendant. My mother became a nurse there, and learned to deal with refractory patients. This gave her a sense of quiet authority. And if anybody had trouble in the street, any accident or misfortune, they all used to say, "Send for Mrs Baines." And if Mrs Baines told you, it was so.

'We were strict churchgoers. I belonged to an age when you did as you were told at home. It was no compulsion to me. I never went out to the theatre, anything like that, that would have been beyond me. There was the Opera House, they did things like "A Royal Divorce", all that sort of thing; Napoleon, "Josephine, I have no son", all that sort of tripe, melodrama. We shouldn't have been encouraged to go to the theatre, not likely. It wasn't quite proper. When I was about 17, 18, I told Dad that I was going to a church dance. And my Dad said, "Well my boy, where there's fiddling and dancing, there's playing with the Devil. You mind what you get up to." Fiddling and dancing – well, it was a Sunday School teachers' dance, something of that. The only dance I should dream of going to would be connected with the church. I would hardly be going to one of the threepenny hops. They were looked on sideways.

'I was never given any detailed instruction in sex or anything of that kind. I'll tell you what happened.' And he acts out the scene, word for word, playing both the role of his father and of his younger self. 'It took less than five minutes, the instruction I had.

' "You know what these things lead to my boy?"

' "Yes, Dad."

' "That's all right then. You look after yourself and don't be silly, that's all."

' "Yes, Dad."

' "If you step over the mark, it'll be you as 'll suffer."

' "Yes, Dad."

' "That's all right then. If you understand it, I needn't tell you any more."

' "No, Dad."

'That was it. To a large extent there was a reticence between children and their parents. Of course, when you started work, there were all sorts of sideways references to it. When your voice broke, the senior clerk in the office would turn round and say, "They've dropped then?" They used to say, "Have a feel of his ears, see if they're all right." They used to say it was your testicles dropping when your voice broke. But there was never any open discussion between the sexes. You wouldn't think of talking to a girl about it. I mean, you knew there were some girls who used to indulge in what we used to say was loose talk with fellows, but those were the girls we avoided.

'I remained under my parents' control till after I started work; but I never felt constricted by it. My schoolmaster wanted me to be a teacher; but I preferred my father's idea of the railways. It was safe; to go there meant you had a job for life. Whether they thought education was only a flash in the pan and not secure I don't know. I sent in an application form to become a railway clerk. I had a letter on the Thursday which told me to report to the Castle Station Goods Department at 6 a.m. on the Friday morning.

'I got up at half past five, made myself a cup of tea, had a bit of oats or something in milk, and walked down to the station. I went to the delivery office; and there were about half a dozen fellows there, papers all over the place, everybody seemed busy. "Go and sit up that corner." There was a boy a bit older than myself, and he was recording and putting a number on the invoices for goods. I helped him to get on with that till eight o'clock, and then it was breakfast time for us two lads, but the others had to go on working. We went over to the platform and sat in the waiting room and undid a bit of lunch out of our pockets.

'I did that for a time, and then I became messenger boy, delivering advice notes. You had to take these notes round the town to various merchants, saying that a full load of a certain commodity, grain or leather, was at the station, waiting for them to discharge it; and they'd got two days, and if they didn't do it within those two days, they'd be charged demurrage on the waggon . . . You'd go to the grain merchants and the corn exchange, the leather firms or maybe wholesale fruit merchants – it might be a load of oranges. Then you'd go home for your dinner, be back by a quarter to two, and then you'd sort out all the invoices in number order, so you could always trace the invoice if it was needed. When you'd got a full batch, you pierced them, threaded them with a firm back stitch in hundreds and put them away. There were six or seven delivery clerks in that office. As a boy of 14, I went at six in the morning. The office closed at six, but with me being the boy, I had to wait and put the letters in the parcels office to be taken by train. I left at six-fifteen; eight shillings a week, less threepence deduction for provident and pension.

'As I had to get up at half past five, I was in bed by half past eight. I did join an evening class in shorthand; the ambition was to become a letter writer. In those days, there were no girls in the offices, oh no. There were lads of various ages, some of them up to 20 or more, and they would be taking letters in shorthand and writing them. A few were typed, but not many. You were only allowed to type letters to the general public or head office at Euston. But station letters were all written. Office discipline was strict. If you had to absent yourself for necessity, and if you were a bit too long about it, you'd soon be asked where the hell you'd been. You didn't speak out of your turn. You were the boy, and you spoke when you were spoken to. You didn't get saucy and join in or originate conversations. No. You answered questions, or you might ask them if you needed information. Relationships were formal. It wasn't until after the First War that you saw the difference. They even began to smoke cigarettes in the office then.'

4

MEMORIES OF THE COUNTRYSIDE:
MISS RENSHAW, 90

IT IS SURPRISING how many old working-class people have recollections of the countryside in their childhood memories. In part, this may reflect the higher proportion of the population still working in agriculture at the turn of the century, but it wasn't *that* much higher. The theme of the countryside goes much deeper. Richard Hoggart describes, in *The Uses of Literacy*, how his grandmother came to Leeds in the 1870s, and although she learned to be a city dweller, 'yet in every line of her body and in many of her attitudes her country background spoke. Her house, still rented at nine shillings a week in 1939, was never truly urban. Newspaper packets of home-dried herbs hung from the scullery ceiling; a pot of goose-grease lay always on the shelf there, in case anyone "got a bad chest".' It took a long time for the people to forget that the industrial cities grew out of those migrations from the land; and they continued to be haunted by memories – the relatives too old to uproot themselves from the villages, and the visits to whom were always associated with holidays and summer, the dream of the return home; this all echoes the hopes of many migrants from peasant cultures in Western society today. For a long time, the working class in the industrial towns was like an unhappy stepchild, longing for a return to its true parentage. It is impossible to exaggerate the influence of the countryside on the early towndwellers, and how this was transmitted sometimes through several generations; it sharpened the resentment of industrialism, even though life on the land had often been even harsher for some of them than it proved to be in the towns. It certainly isn't chance that the myth of the happy childhood is bound up for so many people with the persistence of rural memories. These have only really faltered in the last half century or so, as the sense of continuity has been broken, the transmission of values between the generations more decisively interrupted. The working class has become more completely detached from its own traditions as it comes to depend increasingly on the values of the market-place. It is this process that has caused the excision of memories already growing fainter with time.

Miss Renshaw is 90. She sees her childhood as a lost paradise, and she knows why. The years have brought her leisure to reflect on the early happiness and its passing. 'A marvellous life I had till I was 13. Oh, I loved my father. He was a god to me.' She sits in her armchair with its crocheted covers, her tray with its knife and fork on a table beside her. She is crippled with arthritis and cannot move without help. A crystal brooch shines on her white lace blouse. In a jug over the mantelpiece some desiccating stalks of lavender fill the room with a rich sweet smell. The sounds of the adjacent farm come through the open door. Hot white sunlight lies across the stubble that is burning in the fields with a crackling, almost invisible flame. The curtain stirs soundlessly in the slow-moving air. The village clock chimes the quarter, two brief notes that die so quickly you almost doubt you heard them.

'He worked on the farm. He was only an ordinary labourer. He had nothing special as other folks would notice. But he loved me. He loved all six of us, but I was the oldest, and I was his favourite. He took me everywhere. On holidays from school he would say, "Come on gal, we're going somewhere." He made everything we saw so alive and vivid to me. Life was always an excitement. My mother was an invalid. She had consumption, and he took on a lot of responsibility for the children. To me, he could do anything. If the farmer had a churn of milk go sour, my Dad would hang it up in bags to dry out, mix it with a bit of rosemary, you had the most delicious cream cheese. Many a time I've been out with him by moonlight at hay-making time; and I'd take his breakfast out soon after dawn, and he'd already been working for hours. Oh, I can see his face now as he stood in the field, in the first sunshine, he was like a man of gold. Which he was to me. He'd go out shooting rooks, and we'd have rook pie. He used to catch sparrows by going round the eaves; of course all you could eat of sparrows was the breast, you needed a lot of birds to make a pie. Everything went into pies; lamb-tail pie, I wonder how many people have had that? The man who came and cut the lambs' tails used to charge 1s 6d a dozen. They were very tasty, but there was a lot of bones in them . . . And he'd fry up chitterlings with bacon. And the mushrooms, we'd gather them in clothes baskets, great wicker baskets, and we used to sell them 3d a pound. You couldn't walk without treading on them, early September morning, the dew was like jewels in the grass. They had to be gathered early, before the sun got on them. Those we didn't sell he'd make into mushroom ketchup . . . Then cream with the first tea of morning, what a luxury. He had a little pump that would turn butter back to cream, and he always made some for mother before he went to work. The wine he made, elderberry, potato, parsnip. Sloe gin; skips full of sloes. You wouldn't find them now, they keep the hedges too low. Once I made some dandelion wine; only the sugar and the washing soda came in big sacks exactly the same, and I must've used soda instead of sugar. So just before it was time to bottle it up, he said he'd try the wine. Oh, I can see his face now as he tasted it; of course it was all ruined, but we laughed and laughed. We laughed all the time.

'Life was a feast then. Jugged hare at harvest time; the men went round the fields with scythes. They started at the edges and worked inwards. The rabbits and hares were so dazed, you could just pick them up. The woods were always full of nuts, hazelnuts, filberts, sweet chestnuts. There were two spinneys near where we lived, one of pine trees, the other mainly elm. In that pine spinney, dark and green, it was like walking on a carpet, all the pine needles, soft and silky. We used to build houses with the branches that fell off. The fields were full of flowers. I think a lot of farmers have killed them off since then. We gathered campion, and the little wild pansies we called pink-eyed johns. We picked water-blobs at the mill, and you had to stand in three feet of water to reach them.

'My mother was always apart from us. I grew up knowing she hadn't long to live. Of course, nowadays, they would never have dreamed of having six children, with her suffering like that. I never felt close to her as I did to my father. She sat on an old sofa, whipcord, hard horsehair, and she coughed and she was always dreadfully pale, poor thing. She always seemed to have the mark of death on her. I know it sounds dreadful, but I was afraid of her. I used to avoid her. I loved to be out of doors with my father, or I'd help him in the house. He was a beautiful person. He treated her so tenderly, he waited on her. I know he loved her, even though I didn't. I think children work things out. I knew it was no good letting myself grow too attached to her, because I always knew I would lose her.

'She died when I was 12. And then, being the eldest, I soon had to go out to work. And work, in those days, if you were a country girl, meant service. So at just 13 I left school, and I went on the carrier's cart to Kibworth, about 16 miles away. It seemed like going to the end of the earth. I went to a woman, a Mrs Pettigrew. She was a widow, and she lived with her bachelor brother who owned a factory in Peterborough, where he made jam I believe. But there was nothing sweet about either of them. This Mrs Pettigrew had a grown-up daughter, also a widow – or so they said – and this daughter's little boy lived with them. He was about 7 or 8. But they were unkind to me. They must have been delighted in having me, a poor 13-year-old, living in a freezing room at the top of the house. I was like a mouse in a cage. The missis put me in a room that had no window. She said, "Young girls spend too much time dreaming and looking out of windows." It was really a sort of loft. In winter it was so cold I'd wake up with my teeth chattering, and I had to be up before six, getting everything ready for them all. I virtually waited on all four of them. When I sat down of an evening, I'd have a pile of darning to do; and this missis would come and thrust her hand into the sock I was darning, to make the holes bigger on purpose, so it would make more work for me. I knew it gave her pleasure. I could tell from the way she set me tasks to do. I had to scrub the floors without soap, only a bit of soda, and oh, my hands, all the winter were red and raw. They cracked and bled, all winter long they never healed. It was agony to put them in water.

'This little boy, I had to take a ewer of water, boiling water, up for him to wash every morning. There was a day girl who actually washed him, but it was one of my jobs to take the water up. And one morning, he was running around, and as he rushed past me on the stairs, I accidentally spilled some of this water, it went over his arm and shoulder. I suppose it burnt him a bit. It couldn't have been too bad, because by the time the water had been poured into the pitcher and carried upstairs, it was nowhere near boiling. Well, he put up such a performance. He made out I'd done it on purpose, as though I'd thrown the

blessed stuff at him. And the missis got really angry, as though
it was my fault. Do you know what she did? She put the kettle
on the range, to boil it up, ready to do the same to me. I couldn't
believe it. She was going to throw boiling water over me as a
punishment. I watched this kettle, the steam started lifting the
lid. She must have seen the terror in my eyes . . . Anyway,
whether she hadn't really meant to do it at all, or whether she
thought better of it, she didn't do it in the end. Perhaps she just
wanted to scare me; if so, she succeeded. I was only a kid
myself, I was 13.

'I was so unhappy. After my life at home, I'd no idea there
could be such cruelty. I would have run away, I'd've done
anything, but I knew my Dad needed the few shillings I got, he
had to bring up the others. So I didn't say anything. I used to go
home once every four weeks, on a Sunday. I lived for those
Sundays. But when I got there, I couldn't say anything to my
father about what life was really like. I said it was all right. But
he knew. After about eight months, he said to me one Sunday
afternoon, "How should you like not to go back to your place?"
I couldn't believe he meant it. He looked at me and said,
"You're not happy there are you?" And I broke down in tears
and told him all about it. The next day, he got me a job as a day
girl with a farmer, so I could come home at nights. They were
kind to me there, because they knew us. I thought nothing of
walking the four miles there in the morning and back at night. I
was able to help my Dad look after the house. I think I replaced
our mother. And that says everything about me.

'I've thought about it a lot as I've got older. I loved my father
with a love I've never felt for anyone else. And he loved me too.
I was more of a companion to him than my mother could ever
have been. He used to say I was his little sweetheart. He used to
call me his little woman when I was ever such a girl, and his
eyes used to light up whenever he saw me. You think about it,
years later. I've often wondered if I wasn't spoilt for being a
wife myself because of the love I had for him. Nobody could
ever come near him as far as I'm concerned; nobody I've ever
met all my life.

'I nursed him through his last illness, and I was proud to do
it. I was 31 when he died. By that time, I wasn't interested in
getting married, looking for boyfriends. I've always been a bit
of a mother to my brothers and sisters. They've said as much.

Only to my knowledge, there's none of them knows what passed between me and my father. We had only to look at each other to know what the other was thinking. After him, what sort of a life would I have had with anybody else? He spoilt me, bless him, but to this day I love him, and I can feel him close to me, in the fields, in the lanes. If I see something – a field of flowers, a flight of birds – I tell myself, "Oh, I must tell our Dad, he'll love that"; and when I'm on my own, in the night, I talk to him; and I believe he hears me yet.' Miss Renshaw, 90, Leicestershire.

5

THE POOR WORKING CLASS: MRS McIVER

BOTH MR BAINES and Miss Renshaw were children of the respectable working class. Part of the discipline and control which such children knew was an attempt to provide them with skills that would prevent them from falling into the stratum beneath them – the unskilled, unemployed, those who lived in constant fear of the workhouse. Robert Roberts in *The Classic Slum* says it was 'parents of the most respectable and conformist families who were the staunchest upholders of discipline'. Those who knew only poverty and squalor had a vastly different view of childhood. For Mr Baines, the strictness of his early years was part of a profound and loving attachment to his parents. The childhood of those destined for rougher labour was not so well regulated. Harshness of living conditions sometimes did the work for those parents unable to temper the cruelty of life with care and love.

Mrs McIver is in her 70s, and lives in a terraced house in Wigan. There used to be a colliery opposite, but it has been closed for a long time, and the area in front of the house is now open ground. The houses were formerly all pit cottages; but most of them have passed into individual ownership, and the redbrick uniformity has been broken by bright paint, extensions and alterations to the property.

'Oh yes, we had a rough time. There were 17 of us; 17 children. They didn't all live. My brothers had to pinch food from shops to help feed us all. They would distribute it around, and they used our cellar to store it all. They used to get tins of corned beef, fish, ham, everything. Once they took a whole sack of flour from a shop. They didn't realize there was a hole in it; so of course the police could follow this trail of flour from the shop right to our front door. They knocked on the door, and our mother opened it. They said to her, did she know anything about any flour? She said, "I've got no flour apart from what I use for my baking." But of course, when they looked, they found it, and all sorts of other things as well. My brothers were sent away for that, they did time. It didn't stop them though. It was the only way to get enough to eat. My brother broke into a shop once, and there was this cat started mewing. He strangled it to shut it up, so it wouldn't give him away. He'd got gloves on; he filled his sack with ciggies and tobacco, and a great roll of bacon. We had a big dresser with a top that opened. It was all stored in there. He didn't get caught that time.

'We used to get our food on credit, go and pay on Thursday; and then stock up with a fresh supply for the next week. You had to pay all you owed before you could start again. Once my mother sent me to get the groceries. She hadn't got enough money to pay for them all, so she said to me, "Now make sure you get all the stuff before you pay." She gave me what she had, but we knew it wasn't enough. So I got all this stuff, potatoes, tinned stuff, cheese, whatever it was. Then I gave him the money I'd got from my mother. "Me Mam sent this." He said, "You leave all that bloody stuff on the counter." He was going to take it all back. I went mad. I started throwing everything around, all the tins, I threw them at the shelves where everything was all stacked up; the whole lot came crashing down. I threw the jackbut all over the shop. I was that mad, he thought I'd wreck the place. He let me take the groceries.

'I was the fourteenth child out of the seventeen. There were twins after me. The youngest child only lived six weeks. When the twins were three – I was about 18 months older, so I'd be four and a half by then, and one Sunday afternoon our mother left us in the front place together. At that time she had a bit of a shop, sold ciggies and papers, and she left me to keep an eye on the twins in the front place. There was a coal fire; and as I sat there on the hearth, I was taking pieces of paper and lighting them at the fire until they burned my fingers, and then I dropped them into the grate. One piece of paper burnt me suddenly, and I let it drop, and it fell onto Edith's pinny. Her clothes all started to burn, and she screamed out. I panicked, and I ran out the front and went to hide on the piece of spare ground. I was frit to death. It didn't occur to me to go and fetch somebody. She wasn't too badly burned. My sister came out to look for me. I got a real battering for that. My father never hit us; it was always mother who took charge of correction and punishment. Well, even though this child wasn't badly burnt, she got pneumonia and died as a result of this some little while after. The other one fretted for her, and a few weeks later, she was dead too. So that made me the youngest child.

'My father used to paste my mother. He was a miner, when he got work. Most of the family went in the pit. My father had a brother who was killed in the pit. There were three brothers; when this lad was killed, my grandmother got word from some of the neighbours that one of the lads was hurt. When my grandfather got home, she asked, "Which one is it? It's not our Joe is it?" "No, it's our Ted." She said, "Thank·God." He was more of a weakling. I suppose she felt if one of them had been killed, it was better it should be him, because he wasn't as strong as the others.

'We were so poor. We used to go up to the Convent, cadging leftovers, bits of bread and cheese, bacon bits, anything that was going. We used to go to the soup kitchen. Mother used to tell us to say there was even more of us than there was, so we'd get a bit extra. Later on, as I was growing up a bit, my mother got on her feet a bit more, selling second-hand furniture. We really thought we were somebody when we got oilcloth for the floor instead of bare stone flags. You accepted it though. Everybody was the same; we were all in the same situation, no money. There seemed no way out of it; you had to get on with it, and not expect too much. All my brothers went into the pits. They had no choice.

'I left school when I was thirteen, and I started in a factory. I had to go at seven forty-five in the morning till five-fifteen, and during your dinner-break you had to keep the machines going. Then when you got home at the end of the day, you had housework to do. On Mondays there was always the washing to help with, then Tuesday there was the ironing and the two bedrooms to clean. I worked in the factory for three years; 8s 3d a week.

'My mother died at 62. She used to weigh 17 stone, but she shrunk as she got older. I think they cared for us in their own way, but with so many of us, you had no chance to show it. My mother was the boss inside the house, as far as the children were concerned. She was the one who hit us when we had to be hit. I sometimes wish she'd shown us a bit more love, but there you are. She had so much to do. You'd be as like to get a slap as a kiss; but sometimes that was their way of saying they cared. No softness, nothing that looked like weakness. You couldn't afford the luxury of the deeper feelings. "Don't be so bloody daft", they might say and give you a sort of slap, half-joking. That was as near as it came. Affection. The only time I had any real show that my mother cared, she did put her arms round me once, when I'd just met my husband and I was madly in love with him; we'd had a quarrel and fallen out, and I came home heartbroke. She tried to comfort me. "Never mind him."

'My mother and father never spoke to each other for five years. Father and the lads lived at the back, mother and me at the front. He didn't dare come into the room. Whatever it was he'd done, she never forgave him; whether he'd been unfaithful to her I don't know. They only communicated through the children. It carried on until my mother died. When she was lying on her death-bed – I was 18 – all the children were gathered round, and my father was sitting in the rocking chair with his head in his hands. The priest came, and he said to my father "Go in to her." Father said, "She doesn't want anything to do with me." The priest went to mother, and he said to her "Can you say the Lord's Prayer?" And she said she could. So he asked her to recite it; and when she got to "Forgive us our trespasses as we forgive them that trespass against us", he stopped her and said, "Do you know what you've just said?" She said, "Yes." And then the priest sent my father in to her. That was the first and last time I saw them so close.

'Even when my father was dying, he never told us what it was that had made them quarrel. I loved my father better than my mother. She had a hand of iron. But our father never told us why she had been so unforgiving. He took his secret to the grave.

'My mother was once told by a neighbour that my father was in the Blue Bell pub with a woman who had a reputation. My mother just said, "Oh is he." She went down to the pub, and found them just coming out the door. She got hold of this woman and threw her under a hansom cab. My mother was a powerful woman. People always used to send for her when there was trouble; at times of confinement, dying. They always said they knew they had nothing to worry about if my mother was there. The neighbours would always be looked after by the neighbours.

'Life was rough in our neighbourhood. Every Saturday night there'd be fights, and the kids would come rushing in, saying,

"There's a good one up at Number 24", and off we'd all run. It was a kind of excitement, finding out where the bloodiest fight was. We thought of it as free entertainment; as a kid, you don't think of the pain and strife that might be behind it. There were three families of us all in a row, Mrs Rose lived next door to us on one side, she had 21 children, our mother had 17, and then there was Mrs Donnelly with 19. Three houses, all next door to each other, two up, two down, 63 people. And to think children expect a room of their own now.

'When I was married, I had to use the same room as my Dad and the lads who were still at home. I had to put a nightie on on top of all my clothes on my wedding night, because there was no room to change. I was already pregnant as a matter of fact. We had straw mattresses, not beds, just bug-infested mattresses. On the wedding night my Dad fixed up a curtain down the middle of the room, so we should be a bit more to ourselves.

'A rough childhood prepares you for a rough life. You learn not to expect too much. I grew up knowing nothing, even though people lived so close together. I had to get married when I wasn't much more than a child. I'd only been with my husband once. He liked his women. In those days, when you got pregnant, you got married. He'd got VD when we were married. I'd no idea. He'd got, what's the worst one? – syphilis. One week he was on night turn. He came home in the morning. I was just putting the boiler on to do some washing. He said, "I want to talk to you." "Wharabout?" "Have you got a discharge?" I had, but I thought it was because of being pregnant, so I said, "Yes." He said, "Because I have." I said, "Is it not natural then?" I didn't know. I was very ignorant. He said, "You'll have to come with me now to the doctor's." He went in first. Then the doctor sent for me. Had I been with anybody else? Of course I hadn't, I was heart and soul wrapped up with my husband. I was told we'd have to go to the Infirmary. I was told not to have sex with him on any account. He didn't put it quite in those words. We went up to the Infirmary. He said to me, "If you've got anything, I'll leave you here and now." I sat in that Infirmary, trembling from head to foot. Do you know what I thought? I believed if you'd got it, they couldn't cure it. I thought they smothered you if you'd got the worst, syphilis. Old wives' tales. I went in and I was examined, and the doctor said to me, "You're quite all right."

The baby wouldn't be affected, but I was not to let my husband near me. I said to the doctor, "Will you give me a note to say I've not got it?" When I got outside, he said, "Well how have you got on?" "I've not got it." I gave him the note. I wanted to go and tell my father, but he insisted we should go home and talk it over. He was going to the Infirmary in Bolton, away from home. He had to keep on going for ages. I don't know that he ever did get completely cured. He never said who he got it from. He told me he'd been kicked in the groin by a pony in the pit. I believed him. I even said it in court when we got divorced. They all laughed at me.

'All this was when I was pregnant with the first child. I didn't know anything. You had no knowledge. I didn't know how a baby was born. I always said I was terrified of blood, so I didn't know how I'd go on. I thought they cut open your stomach from the navel to get the baby out. I couldn't imagine it somehow, but that's what I thought happened. We were so innocent. Well, when the labour pains started, I didn't know what they were. My Dad said, "I think you've got the flu." So they put me to bed. But I felt uncomfortable, and I was in pain. I got no sympathy from my husband. He went to sleep and that was that. In those days you used to have a bucket, a zinc pail to use, if you needed it in the night. Well, I felt ill, so I sat on this bucket, and I didn't know what was happening to me. The baby started to be born, and even then I didn't know. I said to my husband, "Wake up, there's something wrong, ee, I've got a bladder coming out down here." I thought my insides was all coming out. Then I put my hand down and I felt the profile of the child, the nose and the eyes. I said, "It's the child, the child's being born." Then I felt again, and I could feel the back and the bottom coming out; there was no difficulty; only the surprise and the shock. My husband said, "Well put it back till morning."

'When the baby had been born, I lay back on the bed, and he went out to knock up his sister, the baby just lying there on me. The cord hadn't been cut or anything. I felt champion. Then his mother came and the midwife, and they helped clean me up, do what was necessary. The child had to be baptized straight away, because she was very weak. She lived six weeks. That was how I learned about childbirth. And that was when I stopped being a child.'

*

Those who grew up in the old 'respectable' working class often talk now of how unimportant money was to them as children. They grew up proud of how much they could do with very little money; whereas their counterparts today are ashamed of how little they can do without a lot. This is how those things which should represent gains in working-class life are balanced by loss; and how the improvements anticipated by many of the leaders of the old working class have been neutralized. In many ways, the dominant model within the contemporary working class is shaped out of elements of the older 'rough' way of living: what were regarded by a majority as improvidence, irresponsi-bility, selfishness, living in the present, an absence of moral values, have all been transformed, if not into virtues, at least into general norms; whereas the older prevailing way of life – with its endurance and frugality, self-denial and deferring of joys and pleasures until they disappear – become a deterrent, the worst thing that can happen to you, a sign of failure. These things have been devalued, because the possibility of human resources as a substitute for money would severely interfere with the dynamic of the economy, which is all about selling things to those who were recently poor. In this way, what look like profound changes in society are really only slight shifts of emphasis, the conjunction of already existing aspects of the culture, which create an illusion of radical change in a system that is constant in that it always takes from the working class. When you talk to older people, there is still a memory of the last vestiges of an alternative way of living that didn't depend on money – the development of skills and abilities to answer human need, all the things that have been squeezed out of an experience of childhood that depends more on the influences of the market-place than on the development of autonomous and self-determining human beings – a culture which not only denies that the best things in life are free, but which, unless it can sell some travesty of them for money, denies that they exist at all. In this way, a debased version of the old working class becomes the model for the new poor – a sorry caricature of the way many of the old poor managed to live in dignity and hope. Dignity and hope are denied them now, because they reside not in human resources, but in money alone and what it can buy. Although when the old remember they are sometimes queru-lous and moralistic about the changes they have seen, the phenomenon is really neutral; part of the continuing dispossession and loss and violence to the working class, which remain, as ever, indispensable to the cold purposes of capitalism. If the material gains had not been neutralized of course, we'd have seen something much closer to socialism; and such a concession is not likely to be yielded so easily.

6

ABIGAIL RAGLAN, 82: A DISPLACED CHILD

ABIGAIL RAGLAN, 82, acknowledges these changes when she says, 'I've always been as poor as Job, but that's only in material things. I feel sorry for children today. They have nothing to challenge them, there's nothing that will bring out the best in them. They don't know the meaning of struggle, it's all given. We had a poor childhood, but we didn't know we were poor. We didn't suffer for it.'

Because of the uniqueness of Mrs Raglan's experience, she has some rare insights into the way we live. It sometimes needs people who grow up on the margin to gain an understanding that is denied those who live in a more spontaneous and less reflective way. Although she has always lived in the working class, she was never of it. To see her now in her council flat in a Southern country town, you could well imagine she has a tale to tell. You would think it was a story of hardship and poverty; but not the epic, of which nothing is discernible in the plain furniture, the photographs, the plants, the books – except that the copy of *Roots* and the collected works of Alexander Pope strike a slightly unfamiliar note in an old person's flat. A bowl of sweet peas scents the air. The children going home from school pass the open window. They are all eating, ice-cream, sweets, crisps, cans of Coke. Mrs Raglan looks at them and says, 'Comforts for all the things they will never know, never learn.'

'I lived with my brother, mother and grandmother in a little cottage in Dorking. I was always told that my father was dead. He was said to have died of consumption. Only I learned very early in life not to take anything for granted, not to accept what other people told me uncritically, but always to doubt. One day, it wasn't until I was in my 50s, I was speaking to my father's sister, and something she said made me suspicious. I said to her, "Is it really true that my father died of consumption?" And she said, "You should believe what your mother told you." Well that convinced me that he was still alive, and that it was my duty to find him. One thing I'd been told was that before he died, he had been living in Luton. I thought, "Well, if he is dead, I would like to place some flowers on his grave." I didn't like the idea of my father disappearing without there being a place where I could visit and pay my respects to him. Our mother had always talked to us of him with love, and it seemed strange that no one should know where the grave was. If you love someone as my mother loved my father, you want to keep up a shrine, a place where you can think of the loved one as resting. I wrote to the Citizens' Advice Bureau in Luton, asking if they could locate his grave for me. They wrote back saying they couldn't give me a grave number, because he didn't have one; he was alive and living at the following address. Well, I stood looking at this piece of paper for half an hour, I couldn't take it in. If you've been brought up with the idea of someone being dead, it comes as a terrible shock to find out they're alive after all. I made up my mind I'd go and see him. I went to Luton, found the street, and knocked on the door. He knew me at once, even though he hadn't seen me since I was two. He said, "I knew you would come. It's taken a long time, but I knew no daughter of mine would fail to find me." It took me to the age of 54 to find out that I had a father. And do you know, the five years I knew him before he died were five of the happiest years of my life. He introduced me to a different world. He took me to all the places I'd never been, the art galleries, the Tate, the Wallace Collection. I never knew such wonderful things existed as those he opened to me. He took me everywhere, even though by that time he was nearly 80. He was interested in literature and learning. He was descended from the same family as Alexander Pope.

'My mother had left him, he hadn't left her. She left him because of her pride and bitterness. She just went one day, took my brother and me with her. He came home and found us gone. He knew that when she took an idea into her head, she'd never go back on it. In fact, we'd only gone from Guildford to Dorking, but he wasn't to know that. It was a very brave thing for a woman to do: in 1899 women didn't just leave their husbands and take the children with them. But even so, she wasn't nearly as brave as her mother had been.

'We never saw anyone as children. No one ever came to the house. We had no visitors, no real friends. My brother and I were constant companions to each other. He was a year younger than I was. We quarrelled a lot, but we were always together. We used to go and gather turnips out of the fields if we felt hungry, we used to help ourselves to pig-nuts. I don't know how we found out what you could eat and what you couldn't. We ate cow parsley, the root, and even yew-berries, which are supposed to be poisonous; but if you eat the berry and throw away the pip, they're lovely. We'd gather bluebells and anemones in Glory Woods; and I used to love to climb trees. What a wonderful feeling it was, to be at the top of the slenderest trees, with the wind swaying them as it came across the open fields. It gives you such a sense of exhilaration. Children who've not had such a childhood don't know what they've missed. We used to wander the woods and fields freely.

'We loved and respected our mother. She didn't have to discipline us. She always kept a dog-whip above the door, but she never had to use it. My brother and I had to work at home, help with the chores, clean the knives, do the hearth, sweep and scrub. She was very open with us. She always encouraged us to tell her everything, which we did; and then she would patiently explain to us anything we didn't understand. We once saw a man and a woman in the fields together; they seemed to be fighting and struggling. We said to her, "Was he trying to kill her?" She said, "No. Sit there, and I'll tell you." And she told us, quietly, very straightforward, very frankly. There weren't many children who received instruction like that, because at that time people were very closed and reticent about such things.

'You can judge how brave my grandmother was when I tell you what happened to her. She was very religious, a Methodist. One Sunday, she went to a Methodist Hall in Croydon, and she heard the preacher there, a lay preacher; and she was so moved by him, his words, his face, everything about him, that she fell in love with him on the spot. She said to herself, "This is the man for me." And she stayed behind after the service, to meet him; and her feelings were evidently returned, because they were married not long afterwards.

'This man, my grandfather, was the son of a member of the ruling caste in Zanzibar. Of course, as a result of her love for this man, she was completely cut off from the rest of her family, isolated from all the life she had known, the respectable background she had come from. This was in the middle years of the last century, when even the sight of a black face was a remarkable event in the quiet streets of Croydon.'

From an old envelope Mrs Raglan takes a copy of her grandfather's marriage certificate. It is dated August 18th, 1870; faded dark blue paper, the handwriting in perfect copperplate. It reads: John Springfield, age 23. Father's name: Jumbaloowalee. Father's occupation: a chief in Zanzibar.

'We heard the story from my grandmother when we were quite small. My brother was always darker than I was, but we knew we were both set apart from other children. Of course when we knew the story we were thrilled. The only thing that makes me sad today is that my son doesn't want his boy to know about it. I'm sure he would be as proud as I am if he knew; and I'm sure he'll find out, although of course I can't say anything.

'So my grandfather was the son of a chief of the island of Zanzibar. All the children of this chief had been warned about playing outside of the compound, because of the danger from slavers. But there this boy was one day, picking fruit, when darkness suddenly came. Some hands reached out of the darkness and grabbed him, and he was taken off onto a slave ship. It was a Portuguese vessel. He remembered lying there in water and filth with a lot of other young men and children, all chained together. But he realized that for some reason, he hadn't been shackled like the others. He was wearing his linen robe, and they must have guessed from that that they had made a mistake, he was the son of a chief. He had also been warned that he must never, never eat white man's bread, because to do so would be to break caste. But while he was in this miserable state, he did eat a crust; he was more or less forced to do so; which meant he would never be able to go back home again.

'When they discovered they had the son of a chief on board, they knew they couldn't take him as a slave. They ripped open his stomach, from groin to chest, and then threw him out on the mud of the riverbank or the seashore, wherever it was, to die. But an old woman from the household had seen him be taken. She had followed the ship upriver to the spot where they threw him out. And she took him up from the water, and stitched up the wound in his stomach with fibre, and bound it with leaves, so that he didn't die. She fed him and looked after him until he recovered. For the rest of his life he had the scar – one side of his stomach was half an inch higher than the other. But it saved his life. It happened that Dr Livingstone was sailing round the island at that time, and he heard of this boy and his story, and he took him on board with him. He could wave to his people from the boat, but because of that crust of bread, he was cut off from them for ever.

'Dr Livingstone was a missionary and a Christian as well as an explorer. So my grandfather became a Christian and was brought up as a Christian. He went round with Livingstone for a while, but the doctor was growing sick, and not long afterwards, he fell ill and died. Grandfather was put into the Royal Navy. It was very rare for a coloured man to go into the Royal Navy at that time; but he was trained there to be a captain's valet. In spite of his status, the only thing that a black man could conceivably do was be a servant. It would never have occurred to them that he was fit for anything else. But at least a servant is a step higher than a slave.

'The ship he was on was the *Victoria*. He went to America with it. The ship docked at Springfield – and I think this was very unjust – when it arrived there, the captain said "Now John, I'm going to name you John Springfield." They even took his name away from him. There it is on the certificate – Jumbaloowalee. From then on he became John Springfield. He remained in America and became a preacher. He went all over America preaching against slavery, at meetings, missions, everywhere. Eventually he was brought back to England by Wilberforce, and he went all over this country as well, telling his story. He did live to see slavery abolished of course, while he was still young. I think my grandmother fell in love with him because he was so alone; I think she gathered him to her out of pity as much as anything else.

'But she adored him. In due course they had a daughter, my mother. She went to a good school, but she was a most unhappy person. As long as her father was still there, yes, she was all right. But after her father died – which he did when he was 44 – she turned against everything and everybody. She had been very badly treated by people here because of her colour. She used to go home and cry at the treatment that had been dealt her at school by the other girls. She was obviously an object of great curiosity; and she always retained this sense of being apart. A lonely person, so cut off; she had no companionship as a child. She died when she was 44 – the same age as her father.

She died of cancer. I believe she worried so much, it's as if the cancer came from all the bitterness inside her.

'I hear people around here, there's a lot of racist talk. They don't know my story. But I never let it pass, I always challenge them. My grandfather never wanted to come to this country. He was quite happy where he was. He should have inherited his father's position. He was to have worn the robe after his father died, but of course it was denied him. He wasn't an unhappy man. He'd been taught to make boots and shoes, and he had his workshop in Guildford where he used to make ladies' shoes and button boots. The ladies would come to his shop, they loved to listen to stories of the beautiful land he'd left, his childhood and how he used to play with lion cubs.

'He was a lovely man. Their door was never shut. My mother worshipped him. He would always invite any old tramp or traveller in for a meal. She was always getting home and finding some poor scrap of humanity at their table. One day an old tramp came to the house; it was a freezing cold day in February. My grandfather said to him, "Have you got a shirt on?" And the old man said, "No." So he said, "Have mine, it's clean. It'll keep you warm." It was a flannel shirt, and the tramp put it on. Grandfather put another one on, but it was still damp from the wash. He got a chill, it turned to pneumonia and he died. He gave up his shirt to a white man, an outsider; and he died.

'My mother was bitter. You can't get through to a person who is bitter in life. Unhappy people you may, but never a bitter person. She adored us children. We were only babies when she left our father. After I'd found him again, I said to him, "Did you ever say anything to her about her colour?" Because she was so proud. She was a darling really, my mother, she had a heart of gold. But nobody liked her. I think she may have feared the children might not like it if she shared us with her husband. That was why she left. It was a sacrifice. As a child, she used to go home sobbing to her father, "Why was I born, why was I born?" If you've been lonely as a child, it isn't easy to get close to people when you grow up. I think it was people's unkindness that killed her. She didn't want to live. When my brother and I were 14 or so, she said to us, "You can look after yourselves now. I've done all I can." And from that time, she gradually went down and down, until she died.

'It didn't hurt my brother and me. We were proud of our

blood. We fought it out if anybody said anything to us. I've had fights over it, pulled girls' hair, rolled on the ground. The first day my brother went to school, he'd had three fights before dinner time.

'I love my grandfather, even though I never knew him. I can almost see him. It's very strange, these last few years I've thought more about my grandfather than anyone else . . . I can picture him, I can hear his voice. He's very real. He lived for us children, even though he died before we were born. Love that is set free into the world, it lives on long after people are dead.

'Although my mother brooded, and we grew up in a solitary way, my brother and I became very independent, self-sufficient. The only time my mother was really happy was when the minstrels used to come to the local theatre. Everybody in the town knew about her, and whenever the minstrels came, they'd always come and look her up; and within a few minutes, she'd be playing the piano and they'd all be singing together. Then she was like another person, she was transformed. Them Golden Slippers, There Once Was a Nigger his Name was Uncle Ned, When the Roll is Called up Yonder . . . And then of course our mother would sing to us . . . I bet you don't know this one

> (Sings) There's a coon and a yaller gal a-sitting on a rail,
>   Underneath that ole umbrella,
>   And the coon to the yaller gal is telling of a tale
>   Underneath the old umbrella . . .
>   That coon done put his umbrella away,
>   The niggers ask why, that coon don't say,
>   But he can't forget the fun he had that day
>   Underneath the old umbrella.

'I feel convinced that my grandson will find out the story of his forebears. He and I get on well. I'm sure he'll be like me, he won't just accept everything he's told. He'll be proud to know one day, just as I am. I'm proud of my heritage, I'm proud of my grandfather and my African blood.'

7

LILLY, A PERMANENT CHILD

LILLY HAS BEEN a child all her life. She is now in her 60s. Her mother, full of an aggressive energy that had no outlet, reduced her husband to subservience early in the marriage. He worked for 50 years in a tannery, a countryman who always spoke with regret of harvest and pig-killing time, of his father, 'who could turn a pig's belly in three minutes', of his mother, carrying great wicker baskets of purple elderberries at wine-making time. He continued to work until he was well into his 80s, when the only way he could get to work was on the bicycle he had ridden all his life, because arthritis made it impossible to walk to the pub, where he cleaned the lavatories twice a day. Silent, frugal, self-effacing, he was loved by his daughter; but their relationship was invaded, commuted by the power and violence of the mother.

Lilly was brought up to be frail, and therefore completely dependent on her mother. There was always something wrong with her, never defined, but which, it was understood, only her mother could deal with. She was a shy and confused child, afraid of other people, tongue-tied and secretive, slow but not stupid. Her mother annexed her emotionally, and all her perceptions of the outside world were filtered through her mother. She became an extension and, later, a sort of emissary of her mother's feelings. From the start, she was her mother's companion, servant, scapegoat and support. Her mother had been the eldest of 11 children. Lilly was an only child; born just when the majority of the working class had discovered birth control. This change was to have an important bearing on the lives of working-class children (or perhaps it was a symptom of deeper social changes anyway), just as it had had on the children of those in higher social strata previously. Where children had grown almost casually, and the death of children could be greeted with grief but acceptance ('They were too thick to thrive,' said one old lady in Gloucestershire, talking of her 15 children, seven of whom died in infancy); where the differentiation of their character had seemed sometimes rather rough and ready – one child the bright one, another the wrong'un, another soft-hearted or jealous, and one the 'dilling' of the family, as my Grandma called my mother (a term meaning the weakest one, a term used generally of a litter of farmyard animals), now their unique and irreplaceable features began to be of major importance.

Between Lilly and her mother there grew a profound (and, later, resented) dependency, from which the father was excluded. He always circled anxiously around them, finding no way into the mysterious bond which seemed to unite the two women. It was a powerful collusion, on the mother's terms. Lilly looked to her mother for all cues and responses and feelings. The mother secured the daughter to her more firmly by the threat of her own ill-health: she claimed she had a bad heart, and any gesture of independence on Lilly's part called forth the threat of an immediate attack. She lived well into her 90s.

Mother and daughter lived in a male-dominated society. There was always felt to be something 'masculine' about the mother, with her love of pubs, racing, darts and beer. Lilly's schooling was intermittent; she seldom completed a full week at a time. This was also to be the pattern of her working life, a succession of unskilled and casual jobs – pea- and fruit-picking, lifting potatoes, cleaning, work in laundries and service jobs. The work was generally cut short by the mother's need of her; and in aggregate she spent many years unemployed. In her early life she was like a premature adult, with no childhood companions; and later, she seemed like a retarded child. Somehow, she was neither child nor woman, but lived in a twilight between the two, from which her mother made sure she never emerged. It was this uncertainty about herself that everybody noticed, the confusion if anybody spoke to her, the inability to respond to anyone as an equal. If she saw anyone coming, she would cross the street rather than talk to him or her. She wouldn't go out on her own.

Mother and daughter didn't acknowledge their private dependency. It was still concealed by the absence of any need for social emancipation of children from their parents in that generation. There were in many working-class families unmarried middle-aged men who could still say quite unself-consciously that their Mam was their only sweetheart, and married daughters who wept bitterly when they had to leave their mothers, even if they were only going two or three streets away, and who spent much of their time back in their childhood home. Relationships remained close and unexamined. Poverty still guaranteed that what bound people was stronger than the things that divided them. Even though people quarrelled frequently and violently with their nearest kin, the ties were seldom broken.

The life Lilly and her mother led was a public one: the pub and the street. Their great delight was the racecourse. They went on coach trips to the races all over the country. Reckless and improvident, they would win a few pounds one day, lose it the next, stop at a pub on the way home for a few drinks and discuss the next day's race card. The interior of their house was barren and cheerless: patched leather chairs, a deal table covered with newspaper, bare lino with a greasy rag-rug, a bag of coal in front of a hearth covered with coal-dust. Lilly's mother would sit with a magnifying glass over the *Sporting Life* or *Daily Mail*, cutting a raw onion with a pen-knife to eat with a bacon sandwich, while Lilly ran up to the bookmaker's to place a couple of bob each way on whatever they fancied. Whenever they could afford it, they went for holidays to racecourses, Wetherby or Plumpton, in company with all the people who shared their semi-public existence, 'pals', Lilly's mother called them, the easy intimacy of people without surnames whom they met through drink or the races. They continued an archaic, and probably quite ancient, form of popular social life.

Whenever they went away, Lilly's father would clean and decorate the house, spread fresh newspaper on the table, clear out the ash from the clogged grate, scrub the step and clean the cracked red flags of the kitchen floor. Sometimes he would take his bicycle out into the country and visit the Saxon Church at Earl's Barton, or the site of the battle of Naseby, the village where he was born.

Lilly grew up with no opportunity to express herself at all, subservient in everything to the stronger woman, included as a matter of course in all her activities, with no concession to her childhood – an ancient attitude which persisted until quite recently in the poorest working class. She failed to develop a personality of her own, but imitated her mother's responses, her attitudes, even her way of speech and walking. Even in the less dynamic section of the working class, she looked slightly quaint in the 1920s; they said she was 'an old-fashioned child'.

As Lilly grew older, much of her repressed energy went into copying sequences of popular songs in close handwriting in Woolworth notebooks. She did this throughout the '30s, transcribing the lyric of each song like poetry, until she had filled hundreds of books. She sat under the yellow gas-mantle of the little rented house, solemnly copying

> Little bits of powder, little drops of paint,
> Help to make a gal, look like what she ain't.

She went with her mother to the local cinema every Friday for almost half a century, the same cinema, whatever film was showing, at the same time every Friday, with no regard for the scheduled programme. They loved the music hall, and went into the pub which the theatricals used; they applauded every show until the theatre closed in 1958, by which time it was showing revues called 'My Bare Lady' and 'Yes We Have No Pyjamas'. Lilly's mother loved scandal, and she knew of all the murders and attempted murders of the neighbourhood stretching back to the early years of the nineteenth century. She would hold her pub audiences spellbound with her accounts of brutal slaughter. 'And when they went to arrest him, he was working in the meat-market, and cutting up the meat with the same bloody knife he'd disembowelled his missis with . . .' 'Anyroad, it turned out, they buried her in the wrong grave. And the real Mrs Kingston was walking through the churchyard one day, and she saw the headstone that told of her own death.' And years later, Lilly would repeat them, word for word. 'And he buried her in the orchard; only the dog used to go and howl on her grave, until at the finish he killed the dog as well; and that was how they found him out.'

When she was in her 40s Lilly played for one of the local pub darts' teams; and she even went on one or two excursions to away matches unaccompanied by her mother. It was on one of these outings that she met the first man with whom she ever had anything like an independent relationship. He initiated her into sex. Her mother found out that this man had been in prison, and that he already had a wife. More than this, she caught pubic lice from the encounter, and the mother so terrified her with stories of the consequences of sex, that Lilly willingly abandoned her one attempt at an adult relationship. She couldn't overthrow the control that had crushed and comforted her for so many years.

The last 15 of the 60 years they spent together saw a decline into demoralization. Lilly's father died. They had gone away for a weekend to the races, while he papered the living-room. He fell from the trestle, and died a few weeks later. When he was gone the house was no longer kept clean. Lilly's mother became deaf and more frail; and she kept up a monologue, not about the old days, but about anticipated excursions and new pals. As she became less mobile, Lilly was even more obviously an extension of her mother's will, doing her bidding, fetching and carrying. Lilly grew fat. Her mother got dirtier. The house fell into greater disrepair. It had once been a substantial house, with three steps up to the front door and an ornamental grille at the window, a letterbox with 'Letters' in Gothic characters on the flap, a white china door-handle and a wrought-iron shoe-scraper in the form of two storks facing each other. The waxed paper in the hallway was torn, and heaps of plaster crumbled from the wall and gathered on the worn lino. Some engraved panels in the kitchen door filtered a red- and blue-coloured light into the dark back kitchen, where there was only a shallow fireclay sink and an old gas-stove. The kitchen opened onto the lavatory, which was simply an enamel cone through a deal board, and which had to be flushed with buckets of water.

The old woman sat in her chair, pinafore and hat always on. At times she became confused. The grime never left her neck and fingers. The outings ceased, except to the pub and betting shop. They spent more on drink. The old square clock was sold to a man who happened to knock at the door one day. Mother talked with gusty enjoyment about death. She had seen the undertaker in the churchyard, and he had raised his hat a little higher than usual, but she realized he hadn't raised it to her, but to death whom he had seen grinning over her shoulder. She quoted epitaphs she had read and remembered:

> Time was I stood where thou dost now,
> And view'd the dead as thou dost me;
> Ere long thou'lt lie as low as I,
> And others stand and look on thee.

The mother embodied residual aspects of a radical working-class tradition. She hated parsons, employers, authority and charity. She and her daughter lived out a primitive hedonism – very much out of keeping with the philosophy of the aspiring and respectable working class, but in certain ways the model which was modernized and made more general by the coming of the consumer society. But if Lilly's experience anticipated the future in one way, in the repressed relationship with the mother, she belonged to a much older tradition of poverty.

When she was 92, the mother fell in the street and broke her thigh. She was taken to hospital and not expected to live. She was cleaned and fed and, against all expectation, recovered. She began to sit out of bed for a few hours each day, enjoyed her meals, drank a Guinness. Lilly began by visiting her every day, but gradually her visits became less frequent. It was clear that her mother was not going to die. Lilly had her mother's pension book; she began drawing her money and spending it. At last, there was no longer any reason for the old woman to remain in the hospital. Lilly was asked to make arrangements for her mother to come home. Lilly said she wouldn't. This was the first time Lilly had ever been alone. She was over 60.

Her mother's younger sisters were outraged. The hospital social worker was concerned. Of course she must return home. There was nowhere else for her to go. Her mother's surviving sisters were too old to look after her. But inside Lilly, a belated and doomed flicker of independence moved. She said, 'Why should I? She's had her life, and she's had mine as well. Now it's my turn. I've never had any freedom. I'm glad to be away from her.' She caught something of the changed feeling of the time, and it caused her to see her life in a perspective she had never known. Until this time, she had never spent a single night apart from her mother. She was going to the pub every day. She had met people on her own account, even some men, Irish and black workers who lived in lodgings, many of them lonely and unsettled. 'What life have I had?' she asked plaintively, 'I've never had a boyfriend before. I don't care. If people think I'm wicked, let them. I can't look after her, I can't nurse her. I've got no experience of nursing. I haven't got any experience of anything.' Her mother was removed to the geriatric hospital. In the now elderly daughter, with her hair grey and in a roll round her head in a style fashionable in the 40s, her pebble glasses and sad wounded eyes, the fire of adolescent revolt seemed to have been kindled. She had had no conception of growing up, but had lived all her life in the terror of a loss that would have delivered her.

There was something desperate and clumsy in the late attempt at independence. She was doubly victim: not only had she been caught up in an already archaic culture, but her belief in it had been destroyed.

The mother remained in the geriatric ward until she died some months later. Lilly was with her when she died, and held her hand. During her time in hospital, the mother had begged her sisters not to publish the news of her death in the local paper; she had requested them to have the funeral from their house, because she didn't want the people Lilly was mixing with to discover her address. She feared they would prey on her, even for the sake of the pension and the few pounds of burial money she had put by, and the small insurance policy.

On the day of the funeral Lilly arrived at her aunts' house only just before the funeral car was due. She was a little tipsy, aggressive and confused. 'When the funeral's over, I'm going to have a drink with her. That's what she would have wanted. I'm like her, I'm a chip off the old block. She wouldn't have wanted a lot of fuss, a lot of weeping and wailing. I'm doing what she would have wanted. I'm just the same as she was. I like life.' 'It's a pity you don't take after your father', said her aunt. 'Don't you try and tell me what to do. I've been told what to do all my life.' Lilly was wearing wellington boots and an old coat over her house-smock. Her hands were grained with dirt, the nails black. She was carrying an old raincoat. 'You won't need your raincoat,' the aunt says. 'Oh, is it indoors?' To me she says, 'I know you're on my side. I don't care what they say, there's been too many bossy women in this family. I don't care about any of them now. Anyway, wherever she is, whether she's looking up or looking down at me, I know she'd approve, my dear old mother. She went to the races the day after Dad died, and I'll do the same. I don't know where she's gone, but wherever it is, she won't mind. When I see her again, she'll tell me I done the right thing.'

The limousine stops outside the house. Lilly gets in with difficulty. There are no flowers. At the crematorium, the service is brief. The undertaker sits in a kind of pew at the front, facing the scant group in the chapel. The coffin is committed to the flames; and the door of the chapel is opened immediately, to indicate to the participants that the ceremony is finished. As she gets into the car, Lilly says to the undertaker, 'You're a good man. You must have helped many a lame dog over the stile.' To the minister she says, 'Thank you for all your kindness,' even though he has not until now spoken to her.

The car drops her at the bottom of the street where she lives. I walk home with her. She lets her arm rest limply in mine. She reaches for her key, which is tied on a piece of string round her neck. She doesn't want to leave the house where she has lived for 40 years, even though the lavatory is blocked, and there is a hole in the roof, which makes the upper part of the house uninhabitable. At least it is close to the betting shop and the pub. Inside, the cat has given birth to four kittens, which have the run of the house. They have not been trained, and the smell is overpowering. 'They are my family,' she says. The budgie has died in its cage. 'What shall I do with it?' Lilly asks.

Lilly is old without having ever been adult. We kiss awkwardly. The door slams, and she disappears into the sombre shell of her mother's house.

If Lilly's experience seems appalling to us now, this partly reflects our tendency to colonize time in such a way that the latest moment appears to us to be the moment of greatest enlightenment. We look back at her, and she becomes a useful reference point for us to measure the distance we have travelled. We can only pity her for the extinguished spirit and limited life. And it is true that she was mutilated and reduced. But it was far less painful to her when she was a child and young woman, because she grew in a context in which self-expression was no part of a child's purpose. She lived in a wider and more secure network of people. She grew up without self-awareness. She was simply a girl who stayed close to her mother. What is wretched is the combination of having been crushed then and being alone now. To have lived through the decay of the values in which she was brought up is what gives her experience its poignancy. She grew up in an atmosphere in which the needs and wants of children were not considered important; but to have survived into a world where these have become a source of

endless anxiety and concern – not to mention profit – gives her
the sense of being an archaism, a sort of human fossil. As the
sense of inescapable destiny of work and want relaxed its hold
over working-class life, so the raising of children became less
concerned with schooling them for hardship and struggle, and
permitted the emphasis on personal and psychological satisfactions. It seemed to be all gain; but the context in which these
changes occurred was not neutral. The determinants of identity
only appeared to change from outside forces – i.e. work and
poverty – to internal ones – appetites, personal needs, individual wants. It is essentially a *social* change, and it is an illusion
to think it represents freedom, because the context in which it
has happened ensures that self-expression for many working-
class children means the expression of a self that has been
defined by the market-place and by what can be bought for
money. And that is as inescapable and destructive an influence
as the old culture of work and poverty ever was. But because it
seemed to promise an answer to all the earlier hardships, an
end of the disciplines and denials working people have always
known, the change looked like a liberation. People were all the
more ready to efface themselves, give their children over to the
influences of a culture that appeared to be the opposite of that
which parents had previously done their best to shelter them
from.

Of course these changes are part of a long-term process
which continues, they are not simply an event that can be
dated. Some sections of the working class resist them longer.
Some families embrace them only reluctantly and partially; for
many, older satisfactions remain. But they spread, and the
market-place usurps more and more of those areas in which
people had been sufficient to each other. It creates dependency
on its products, undermines autonomy and devalues all that is
valuable in the working-class tradition in a way that poverty
could not, because poverty created resistance and opposition.
The seductions of the market-place are immediate and appear
benign, and parents come to seem, not protectors, but irritants,
obstacles with their never adequate money, who prevent the
enjoyment of all the good things that the market-place holds
out to the children. This is not, of course, to argue in favour of
that older poverty: the disregard of children and their sensitivi-
ties was too cruel. It is the oscillation between these extremes

that is damaging: from the paralyzing disciplines of the old poverty to the numbing and impotent liberation of the new dependency on the market-place. All balance is lost, and the real needs of children are obscured by the one thing that survives – the system that subordinates human life to the power of money, and the tributes it exacts according to the changing context. The other thing that endures is the extent to which children are loved; this continues now, as ever, to shield children from the ravages of capitalism on human lives. It doesn't redeem, but it tempers, and that is constant. The effects of brutalizing social values – whether primary poverty or over-reliance on the consolations that money buys – scar more seriously those deprived of parental affection.

8

JERRY WALSH: THE REPEATING PATTERN

JERRY WALSH WAS born in 1920. He lives in a maisonette, an enclave of new building scooped out of a gap in a decaying Victorian suburb of North London. The housing development is a series of identical blocks in dark red brick, with staircases of concrete, bleak and functional. Inside, however, the flat is a surprise. Mr Walsh has painted all the walls with a scene of beechwoods, so that it looks as though he is living in the middle of a forest; great tapering silver tree trunks with autumn foliage; badgers, red squirrels and deer look out from the grass. The paintings cover the whole wall, so that even the light switches are incorporated into the picture. Mr Walsh has retired from his job early. As well as the murals, he paints on velvet: flowers, woodland scenes, birds, all executed on black velvet, which gives the pictures an extraordinary depth and dramatic effect.

'My mother died two years after I was born; as a result of complications that set in with my birth. I don't remember her at all. All I know is that round about 1923, my father was knocking around with a woman who was a cook in domestic service, and he married her. This woman already had an illegitimate daughter – it was said, by a previous employer – and she married my father to give this daughter a home. This girl, Olive, was 18 months younger than I was.

'I was the youngest of our mother's six children. At birth I had pneumonia and pleurisy. Although I was born in January, they didn't register my birth until some months later, because they didn't think that I would survive.

'My father and stepmother had a child, a boy, a year after they were married. For me, that was when the trouble began. The oldest ones in my own family were already grown up – the oldest brother was almost the same age as the stepmother. He joined up – I think my father wanted him out of the house. I don't think the stepmother had a very good reputation. The next brother had been adopted by a wealthy woman. He was a good-looking boy, brainy, and this woman was going to put him in a public school; but when he knew our mother had died, he came home and took a job in a bakery to help out. Then at 16, this woman sponsored him to go abroad, and he emigrated to Canada. He never actually lived with the stepmother, so he had no idea of what I suffered. Then came my sister, and another brother just starting work, and a brother four years older than I was. Then came the stepsister Olive, and then my half-brother. But to all intents and purposes the family consisted of my older brother, me, the stepsister and the new half-brother.

'When my father married my real mother, he was a serving soldier stationed in Salisbury. Her parents disowned my mother. They were rather respectable, and my father had already been charged a couple of times with being absent without leave. He was a bit of a black sheep, and anyway, the army was considered the lowest form of life, even though he was in the Third Hussars. He just used to go absent: he'd go and join a travelling circus that came to town, anything. Basically, he could never accept his responsibilities, and that's how he stayed all his life. Whenever he went off, he would just disappear, and of course his allowances from the army stopped and my mother half starved. My father was a rogue.

'He had a Crown and Anchor board: that is, a board with six squares on it, with the emblem of a crown in one square, an anchor in another, and the four card suits in the others. People used to put their money on one of the squares, and my father shook a dice, and the number on the dice corresponding to the square took the money on it. It was illegal, of course. But my father fiddled it as well: he used to hide the dice in his hand, outside the shaker; and he would shake his hand and make the dice rattle as if it was inside the container, although it was really striking against the outside. People would place their bets – I think it was 3-1 on the crown, 2-1 on the anchor, and the rest even money. And he made sure that the square which had the least money on it always won. Occasionally, to allay suspicion, he would let somebody else win. But all the money he made out of it was spent in the pub. He was a boozer, like a lot of the men at that time.

'My father had a favourite phrase. He used to say he believed "in stock before money". That meant he believed in having kids before he had the money to feed them, because as soon as they came to working age, they would keep him. That was the illusion of a lot of working families. My old man was an idle sod. When he was left with six kids, he got his discharge from the forces. But there was no money. He did casual jobs. He would go and buy chestnuts and roast them, and sell hot chestnuts in the market. Or he'd go to Woolworth's and buy cheap jellies and sell them as hot drinks. The family never saw any of the money. He was a spiv.

'I heard this story from the others – it was before I can remember, while my mother was still alive. Friday used to be pay day for the workers then, and that was the night he used to do his Crown and Anchor board. He used to win quite a lot of money – naturally, he'd fiddled it. The first thing he'd do is come home and shove a load of notes in an old shoe of my mother's, and then he'd hide this shoe, and take out just as much as he needed for his boozing. He used to come home blind drunk. My mother would go round his pockets – anything he'd got left, she used to have it, it was practically the only money she saw. He'd always acted a bit mysteriously about this bloody shoe; my mother didn't know what he used it for, but she often wondered. One day he came in and she watched secretly. When he'd put his money in it, he hid it in the copper. This was Friday, and the copper was lit up only on Mondays to do the washing. It was never used over the weekend. When he'd hidden the shoe, he went off drinking. Mother took out this shoe, took out the money and lit up the copper. The shoe was burnt. The old man comes home drunk as usual. Next morning he goes to the copper and finds it full of dead ash, and she says, "What you doing?" He said, "Nothing. I was just surprised that you did your washing on Friday instead of Monday." Years later one of my brothers let it out, that she had burnt the shoe and kept the money. They had decent food for a week or two after that. It was the first time my mother had ever watched what he did with his money. And he never mentioned it afterwards.

'My mother died in the workhouse. She died of cancer of the womb. Now she would have had a hysterectomy, and she would almost certainly have survived.

'I was consistently mistreated by my stepmother. I was disparaged, rejected and set apart, not only from my stepsister, but from the half-brother who was two or three years younger than I was. They were always given preferential treatment over me. I was an outsider. So was my older brother, but I was only concerned with myself at the time; and he was old enough to go out and find his own friends. I had to do all the chores. I had to wash up after every meal. I had to go and gather dandelions to feed the rabbits my father kept – he used to sell them as one of his side-lines. I had to do the shopping on my way home from school, I used to go and get 4 penn'orth of bacon bits, the pieces that fell off the bacon cutting machine. When I was ten, I was getting up at six o'clock to go round to the baker's for a sackful of stale bread, which was sold off cheap in the early morning.

'I was a puny kid. I always had ill health – that's why I've retired early; and it's all because I was so badly treated as a child. I used to get impetigo and had to go to hospital for treatment. They used to tear the scab off till they got to the raw flesh, and then put powder on the sore.

'The walls of our bedroom were bug-ridden. One night my brother lit a candle, and we counted 15 bugs in the bed. When we told our stepmother, she wouldn't believe us. We kept the dead bugs in a matchbox. We had dirty old army blankets on the bed which were never cleaned.

'If ever I went out, I had to take this younger brother with me. He was a rotten sod. He used to report everything I did to my stepmother. I got a hiding every time, however trivial his tales were. Once she hit me because he told her I'd picked up a piece of coloured glass in the street.

'I was made to feel inferior all the time. My stepmother's parents had a shop in Canterbury, and they used to send a parcel of goodies every so often, but they were only for her children, not for me. In these parcels there'd be Ovaltine, butter and sweets. And at suppertime, the Ovaltine would come out, while I was given the old cocoa. My father and the stepchildren had butter and I had margarine. I always felt there must be something wrong with me. I was always ill, my teeth were bad. I always had the free treatment at the dentist's, which meant teeth were taken out without anaesthetic, and I remember the nurse was as brutal and indifferent. I was segregated from my stepmother's children. The clothing I had was the cast-offs of her former employer's children. She went up there occasionally when the master was away, and the other servants would give her some of these old clothes. These children went to a posh college; and so the clothes I wore were the worn-out uniforms of this school I never went to. I felt conspicuous. I thought it must be obvious to everybody that I couldn't possibly go to such a school.

'She would give me a bashing if I got a hole in my clothes. She kept a stick in the cupboard. If the half-brother's report was serious, out came this stick. It was only used on me. I became so that I couldn't cry. However painful it was, I never cried. Sometimes, after I'd been beaten, my half-brother would kick me to make me cry, but I didn't. I used to wet the bed. I even used to wet my trousers at school. When I got home she would say, "Let's have a look at your trousers," and if they were wet it meant another hiding. I felt that my half-brother was always watching me. My older brother used to get bashed by my father. But he could always avoid the worst of home by going off with his friends. When he was 14 my brother had a serious accident. He was always fascinated by traction engines. Near us was a flour mill, and he used to go off and watch these engines in the mill yard. One day he was standing by the wall, and one of these engines mounted the pavement, and he saw it was coming towards him. He was so terrified, he couldn't move. The engine caught his hand against the wall and took half his hand off, two fingers and half the palm. He had it stitched up, and the company admitted liability. He got £250 in trust in compensation for when he was 21. The stepmother had access to the interest on this money, she talked the solicitor into it somehow. The idea of the money was so that he should have special schooling to help him overcome the disability and learn a trade. Needless to say, he never got any special training. When he was 21 he went to get the money. He had to sign a document, and he didn't find out till afterwards that he'd signed away £50 to the stepmother and £10 to the solicitor; that was on top of all the interest he'd been done out of. So all he got was £190. He left home and went to work on the railways. Eventually, he became a draughtsman. He was still called up for service, in spite of having only half a hand. He worked on demolition in the Royal Engineers, and his job at Dunkirk was to blow up bridges; he got out on one of the last ships to leave Dunkirk. He was clever, and had a good brain. He managed to make a success of his life.

'My stepmother always wanted to humiliate me. Little

things, but to a child they can poison your whole life. My eldest
sister was married, and her husband always felt sorry for me.
He gave me a cricketer's cap; but the stepmother decided I
should wear it for school. The boys all laughed at me. I got
mocked without mercy. In the end I refused to wear it. So she
made me wear one of my sister's hats instead. She stood in the
street and watched me all the way up the road. That was the
only time my father ever intervened and took my part.

'My father always claimed to have heart trouble. He was
permanently on the panel. The panel man used to come once a
month to make sure he wasn't faking. The stepmother would
say, "Oh, he had an attack a couple of days ago." He used to
feign these heart attacks, it terrified us all. He would clutch his
chest and faint. My brother always knew he was shamming.
One day when he was in the middle of one of these attacks, he
stuck a pin in his backside. He jumped up in the air, the most
miraculous recovery you ever saw. But we were always told to
keep our mouths shut whenever the panel man came. Occasionally my father took unofficial short-term jobs. He got about £1
a week from the Public Assistance. But before you were allowed
even that you had to get rid of any decent stuff in the house; half
the furniture went before we got a penny.

'I was always artistically minded. I won a contest when I was
14, to be apprenticed to a signwriter, grainer and gilder. I was
overjoyed. I ran home and said, "I've got an apprenticeship."
"You can't take that. I can't keep you on five bob a week. I've
seen a job going at 7s 6d a week as an errand boy to a florist." I
had to take it. The man who took the apprenticeship I should
have had owns the business now. The signwriter had no sons;
and he left the business to him.

'I was a frail kid, and I set out on this bike with boxes of
flowers for delivery. I had to go to the station, collect the flowers
and take them to the shop. One of my jobs was mossing
wreaths. There was a didicoy who used to bring a sack of moss;
a lot of it was wet grass and leaves, and I had to sort all this out
and put the moss in the wreaths. I'd always got septic fingers
and blood-poisoning from it.

'I was always a nervous child. I was afraid to come home
from school, because I never knew what the half-brother might
have told her. I used to stay out all day when I could, and steal
food from market stalls and bakehouses. One night the

stepmother hit my brother over the head with her shoe, and the wound needed five stitches. He had to tell father that he had fallen and hit his head against the bedpost. He was 14. The next day he went to work. He was working as an errand boy, and his boss sent him home because he looked so bad. When he got home, the stepmother made him go back to work, because she was afraid he wouldn't get paid for it.

'When my father was in drink, he got very sorry for himself, and sometimes had suicidal tendencies. "I'm going to drown myself in the docks," he used to say. When he didn't come home, I'd be dragged out of bed and be sent to look for him, through the docks. I'd be terrified I was going to see his body floating in the water. I'd generally find him crouching in one of the shelters by the cliffs.

'One day, coming home from school, I picked up a bit of green glass, to look through it. My half-brother reported it. By the time I got home I'd thrown it away, but I got such a bloody crash round the ears for it, straight to bed with no supper. I remember running up the stairs, with her running after me and hitting me. I was always terrified of the dark whenever I went upstairs. We had gas only on the ground floor, and a gas mantle only in the front room. Normally I went to bed with a candle; but on days when I was punished, I was sent off in the dark with no light. I always used to wait for my brother to come to bed before I ever dared go to sleep. I can remember what a cold draughty room it was. The curtains were always moving in the draught, and I was scared there was somebody trying to get in. One night, my fears got the better of me, and I screamed out. She came rushing up. I said, "There's someone there." She said, "That's the bogeyman coming to get you."

'Naturally, that does you damage. When I left school I didn't stop in one job. I worked in a flour mill, I worked in pubs, doing the cleaning and emptying the spittoons, I worked for a baker, working 12 hours a day, five and a half days a week. When the herring ships, the drifters, came in, I went down to the docks to pick up the fish that fell off the skips and overflowed the boxes. I could bring home up to two dozen herring each time. I used to go and get half a hundredweight of coal from the merchant's, which I had to carry home on my back. Often my back got skinned with the weight of it. At home, I was given a couple of slices of bread and marge in the morning, and then told not to come back at dinner-time, because there'd be nothing for me. I went down to the soup kitchen in wintertime. I got a bowl of soup and a hunk of bread. My parents never knew where I went.

'It has all left me with a feeling of inferiority that I can't overcome. When I was 16½, I went down the coal mines. She told me to tell them that I was 18, which was the youngest age at which you were supposed to go underground. I did what she told me. I was afraid to do anything else. There didn't seem to be any chance for me to survive on my own. I got a job in the Kent coalfield. I was on haulage, and I got £3 16s 9d a week; 6s 9d of that was water money – what you got paid for standing in water to work all day. I was allowed to keep five shillings of that wage. I was like a little rabbit, terrified of everything. I was more scared of staying at home than I was of going down the pit, and that's saying something.

'Everything contributed to this feeling of being apart, inferior. Whenever her brother came to visit, he always gave her children 2s before he left, and me a lousy penny. She told me that I ought to be bloody thankful I'd got even that.

'My stepsister showed some kindness to me. She would stick up for me on occasion. She sometimes used to comfort me like a mother. But if she gave me a sweet, I got clouted by her mother. I remember at Easter, my half-brother and stepsister had lovely coloured Easter eggs in a cup; I got a plain white one, inferior cheap chocolate. It was the same at Christmas – I got some paltry Woolworth toy, while my half-brother had a clockwork train. I didn't even dare look at his things. The boy used to eat his sweets in front of me. He loved to taunt me. He never did anything wrong. The reason why the stepmother sent me down the mines was to be able to keep him at school. He went into the RAF as an apprentice. He signed on for 27 years, became a pilot officer, and he had a substantial pension and a gratuity to look forward to. I've never seen his wife and kids. I've only seen him twice in adult life, both times at funerals. At the stepmother's funeral, the first thing he said to me was, "I apologize for all the hidings I got you as a child, and if you can find it in your heart to forgive me, please forgive me. It has been on my conscience for years." I couldn't help noticing that he waited till she was dead before he apologized. If he'd done it before she died, I might have been able to forgive him. But he waited till she could no longer hear him. My relatives all say I should forget it now. They say my parents have been dead a long while, they should be allowed to rest in peace. But its influence on me has lasted all my life long; it isn't something I can set aside. It has eaten into my soul. All the jobs I took for years, I fell down on them. I lacked the confidence to carry things through. I did inferior jobs with no skill, labouring.

'I got married when I was 23, and was grateful to get away in the end. But I was called up in August 1939, just before war broke out. I got 14 shillings a week with the Royal Engineers. After I'd been in a month, my stepmother applied for a dependant's allotment. I was still soft then, and I allowed them to stop eight shillings of that money, so with the ten bob they put to it, she got 18 shillings a week. This went on for 18 months, then I was notified that my stepmother was also drawing an allowance from my two older brothers. I was nearly court-martialled over it. I had to pay it all back. I was considered to have been a conspirator with her.

'I've always had misfortune follow me. I don't believe it's just chance. You attract mishaps; it's as if you're always ready for some disaster or other. In 1941 I had an accident, the sort of thing that could only happen to me. I was with the coastal searchlights, and I was in the engine room, unloading containers of paraffin. At two o'clock we went to the mess for dinner. It was the middle of winter, and there was an open fire in this mess room. The heat from this fire was very intense. We sat as far away from it as we could, right near the door. In the warmth, the paraffin on our clothes vaporized. This gunner came in and he lit a taper from the fire to light his fag. We said to him to keep away, but he said, "Garn, paraffin don't catch light," and as he said it, he held out this taper towards me to prove it. There was a sudden flame up and down my body; suddenly I was a big ball of flame. I ran out of the mess, and we were right at the edge of the cliff, so there was nothing to do but jump in the sea, a drop of about 30 feet. I couldn't swim, but I just jumped automatically. It was a low tide. Fortunately, I didn't struggle, I more or less let myself go. I was wearing battledress, overalls and a balaclava helmet. Somebody jumped in, and people on the cliff were throwing lifebelts. Somebody threw a rope, and I caught hold of it, but I was dragged alongside the breakwater, and disappeared from view as a wave washed me under the pier.

They thought I'd gone. Fortunately, I hung on, and they felt me tugging at the rope. They were able to drag me up the pier steps. It was freezing cold, and my clothes – or what was left of them – had frozen to my body. I had no feeling in my body at all. They punched and pummelled me to bring the circulation back. They gave me some rum. Somehow I survived. I got pneumonia, and I was taken to Ashford Hospital. I was discharged from the army, a nervous bloody wreck. But while I was in the water, the only thought in my mind was survival. I think that was what I'd learned in my childhood. Survival is the theme of my life. I know at that time I had little else to live for.

'I know it has had a continuing effect on my adult life. It leaves you with a grudge. When I look back, I feel I've nothing to be thankful for. I'm bitter. I got married at 23, to get away from home. And then I had nothing but trouble from my wife.

'I'd been so downtrodden by my parents, I didn't have the guts to fight the men my wife carried on with. I suffered the humiliation of an unfaithful wife for 18 years. After 20 years I got a divorce. I had married someone whose family thought she was too good for me. She was the daughter of a public assistance officer and they lived in a detached house. We got married for the wrong reasons. I married to get away from home, and she married because her parents were splitting up, she wanted security. That was the last thing I'd got to offer anybody. And then, I was only a painter and decorator. I taught myself the job. We lived in a caravan for a while, a con-verted chicken shed actually. But I did manage to buy a house, very cheap, derelict, for only £250. I worked on it, turned it into a lovely home . . . But in the end I told her to pack up her boyfriends or get out. She went to live with another man. I was left with two kids in 1962, in that bad winter; the children were coming home to a cold empty house. I asked my employers if I could leave off work early, so I should be there when they got home. They said I couldn't, but I did all the same. I was reported by one of the men I worked with, and I got the sack. I couldn't get dole money, because I'd been sacked for what they called misconduct. I couldn't keep up the payments on the house, and I had to sell it. I got £3,250. The wife took the children and I moved away. The balance of money I had was about £1,800.

'I went to a marriage bureau. That was a mistake. The

woman I married thought I had a lot of money from the sale of the house, and she was after it. I found out she was no better than a prostitute. All my life it's been nothing but trouble, trouble, trouble . . . I'll never get married again. The second marriage lasted a fortnight. She locked me out. I came home one night and found she'd fixed the lock. The very first night, when I got home, she ordered me to take my boots off before I walked on her carpet. It wasn't even hers. With her, it was just like my childhood over again. She treated me the way my stepmother had; and once is once too often for that.

'The way I reacted against my childhood with my children was that I was soft with them. I treated them both identically. I spent the same on both of them. I never hit them. I would never treat them as I had been treated. But my wife – she was consistently unfaithful. For years I didn't know what was happening. Even towards the end she had been taking the 15-year-old as an alibi, when she went out with her bloke. She'd been doing it for years. The eldest girl had been brought up with it, she'd known more about what her mother was doing than I did. She turned against me in the end. Do you know what she said? She said, "You obviously don't love Mummy, because if you did you wouldn't mind her going with other men." That was the idea she had grown up with . . . Anyway, my daughter, she too has been through a broken marriage now. I don't see her. I've no contact with her. As a matter of fact . . . she wasn't my child . . . She was like the man my wife was going with, the same colouring, the features, everything. My wife used to pretend she was going to evening classes. The nights she was supposed to be going to class, she suggested I should go to a whist drive; and I like whist, so I agreed. Then one night, I'd had rotten hands, I knew I had no chance of winning, so I came home early. I saw her getting off the bus, and I saw this bloke following her home to the door. They went inside. I caught them. Soon after that, she was pregnant. That wasn't long after we were married. And I now realize that first daughter wasn't mine. But I never had the strength to stop her going with other men.

'I was going to see my brother in Canada recently. But I thought before I went, I ought to write and tell him the truth about this stepmother. When I wrote he was very angry. He wrote back to say, "Don't come." He'd always thought of her as a good woman, taking on six kids. He wrote and said that father was not a drinker, he was a very sick man; and of course I knew that was false. But he couldn't accept the truth. He could not bear to think that the idea he had of father and the stepmother was wrong. He'd rather not know it than be disturbed in the way he felt. But of course he had been adopted by this rich woman, he'd never had to live with the stepmother, he had no direct experience of her.

'It has made me very afraid of rejection. I always get rejected. I always have been. I won't push myself. I'm very unsociable. I won't ask anything of people. All the memories of the way I was treated come back to me. They live in me. As I talk now, memories come back that I'd forgotten. I remember when I was young, the stepmother used to bath us. It was always in the same order, my stepsister first, then the brother, then me. We always used the same water, so it was cold and dirty when my turn came. As I got older, I used to be very embarrassed on bath nights. I dreaded them. She delighted in mucking about with me when I got, you know, more developed; she used to play with me, do what she shouldn't. She kept me away from my stepsister.

'But that's the way it's always been. I've always been picked on by people, bullied. If you are a victim, people recognize that in you. There was a master at school who was a sadist, he used to delight in punishing me. Something that happens to you as a child, it goes into you, and it keeps repeating itself.'

When Mr Walsh married and had a family, it wasn't that he repeated the pattern of his childhood in a mechanistic way. On the contrary, he was at pains to treat his children differently from the way he had been dealt with; but he did re-create for himself a familiar atmosphere, in spite of his efforts to escape from it. There was a strong sense of his own exclusion – the child who wasn't his, the rejecting wife and her lover – other people became for him a ghostly reincarnation of the half-brother and the stepmother and the father; and he was the child again, living through the same terrors and anxieties, even though for years he claims not to have known what was going on. Even though he had consciously reacted against his own experience, he nevertheless by stealth reproduced the feelings: there were the interlopers, the sense of being unwanted and rejected. A weak and mistreated child, his whole life has continued to evoke the same painful responses; but he feels he would cease to exist without them; and only his delicate and painstaking art offers him a place of rest from it.

In the accounts of childhood, a common theme is that of chains and continuities: the impossibility of avoiding the past, the repeat in adult life of behaviour and relationships that were set up in childhood, themselves often transmitted from the childhood of the parents. Allied to this, is the haunting of people throughout their lives of certain crucial events, experiences, emotions that occurred in childhood. Many people continue to enact, often in a symbolic way, a moment of loss, grief or violence. There is nothing schematic about it. It is often something elusive but persistent, something that recurs intermittently. Their adult life is pervaded by a memory of the feelings, and they recur to them compulsively, even though the outer form and circumstances of their adult lives appear to be quite different. Among older people, these personal preoccupations tend to be less insistent, only rudimentarily developed; subordinated to the need to survive, work and want, they tend to be less obsessive. They may say now, 'Of course my father never really cared for me' or, 'He was a wrong 'un', or 'I was always jealous of my sister', but they were not, on the whole, seen as the determining feature of adult life. More often, those relationships were idealized, 'Mother was a saint'. It is only as the pressures of poverty and work have retreated that the working out of emotional conflicts has taken on greater urgency and centrality in working people's lives. In this respect, the lives of working-class people have become more akin to those in other social strata, and the more distinctive working-class style of life has become blurred.

Some families can be seen to have repeated similar relationships over three or four generations, however unwillingly. These can sometimes be very dramatic. I heard of three generations of men in one family who committed suicide by shooting themselves; in the first case, a convulsive sense of failure of a man haunted by his memories of the First War, in his son, a sense of guilt at having contributed to his father's death, and in the grandson, it became an obsession that he must die in the same way.

Jeanine, in her early 30s, was convinced that she had cancer;

and a sequence of shifting symptoms so real and incapacitating led to a long spell in a psychiatric hospital. It emerged that her father had been dismissed by doctors and hospitals as an imaginary invalid for many months, and it was discovered, too late, that he was suffering from terminal cancer.

Enid Bradshaw, 55, Hull: 'I loved my father, and I was his favourite. There were four of us, and I was the youngest. He died suddenly when I was ten. They brought him home from the factory. I was playing in the street, and when I saw the men turn the corner, they were carrying someone and I knew it was my Dad. Oh, I went numb. I grieved for him, I was heartbroke. Nobody knew how much I missed him. After that, there was always something missing in my life. I felt very resentful, he was only a young man, 44. Well, when I got married, I couldn't have any children. My husband, I can't say he reminded me of my father, it wasn't till after he'd committed suicide that I saw any connection. I loved him, but I was always bitter about losing my father, and somehow I saw that I was involved in his death. He killed himself ten years after we were married, almost to the day. I don't know what it was; he had a nice disposition, but somewhere – I was under the psychiatrist for some time because I had a breakdown after it – it was me, putting pressure on him; that old resentment, because there was never anybody in my life like my father, ever again, I felt a terrible guilt, because he was never good enough for me. I must have taunted him with my father, how good he was to me, how he understood, how he'd do anything for me. And that got to him in the end. I didn't know what I was doing; only now, it's taken me years to see it.'

But the repeated patterns are seldom as easy to discern as this. Far more likely is a chain of dominating men or destructive women, and the pattern is not symmetrical, but varies in the way it works through from generation to generation.

Mrs Hancock, in her late 60s, Worcester: 'My mother hated my father. She found him repulsive. Not long after they were married she began to hate his insensitivity. He was, I believe, very brutal in sex. He was never at home, always off drinking and gambling. She often locked the door against him. My childhood memories are disturbed by the image of this man, angry or abject, pleading to be allowed back into the house. As a child I couldn't bear him near me.' Mrs Hancock married a

man just as brutal as her father had been. He was violent and
frequently beat her. They had one daughter; and when this
child was two, Mrs Hancock ran away with her. The husband
followed, and broke into the flat where they were living, and
injured her; and he spent three years in prison. When Mrs
Hancock's daughter married, the young couple went to live
with her in the little terraced house she had managed to buy.
Within three years, the husband had deserted, and mother and
daughter re-settled to their domestic life. The daughter has one
child, a little boy. He is 11 now, and, according to his
grandmother, 'just like his father'. She says that she cannot
bear to be in the house with him.

   Jim is 38. He says that his repeat of childhood was
illuminated for him when he came home from an engineering
contract in the Middle East, and his four-year-old son asked
him, 'Daddy, why don't you live with us, don't you like us?' Jim
had never thought of himself as an absent father. He had
always gone abroad to earn money, precisely so that he could
give his child the best of everything. He had bought an old
farmhouse in the Peak District, installed his wife and child
there, and gone to make money while he was young enough to
do so. But when the child said that, it made him feel that he was
reproducing his own childhood: his father had been emotionally absent, even though he slept at home; he had never been
interested in Jim, had had other women. 'It started me
thinking. I might be repeating what my father had done by
imitation, just as my little boy used to imitate me. I could feel
him copying me saying, "Crikey" the way I did, copying my
walk, looking at me with his lovely little face, waiting to see
what I was going to do next. My life looked so different from my
parents' life. We'd lived in the same council house all the time I
was a kid, and here was I, way beyond the dreams of my Mam
and Dad. But you find you can still be doing the same thing that
was done to you, even if it looks different, beneath the surface.
When my kid said that to me, I knew it was time to pack up and
come home.' Jim, 38, Derby.

9

INSTITUTIONALIZED CHILDHOOD:
HETTY DAY

THE VALUES OF a society and the way they act upon children are seen at their most naked and unadorned in the depersonalized upbringing of institutions. Here, there is neither love nor hate to filter them, but simply a loveless indifference. In such places as that where Hetty Day spent her childhood, the values were archaic and ossified. It was intended to produce boys for industry or the services, and girls for domestic service.

'When I was 18 months old, my father died. He died in an almost casual way. He was doing something to the engine of an old car one day and cut his finger. He wrapped the wound in an oily rag, and he got blood-poisoning from it. Within a week he was dead. The story is that they were due to go out that same night; and his arm was swollen and throbbing and he felt ill. But my mother wanted to go dancing, and so they went. My father fainted and was taken to the hospital, and within a few days he was dead. My sister was six, and my mother was three months pregnant with my brother James.

'Of course at that time, 1929, there was no provision for children, nothing. There was no money. My sister went to Reedham Orphanage. I stayed with my mother for a while, when she got a job as a housekeeper. Then when my brother was born, I was sent to Reedham to join my sister.

'Reedham was originally an "Asylum for Fatherless Children". It had been started in the 1830s by Sir Adrian Reed, who built some cottages for widows with children – no unmarried mothers, of course. It was a religious charity. In fact, we had religion crammed down our throats. It made me an atheist. Religion and charity were our staple diet. Then, about 30 years after it was founded, the school was built, and the mothers could then simply send their children to Reedham.

'I remember the first day very clearly. I sat on the bus, chanting "I'm going to school, I'm going to school". I'd been prepared for it. I'd been encouraged to see it as a great adventure. I went into the nursery, and my mother said to me, "Oh, look at the lovely rocking horse", and although I wasn't particularly interested, I went over to it, to please her. And then, when I looked round, she'd gone. I can still feel the sense of loss I had then.

'I went into the Babies' Department first; children from 18 months to five. I missed my mother so much. We were severely treated. We were punished for talking, we had to sit and hold our tongues between our fingers if we talked when we shouldn't. If we talked after we'd been put to bed, they came and pulled the sheets over our heads, and I was always afraid of the dark. By the time I was four, I was no longer considered to be a child, I had to help look after the younger ones, make the cots, just generally prove useful. The food was inadequate, and it stayed that way all the time I was there. We were fed on bread and butter and potatoes and gravy. I remember having a boiled egg once. I just remember a blur of unhappiness all the time I was in the Babies' Department.

'Then at five, until you were seven, you went into the Infants, and that was when you started school. I was happy only in the classroom. I loved school and I loved learning. One of the biggest wrongs done to us was that we weren't allowed to continue our education. We were clever. My brother won a scholarship to the county school, but he couldn't go. There was no room for Reedhamites.

'It was the times between school that were bad. Once you went into the Orphanage, the mothers signed a contract to say that Reedham should take care of you until you were 15. The only release from it would be if the mother married again. My mother did have a man friend, and it was my greatest wish that they should marry, because that way, I thought I'd be able to get out of Reedham. I worshipped my mother, this idol, this beautiful woman. She was an idealized figure, I invested her with all the opposites of the bad things I experienced in the Orphanage. She came one day, it was a Festival Day, when all the parents could come; and she left one of her blue lace gloves behind. I treasured that glove, it smelt of my mother's perfume. I caressed it and kept it beside me, and whenever I wanted my mother, I would take it out and the smell of it evoked her. I was so lovesick for my mother all the years I was there.

'We had our clothes provided, orphan clothes, rough and

durable. We were inadequately clothed, and always cold and hungry. The food was a penance. There was an unvarying weekly menu. Monday, Wednesday and Saturday, we had watery soup, a slice of bread, and then a suet pudding with syrup. The smell of it was repelling. I often didn't eat it. We used to keep it and put it at the rat-holes, so the rats waxed fat on it. On Tuesday we had a stew with carrots, and you might find a bit of meat in it if you were lucky, and then rice pudding. Thursday we had Irish stew which was all grease, horrible. Friday was the worst – the fish stank. Sunday was foul too, cold meat, because there was no cooking on Sundays, beetroot and prunes and custard. I can't touch any of those things today. All the food was vaguely punishing, reminded you of your semi-orphaned and dependent state.

'But we knew nothing different. We knew that a world outside Reedham existed, but we didn't make any connection between the two. I didn't realize that there was any other kind of childhood. I suppose I thought all children went to places like Reedham. I remember, one summer evening, we were allowed to go into the woods, and I went to the edge of the grounds, to the railings that looked onto a housing estate in Purley. And I realized for the first time that children lived in these houses all the time. I envied them. I'd lie in bed and listen to the sound of the trains, and long to be on one of them. I just longed to be away from there; and that longing was associated with the yearning for my mother which never stopped all the years I was there.

'Our clothes were cotton vests, navy blue knickers, like workmen's dungarees cut off, with bibs and straps, a navy blue jumper, very thin. Nothing was ever ours: it was put on the pile. You never owned any item of clothing, but it was passed on to you. We wore the same jumper for a term, and presumably it was washed at the end. After Easter, you went into a navy blue dress, a thick cotton material. You wore a liberty bodice, and itchy black woollen stockings with garters to keep them up. All in navy blue, the only splash of colour was at the collar, where you wore the red and yellow colours of the school. Even the shoes were never our own. Nothing was ever new. Perhaps they came already used. You were never known by your name, all by numbers. I was G80, my sister G90, my brother B52. B and G obviously stood for Boy and Girl. Your numbers were sewn into such items of clothing as were provisionally yours until you grew out of them.

'The school was kept clean by the inmates. A boy was picked each term, and he blew the bugle. This was a dubious privilege, because he had to get up at six. This woke the whole school. Then we had to get dressed, wash, strip the beds in a special way, fold the blankets exactly right, turn the mattress; everything had to be just so. Then we had our duties – cleaning the stairs or the washrooms. I was in Cavell House. The houses were all named after Victorian reformers, Fry, Nightingale. There was a washroom in each house: basins all round an oval room, and in the centre was a circular metal structure with hooks for our flannels and towels. There were 30 basins, and we had to Bluebell each tap perfectly. Each small girl was under the guidance of a bigger girl who ruled over you, guided you, mothered you if you were lucky. Then when you'd finished your task, the mistress inspected it. If anything was wrong, however minute, you had to do it all over again. Cleaning the stairs was unpleasant because, being wood, it was very splintery; you could drive splinters right into your hands. Each stair had to be dusted and polished.

'The boys were allowed a newspaper, so they could get some idea of what was going on in the world. The girls didn't. I expect they thought it was none of our business. We grew up to be institutionalized. So much so that, when I left Reedham I was afraid to cross the road. I was terrified of going into a shop. Your life was so structured that anything that departed from that particular routine was a frightening adventure. It has left me with all sorts of habits. Occasionally, for breakfast, you might have bread and margarine and a little blob of marmalade or jam; and there was always so little of it, I can only eat a tiny scrape of it on my bread to this day. I'll spread the marmalade and then scrape it off again. I'm a perfect bedmaker, of course.

'We had prayers at nine. We went to church every morning to thank God for His blessings, which were not always easy to discern. There was a strong division between the sexes in everything: the girls did domestic science, the boys woodwork and chemistry. There was more than a hint of service in the training we received. We were brought up to feel how much we owed our benefactors. There were opportunities for modest professional jobs if the mothers were sufficiently concerned for

their children and pushed on their behalf. Our mother didn't.
She didn't deserve the love that I felt for her, this intense,
unrealistic sentiment I kept alive all those years.

'I never understood why we were sent away. I knew; but in a
personal sense, I didn't understand. I felt sympathy for my
mother. The shock of losing my father so suddenly must have
been dreadful. I can feel for her as far as that went. But she was
surrounded by family. There were her sisters, two sets of
parents, my father's brothers. I know that my Auntie Chloe
wanted to adopt me, but my mother said, "No." And then they
seemed to wash their hands of the whole thing and let us be sent
away. I can only imagine that my mother overruled them. She
may have been selfish; but I think she was acting in uncon-
scious repetition of her own experience. She had been sent away
as a child, looked after by indifferent strangers. She was in fact
very possessive of us, in an indirect way. It sounds paradoxical,
given that we all went to the orphanage. But I think she
preferred that an impersonal organization should have the
charge of us rather than that we should become attached to
another person, an individual who might be a rival to her,
especially a member of the family.

'Our mother did work. She did various jobs. She was a
receptionist at a hotel, and was matron of a boarding school at
one time. I can't help thinking how odd it was that she should
have been matron of a boarding school while her own children
were at Reedham. She very rarely visited us. It was a red letter
day if she came. If she was expected, I used to go crazy.

'All the girls had a "mother" when they were eight, a girl of
13 or 14. I had my sister of course, and I worshipped her. But I
didn't really get to know her until quite recently. I looked up to
her, and I protected my brother. He'd never really known our
mother at all. I had to grow up fast, because I realized how
much James depended on me. He arrived at Reedham when he
was two. For the first year, he was fussed over quite a bit; they
were quite good with the very tiny ones. I remember, being
constantly hungry, food used to play a big part in the games I
played with my brother. He used to say, "Tell me a story," and
I made up stories about ourselves. We were two children lost in
a wood; and an old woman found us and took us into her
cottage and made a rabbit stew. If you found a chocolate
wrapper, you would pick it up and smell it, and as you smelled

the chocolate, you imagined that you could taste it too. If anybody got an apple, we would all gather round and beg for the core. Even orange peel, you chewed it to get the taste.

'I think the happiest day of the year was Festival Day in July. For that one day, all the girls were dressed up in shantung dresses, and we lined up on either side of the driveway, and greeted the Lord Mayor of London. We had different food that day. The routine was disrupted; they even put counterpanes on the beds for that occasion. Then, after the day was over, the shantung dresses were all put away for the next year, together with the counterpanes. We had to do our utmost to impress our benefactors.

'When my brother was eight he went into the Boys' Department, and I saw very little of him for a while. Eventually, there was some liberalizing of the policy, and on Saturday mornings brothers and sisters were allowed to meet in the dining-room for an hour. But in the normal course of events, boys and girls were not allowed to talk to each other. They shared classrooms, but they couldn't speak, or even look at each other. We did, of course; we broke all the rules. Girls were always passing notes to and fro from the boyfriend of the moment.

'My adult life has been affected dramatically by the experience. I wasn't really aware of how much, until I was grown up and had children. I was sexually affected by it. The feelings that reached us were that the body was not nice. It was something you didn't talk about. And as you discovered yourself, it made growing up difficult. I was a tiny girl, undersized. That was just as well; for the well-developed girl it must have been very awkward. We had these big white nightdresses, and we had to dress and undress under them, a tent-like affair. We had a bath once a week, two to a bath; perhaps the cleansing power of the water was thought to wash away improper thoughts.

'I was always cold and often ill. Apparently, when I went to Reedham I had rickets. I just remember these pains in my legs, and not being able to walk. At the age of six I was being pushed round in a pram because my legs were so weak. I spent a lot of time in the sanatorium. I was weak and rather sickly; mostly from lack of love.

'Once we had a film show. We were all gathered together to be shown the first talking movie. I was terrified of it. I must have been about six. And then, in the holidays, my Auntie Chloe took us to see *Alice in Wonderland* as a treat. But when I saw the pictures on the screen, I screamed and screamed and had to be taken out. And it took years before I could pluck up the courage to go to the cinema again. And when I did, I had to keep telling myself, "I'm not afraid, I'm not afraid." I think we were so deprived, sensorily, emotionally, visually, that it was overwhelming.

'We never had much spare time. The day was tightly structured. Once when I was about ten, I was sent to bed without any tea; some trivial offence, I can't even remember what I'd done. But food was so scarce and so important that it was a major punishment to miss any. I was upstairs, crying, and Miss Campbell, one of the few kind mistresses, came up, and she gave me a cuddle and made me feel better. Then she sneaked me up some tea. I always think of her with gratitude and love.

'You loved a certain person; someone you chose deliberately, almost coldly. And then you worshipped whoever it was you'd chosen. Those girls who were the objects of love were sitting pretty. They were waited on, they had power. You carried on until you reached that position yourself and you were loved in your turn. Lasting friendships were made.

'We were never given any sex instruction. I received what I learnt from two friends. They were both physically developed, young women really. I was small and undersized. They decided it was time I knew about menstruation. I knew nothing about it. They took me into a corner. "Sit down, we've got something to tell you. When you're a bit older, did you know you'll have periods?" I said, "No." "When you're a woman, you'll bleed once a month. It's the baby that makes you bleed. And when it happens, you have to go to the mistress, and she'll tell you what to do." I thanked them, but it never happened to me while I was at Reedham. I'm glad. Those it did happen to had to go to the mistress and be issued with a towel. But they had to ask for every towel they needed; which could be very embarrassing for a girl who bled profusely.

'We were always in line, marching everywhere. At meal times, at the first whistle, we had to go and wash our hands, and then file past the mistress to have our hands inspected, to make sure our nails were white, our hair perfect. Then at the second whistle, we had to get in line, and then we marched into the meal. We stood at the table and said Grace. We were never taught the words, and in fact, I never did learn them all the time I was there. I learned them after I'd left. You could la-la-la them. It went

> Be present at our table, Lord
> Be here and everywhere adored;
> . . . His mercies blest, and grant that we
> May feast in Paradise with thee.

Then we sat down, and ate our meal in silence. If we talked, we had to stand on the bench, and remain there for the rest of the meal, and were allowed nothing more to eat. After the meal, we sang again. I can't remember the whole verse, but it went, "We thank you, Lord, for this our food, And every other needful good . . ." At tea-time, we were allowed to speak for five minutes before dispersing. The mistress patrolled the whole length of the room throughout the meal. At the end of each day, we all had to file into the classroom for the evening service. We sang, "The day Thou gavest, Lord, is ended." When we were in the Infants, we had to kneel at the foot of our bed and say our prayers. As infants, we went to bed at six o'clock. The mistress walked round the beds, and if anybody's hands appeared to be anywhere near our private parts, she would remove them and place them outside the bedcovers.

'I didn't know the rest of the story about sex until I was 16. My friend came to stay at our house for a few days, and she told me what I didn't know. Until then, I used to think that if a boy kissed you, that was the way you had babies. Anything could have happened to me, and I wouldn't have understood what was going on.

'When the war came, and the air raids, of course Purley was right in the path of the planes. There were shelters built for us underground in the fields. We had palliasses filled with straw on the cement floor, and we slept three abreast on them throughout the Blitz. It was a fairly free time there, because you could choose your sleeping companions, and I chose the girl I loved at the time. She was 15 and I was 11. That was quite a discrepancy in age, which didn't happen often.

'My brother wanted to join the Navy. The Board got him a place in a naval school, but mother wouldn't let him go. She

refused her permission. He was only nine at the time, but he
never forgave her. Whenever we saw her, she would say, "Well,
how are things?" But it wasn't the kind of question that wanted
a real answer. We would say, "The food is awful." She would
say, "Well, you look well on it." She didn't want to hear how we
really felt.

'My sister wanted to join the Post Office, but she wasn't
allowed to do that. In fact, my mother was managing a wool
shop at this time, and Beryl had to join her there. She hated it.
She wasn't allowed to go out or anything, she had no life of her
own. Our mother actually kept a very severe control over us;
and this was something I repeated with my first child:
unwittingly, I carried on what had become familiar to me. You
fight against one aspect of your childhood that you disliked,
only to find that something you hadn't even been aware of lies
in ambush elsewhere.

'Beryl went and signed on in the ATS. Mother couldn't stop
her. When Beryl had gone, my mother wanted companionship.
She asked if I could be allowed to leave Reedham. I was making
good educational progress, I was well ahead for my age. I
needed the education. The Headmaster did me this one wrong:
he put it to me, and gave me the choice. He asked me if I wanted
to leave. Of course, this had been the one thing I'd dreamed of
for ten years. And as I was 14 the day before going back to
school, they said I could leave if I chose. My teacher shed tears
at my going, and said how wrong it was to break off my
education at that point. But you can imagine my excitement,
the thought of being reunited with my mother, the woman I'd
worshipped, from afar admittedly, all those years. I went home.
And then for a year I cried to go back.

'I was broken-hearted. It was the most unhappy year of my
life. I don't know why I didn't leave and run away, back to
Reedham. At least at Reedham you had freedom of thought,
they hadn't been able to control that. I'd been made a prefect.
Life was getting easier there. I was used to it. My fantasy of my
mother crumbled. She gave me no peace. She had never read a
book in her life, and she nagged me every time she saw me open
a book. I couldn't go out at nights. I joined evening classes to do
book-keeping and shorthand typing; and I'd get home at eight
o'clock to find her in a state because she'd been left on her own
for a couple of hours. I couldn't do anything; she couldn't bear

to be left on her own. The whole experience of going home was shattering. I'd always thought that adults were perfect. The only thing wrong with life was being a child. I was frightened and miserable without my brother and sister.

'Soon after that, Reedham was evacuated. The whole school went to Nottingham. I worked in the wool shop for two years and I hated it. Then in the end, I saw an advertisement in a shop window for a cashier; and the woman who owned the shop was the particular object of my affections at this time, so that was an added inducement. The habit of relating to an idealized woman persisted with me; so that when the image of my mother was broken, I had to take my fantasies to someone else.

'I was sexually damaged by my experiences. I met my husband near where we lived. There was a hospital there for burned airmen, and that was where we met. He had been badly burned; but what might have seemed abnormal to them wasn't so to me. I hadn't developed, I wasn't fully grown up at 17, 18. He had been damaged by burns, I had been damaged by Reedham. We were both scarred. I wish I could say it had been good. We didn't know what we'd taken on, either of us. It wasn't successful, and has been traumatic at times. It would probably have been better for us if it hadn't happened. Our eldest son was the chief sufferer by it. I so longed for a baby. In fact, I wanted to be a children's nurse; but my mother deprived me of that. So I wanted children of my own. I had my first baby at 21. I was still mentally undeveloped. Reedham was still too much in me. I thought I wanted a baby, but what it really was was a need to revise my own childhood, to set it to rights; and basically, that can't be done with your child, it has no relevance to his life. You can only resolve those things inside yourself, if at all. And then my relationship with my mother had been rather strange, I didn't understand it. All I had behind me as my childhood experience was discipline. I knew only control, not love. That was all I'd had transmitted from my mother. It wasn't her fault; that was all she'd known really.

'As a result, my first child was damaged. He is an artist. His temperament and mine were at odds. Things couldn't have been worse for him. I think he had an unhappy childhood. We were strict. I even had a stick I used on him. When I look back and think how I was with him, I can't believe it was me. But I knew so little. When I was pregnant, I wanted a girl. I wanted to be able to give her all the love I felt I'd never had. When I saw it was a boy, lying there in the cot, I couldn't believe my eyes. I was shattered. It hadn't even occurred to me that it could be a boy. He couldn't feed properly and I had to give him a bottle. I was so disappointed. I was still very immature. There I was with the baby I'd longed for, and all he seemed to do was cry. I held the baby up and said, "Love me, love me." We didn't like one another; and didn't even start to do so until he was 19 or 20. Now we're good friends. I don't think there is any malice between us. He understands why it was like that.

'It was different with the second child. We'd learnt something by then; and perhaps I'd grown up a little. Only it was too late to prevent the first one from being unhappy. But then, the second one was a different person. You don't realize that every child comes with a certain temperament; they're not blank sheets for you to inscribe your own feelings on.

'I became aware of the damage that had been done, and how it can be passed on from one generation to the next. I think it's worked out now; it all expended itself in my relationship with my first son. That was full of pain and sacrifice. But I think he has overcome it; and if that is so, I can accept my part in the suffering it caused.'

10

CHILDHOOD: THE COMMON EXPERIENCE

The sommers flowre is to the sommer sweete
Though to itselfe it onely live and die.

IN THE SAME way, childhood is sweet to adults. Perhaps there
are no happy childhoods, only happy memories of childhood
which, because they are beyond the reach of alteration or
change, take on a significance and a lustre which they may not
have had at the time. Edwin Muir, in his autobiography, writes
that when he looks back at some of his poetry, he finds it strange
that he ever wrote it. 'I fancy we all have sometimes this sense of
strangeness, or of estrangement when we look back, perhaps at
some moment of our childhood, or at a boy waiting for a girl he
loved, or thought he loved – both gone and almost forgotten,
never in any case to be recovered – or at a young man loitering
in a summer dread beside a river which flows into a different
sea. Time wakens a longing more poignant than all the longings
caused by the division of lovers in space, for there is no road
back into its country. Our bodies were not made for that
journey; only the imagination can venture upon it; and the
setting out, the road, the arrival: all is imagination.' And yet, he
insists, 'Our memories are real, but in a different way from the
real things they try to resuscitate.'

If the idea of the unique individual child is, historically, a
recent one, the idea of the happy child is a very new one in
working-class experience. That isn't to say that people haven't
always striven to give the best of themselves to their children.
Nor is it to deny that people have always looked back and
tended to view the world as declining as they advance in age,
and have seen the time of their greatest youth and vigour
through a golden haze. That has always been. But the self-
conscious provision of a happy childhood for children, as
though it were a rather superior consumer item – that is new.
Happiness as ideology is a by-product of the market-place, one
of the more uplifting aspects of consumer culture, its spiritual

content as it were. 'I was brought up poor', said one mother, the daughter of an East London rag-and-bone man, 'and I made up my mind I was going to buy Kelly the best childhood there is.' She was simply reflecting the culture which vests all good in material products and things that can be bought or transformed into commodities. One of the sad side-effects of this is that it makes many parents feel devalued and unworthy; they feel they have nothing of themselves to offer, and the best they can do for their children is to buy them the best of everything and keep out of the way. This is the trap into which many of the formerly poor have fallen; and they find they are on a treadmill of expiation, never quite able to fulfil the dilating needs of their children, desperately expending themselves to provide, and never quite managing to keep pace. The idea of childhood as a time of a kind of quarantine from life, with its implanted compulsion to be happy (which is merely an emanation of the culture of selling), is as absurd and inhuman as the older idea that children have no individual characteristics, are to be seen and not heard, and that their primary purpose is to be disciplined until they cease to be mouths to feed and become hands that will work. The transformation corresponds roughly to the change from children into 'kids', with all that suggests of happy carefree informality.

But the moments of happiness remembered have a different sound altogether from the manufactured excitements of the market-place. There is an amazing sameness about such moments. They remind us of the common source of our feelings and responses, which we lose sight of when we claim something special or different about our unique experience, crouching over it as though it had to be defended like property, and believing it to be incomprehensible to others. The memories are connected with loved parents, or brothers and sisters, someone who showed us kindness, a flash of understanding, a sense of being at one with our surroundings, family gatherings, celebrations, an achievement, shared laughter.

Most people can recall beautiful moments of childhood which pierce the habits of living, the repeated patterns of relationships, the sense of diminishing possibilities that closes in on us as we grow older; and part of their poignancy comes from their remoteness from the context of our life as it turned out to be. As adults, we can now see that they took place before we became aware of our limitations; that we should have felt such dilation of the senses at something as simple as morning or sunlight suggests to us now our lack of appreciation of the relatively trivial place these things have in later life; and the memory of a grandmother who spoilt us is made more intense by our unawareness of the loss of her that was to follow soon after.

'I've the happiest memories of my Granny, and I loved to stay with her. She was an old countrywoman, and she lived in Barton-le-Clay in Bedfordshire. The things she said to me have stayed with me all my life. I can still hear her voice. She'd say, "When people say to you that there's as many good Christians outside the church as there are in it, don't you believe them. If Jesus could be bothered to walk to His own crucifixion, they should be bothered to walk to His house." She used to wash for all the big houses around. The carrier's cart used to go and fetch the washing and bring it to her; and when it was done, she'd lay it out on the lavender bushes all round the cottage, so white you couldn't bear to look at it.' Woman, 75, Bedford.

'Where we live my father had a house on some land, and he grow cane, banana, plantain, coffee and breadfruit. When me going to school, you could have guavas or June plum; you have golden-apple and mangoes, all different kind, you just burst the fruit and suck out the juice . . . When me was a girl, I get up early in the morning and I had to cut the cane. There was spirit everywhere, but they don't worry me . . . I dream-see me family now . . . When my grandfather died, I knew. I dream-see him in the night. He tell me, "Look how long I gone", and me say "Where you going?" He say, "I have to go somewhere." I see him sitting under the plantain tree, and me see him pull he hat over he face . . . The way I see him, he look so sad, and I know he gone. I not see them for twenty year, but I feel them, all the people me love, they inside me and give me strength when I come here to England.' Woman, 40s, Hackney, talking of her childhood in Surrey County, Jamaica.

'On special occasions I was allowed to go with my Dad on his lorry, and we used to go and deliver the timber, or whatever it was he had a load of. We'd travel from Stoke up to Sandbach or Crewe, and then when he came back, it would be evening. The roads always seemed empty then, and he'd drive fast with the windows open, and we'd both sing at the top of our voices, "One man went to mow"; we'd belt it out loud as we could. There was an excitement, the excitement of going fast, but feeling safe and secure, because I knew he loved me. I can feel the cool air rushing past us, I can see his sunburnt face and white teeth and the dust from the wood in his hair. I couldn't wait to grow up and be like him.' Man, 45, Stoke-on-Trent.

'I worshipped my brother. He was nearly ten years older than me. My Mum used to say I came as a mistake. My brother was more of a father to me than my old man was. I was eight when he went in the War; and he was killed at Alamein. When he came home on leave, I used to wait on him hand and foot. He was a god to me. I'd sit and just look at him while he ate his tea; and he used to get embarrassed and tell me to leave him in peace. And he never wanted to talk about it, what he'd been doing, what it was like out there . . . The last time I saw him, before he was killed, he took me into town with him, and we went into Littlewood's with his girlfriend, and they bought me a sundae, which was the last word in luxury . . . When he died, I kept a lot of his things; my room became a shrine to him.' Man, 50, Nottingham.

'On Sunday afternoons, I used to go with my Dad to his allotment. And if it was sunny, later on my Mam and Auntie would come with a flask of tea and some sandwiches. And I sat in an old chair with no back to it that he kept in his hut, and I watched him lift the earth with his spade, or plant his beans or whatever he was doing. What I loved best was early summer, July. I helped him pick peas, all the pods used to squeak in the basket. And lifting the blackcurrant bushes, it was more exciting to me than lifting a woman's skirts. Underneath there was all the fruit – he had white, black and red currants; all the ripeness under the dusty leaves. The redcurrants were transparent; you could hold little bunches of them up to the sun and see the pips through them . . . The sandwiches those afternoons, they were only fishpaste or tomato, but they tasted so good. If I ever have tomato sandwiches now, it all comes back.' Man, 40s, Birmingham.

'I can remember when we moved from Long Buckby to Northampton. I sat on the carrier's cart at the back. We had all our belongings piled up on it, and our legs dangled behind. The grass was high, and the fields full of meadowsweet and Queen

Anne's lace. What an excitement there was that spring. We were going to live in the town for the first time. Up to then we'd lived in the village. You'd have thought there was a migration going on, instead of a journey of about 12 miles.' Woman, 79, Northampton.

'Christmas, everybody came. It seemed like the whole world. My mother had eight sisters and three brothers, and their families all came for Christmas Day, and those who lived too far away, we all used to muck in and sleep together. There might be five of us kids in one single bed; and nobody went to sleep before about three or four in the morning. It gave you a sense of such security; you felt you were related to everybody. In the street where we were, we had five families related to us, and two more in the next street, you could talk to them over the back wall. Christmas night we used to sing, I should think there must have been 40 people in our little front room, baking hot fire, we all had a drink, we sang together, and then they all did their party piece, a recitation, a song, "They played in their beautiful garden,/The children of high degree,/While outside the beggars/Passed on in their misery . . ." I suppose we were overcrowded; but somehow there was room for everybody.' Woman, 60s, Lowestoft.

'For the Sunday School anniversary, we couldn't afford new shoes like all the other children had. So our mother rubbed the soles and heels of our old ones with lard. And then we went into church as late as we dared, when everybody was in their place. And the lard made our shoes squeak just like new ones; oh, wasn't it lovely?' Woman, 60s, Hertfordshire.

'We played out in the streets all the time. All our games had their season, and the different activities went in cycles – marbles, hoops, hopscotch. At that time I think the streets offered a rich and warm background for a child; the women sitting on the doorsteps on sunny afternoons, the excitement of misty autumn evenings when it started to get dark early and you could get away with all sorts of mischief, then in winter rushing round to make a sledge before the snow melted. Our Mam was always in the house whenever we got home, wherever we'd been. You could set your clock by my father's coming and going. My brother and I used to fight like hell, but we never doubted how much we meant to each other. He's the best friend I've ever had. I know one thing. When they knocked our street down, I was over 40, and I'm not ashamed to say I shed tears over it.' Man, 55, Blackburn.

'At birthdays I knew I would always get 20 or 30 cards from aunts and uncles. I thought it would go on for ever, I thought everybody had crowds of people who cared for them . . . It's a shock when it all starts to fall away . . . You grow up and people follow their own road . . . I feel guilty towards my kids that I haven't been able to give them that.' Man, 30s, Southampton.

'We used to love our mother to tell us about when she was a girl. She always had some new story. We used to say, "Tell about Jacko." That was a pet monkey they had: her brother had brought it home when he went away to sea. She said whenever they went to clean their boots, there never seemed to be any blacking. They couldn't understand it; and it turned out this monkey was eating the blacking. It used to steal butter and sit by the fire and try to eat it; and they used to watch its face as all the butter melted. Then it would climb up the curtains at teatime, and jump onto Grandma's shoulder and frighten her to death . . . The monkey died in the end because it ate a box of matches. But when mother told us about him, we could just imagine the little creature, and we laughed till we cried.' Woman, 90, Lincolnshire.

'I used to think my Mum was the most beautiful woman in the world. She had been a beauty queen, not the big time, but at seaside competitions and that. I wanted to be like her; I copied her, I wanted to be just like her. When I was quite little she used to sit and make up my face and I felt very grown up and proud. I didn't know then how unhappy she was. She shielded me from all that, and I love her for it.' Woman, 28, South London.

'I remember once my sister had a bad ear, a mastoid. And when she suffered with the pain, I cried too, and held on to her for dear life. We identified so strongly with each other that we literally shared each other's feelings. There isn't the sharing now. And human beings need that as much as they need their right to be alone. Privacy. There's enough privacy in the grave.' Woman, 70, South London.

'The happiest time was convalescing after an illness, mumps or measles. You know, all the anxiety had gone, you knew you were going to get better. Your Mum spoilt you a bit, they fussed you well enough to enjoy being poorly. My Dad would buy me an extra comic, and I could have jelly and custard every day.

And my Mum would sit on the end of the bed and talk to me, and she might light a fire in the bedroom, which was unheard of most of the time; and then the chimney would all smoke, but it made you feel good; safe, cared for.' Man, 31, Croydon.

'We all sat round the table for our meals, and when it was over, we didn't all rush from the table, we would sit back in our chairs, talk or sing together. The only thing that happens at mealtimes in my daughter's family is rows and argument.' Woman, 60s, Lancashire.

Mealtimes have great prominence in people's discussion of their childhood. If there had to be one simple index of judging whether a childhood had been generally happy or unhappy, I would ask how mealtimes had been: it is surprising how often mealtimes give some hint of the whole feeling of a childhood. Feeding, nourishment, eating together: moments of great openness and vulnerability. At such times, something very deep regularly comes close to the surface. What were family mealtimes like? Did everyone talk at table, and if so, were the conversations expansive or brief and functional? Was a mother constantly eliciting approval for what she had provided; were the children ignored, or did they contribute to the talk; was the atmosphere tense or relaxed? Were there silences, and if so, what kind of silences were they – did they indicate unexpressed feelings of contentment? Was it a gloomy and oppressive time, were the children always being told how to behave, not to interrupt, to sit up straight? Was it a time of laughter and joking, an exchange of news, or were responses constrained and formal? Did the family linger and share the different activities of the day, or was it a hurried and unpleasurable experience? Did father fold his paper on the table and read as he ate, was the meal sketchy, was the table prepared beforehand? Was the food generous (this was always our family's boast, that what distinguished working-class people from the well-to-do and the very poor alike was that that we always ate well)? Were outsiders welcome or unthinkable? Was eating open and convivial, or something rather hasty and secretive? Mealtimes are a very powerful time of transmission and exchange in childhood; more so perhaps than any other moment of the day, except perhaps preparations for bedtime.

The happy memories cluster round similar experiences in

the common pool of childhood – the sense of being loved, the newness of sensory experience and delight in the world and discovery of others. In the same way, the memory of unhappy moments arises from a shared core of universal experience – fear of the dark, the first hint of mortality, thwarting of the will, the learning of limits, a glimpse of imperfection in loved and loving parents.

'During the First World War, one of us was allowed to sleep with mother in her bed for warmth. I used my pocket money – it was only a penny a week – as bribes with my brothers and sisters to get that coveted favour. I was found out and punished; and after that she made me sleep in a room entirely by myself. The fears I suffered anticipating it invaded my thoughts and play all day. My dread of the night that must come never left me. And this particular shadow has lasted all my life.' Woman, 70s, Buckinghamshire.

'My earliest recollections are of the fear of the wrath of God that was drummed into me. We had to go to church three times a day on Sundays. I had to say prayers night and morning. It was quite unthinkable to close the eyes in sleep without earnest fervent prayer. Sunday, the day of rest, was no rest at all. We walked everywhere, though it involved miles. Such sacrilege to cycle or bus. Quiet was the order of the day; only hymns were played or sung, and the Bible read – not Dickens. The whole family went to all church services, and in addition, children went to Sunday School, morning and afternoon. Prayers were my undoing. To forget meant inescapable punishment, or so I was taught to believe. And I would wait uneasily for God to mete it out to me in some form or another. Many's the time when, weary with sleep, I've knelt with my head bowed over the edge of the bed, struggling through my prayers, in only my nightdress – that was the ritual. Often, I would fall asleep in the middle of it all, to wake up with a start, cold and stiff . . . to carry on again until eventually God was appeased. In winter this could be disastrous, and in fact my health suffered as a result. However, it was something that had to be done; although fear was the driving force, not love. Across my heart was etched, deep and fine, THOU, GOD, SEEST ME. One hot summer's afternoon I had to write these words a hundred times, best handwriting or else . . . I never liked God after that. How could I?' Woman, 72, Halifax.

'I was afraid of the dark, but I never dared tell anybody. I thought it was something in me that was wrong. It wasn't that my parents wanted to make me suffer. My mother would certainly have let me have a light if I'd asked for one. It was the fear of my father's contempt for weakness that held me back. He was always such a stern and controlled person. To this day, no doubt about the rightness of everything he says and does has fallen upon him. He hates people who can't stand up for themselves, who are ill or complain. He's just had a terrible series of operations for cancer; he has known awful pain. In some ways, you'd love to hear a whisper, just a sigh escape him. But nothing. And this was how he expected me to be. I'm not and I never shall be, but I can at least pretend that I am. So every bedtime was filled with terrors for me, right up to the age of 12 or 13. When my mother went out and turned the light off, my imagination used to bring alive all the things in the darkness – the furniture, the shadows, the wardrobe. I'm a weak person, shy, nervous; but I've always had to pretend I was the opposite. There is something terrible being an only child. They gave me a privacy that was like a cell; while they thought they were doing their best for me. I think that's the worst part of it: those who are devoted to you, those who love you best manage to inflict the most terrible wounds. They make no allowance for you being a different person from them: they think you are an extension of them, and they don't see you as a separate being.' Man, 34, Bolton.

Adults' unawareness of what children are thinking and feeling is one of the most common themes in childhood reminiscences; the sense of being misunderstood, not recognized for who you are. George Eliot describes this feeling when she says, 'Family likeness has often a deep sadness in it. Nature, that great tragic dramatist, knits us together by bone and muscle, and divides us by the subtler web of our brains; blends yearning and repulsion; and ties us by the heartstrings to the beings that jar us at every moment.'

'I remember when my father was dying. I was ten. He was in hospital, and I went with my mother and sister to see him. Actually, I'd been in hospital myself, I'd had my tonsils out, and it wouldn't heal. I felt I knew how horrible it was, being in hospital. I was determined to let him know that I understood how he must be feeling. We walked down the ward, and came to his bed. He took one look at me and said, "Get that pasty-faced child out of here." That was the last thing he ever said to me. I had to go and wait outside in a little waiting room. I was angry that I hadn't been allowed to share with him the horror of being in hospital . . . I always felt I was never a person for my father . . . I didn't have any sense of what a father should be like.' Woman, 40s, South London.

'The only time I ever went out with my father, he took me to the Wood Green Empire to see Phyllis Dixey. I must have been four or five. It was a nude show. There was what seemed to me to be this old woman, with huge ostrich feather fans. The comedian on the bill was Arthur English. He came down into the stalls, talking to the audience. He looked at me with what I now realize was pity. He said, "You're a bit young to be out this late, darling." That was the only time I ever went out with my Dad. He had no idea of children, it wouldn't have occurred to him that you don't take toddlers to strip shows.' Woman, 30s, North London.

'When I was a lad, all the women used to come and call their kids in. Summer evenings we'd stay out playing till it was twilight. I wish I could have heard my mother's voice calling me. Not once. They don't realize. I would look at the women on their doorstep and hope that mine would be among them . . . She never called me. I wanted her to call me. I knew that not calling me meant that she didn't care.' Man, 30s, Salford.

'My old lady, she never really wanted to leave her own Mam. She was always round there. We got home from school, the house was always empty. "Where's Mam?" "Round Nan's." She'd be there, they all sat round the fire, her sister, a couple of neighbours, and our Nan – she was a right old witch. I asked Mam to come home. "In a minute." It was always warm round Nan's, scruffy, but it wasn't cold and neglected like ours was. I don't know if it was just our family, but men and women were that different, they might have come from different planets. You'd've thought they were distant acquaintances rather than man and wife, half of them. He went to the pub, Saturday football, down the betting shop. They only met on Sundays, and he was half cut then. I remember feeling pity for my parents. I thought, "Is this life? Is this all there is to it?" I felt not properly looked after, only I didn't know what was missing.

I used to think my mates had a lovely life, I'd go home with them, and their Mam would be in the house like she actually lived there, and there'd be a fire in the grate, and they might have egg and bacon for tea. Bloody heck, it isn't asking much, but we never had it. Then she got mad on Bingo, she used to be there morning, noon and night. My old man one night tied a mattress to the top of the car and dumped it outside the Regal. "Take your bloody bed and live there." We were left to get on with our own life. Carol got pregnant when she was 15. You should've heard them. You'd've thought they were model parents, the way they carried on over her.' Stephen, 19, Wigan.

'My father was good-looking and he had charm, but he was irresponsible. My mother married him for his looks; but he drank, and he didn't care tuppence for the kids. He was a costermonger and he lived by his wits. He had a barrow in Deptford High Street, but he was a bit of a villain. The police were always after him. I wondered why she didn't leave him. I always thought she wouldn't have acted as she did, if she'd known how I felt. I would lie in bed listening to her screaming at my father, and I would be trembling from head to toe and begging God to make them stop.

'She always kept a meal hot for him for whenever he got home; and you never knew when that would be. I've known him in a nasty mood go down to the fish and chip shop before he came home; there were a few tables in this fish shop, and I've seen him sit down and eat fish and chips; and then, when he got home, he'd start a quarrel and end up by throwing his dinner on the fire, all over the range she'd been polishing. But not while he was still hungry. I could never tell my mother what I knew, that I'd seen him go in the fish shop beforehand. It was calculated that he had planned to hurt her, and I had to shield her from the knowledge, when I was the one who wanted shielding myself. I didn't want to know those things.' Woman, 60s, South London.

'I always slept with my mother in her bed. My father was out, supposed to be working nights, but he was with other women. Sometimes, my mother's boyfriend came. And when that happened, they never bothered to move me. This man would say, "What about her?" and my mother would say, "She's all right, she's fast asleep"; and I would lie there, rigid with fright. I was repelled and horrified. But then afterwards I would pretend to wake up. I'd stir and open my eyes as if I'd known nothing that was going on. My mother would say, "See, she knows nothing about it." I had to learn to play-act, to pretend, right from when I was six or seven.' Woman, 40s, Manchester.

It is a common theme that parents don't perceive their own child as him or herself. Sometimes they are re-living their own childhood, or imposing an idealized version or revision of it on their own children: or they may confuse their own feelings with those of their children, seeing them as merely an extension of themselves.

'My mother was always saying that I was part of her, that I was her little girl, that she and I had an understanding. And it wasn't true. She used to tell me how she was disappointed with my father, how thoughtless and selfish he was, what a mistake it was that she'd married him, just a factory worker, when she could have had the pick of Reading when she was a girl. She made me hate him, because all she told me about him was bad. But it went further than this. She held out to me a promise that one day she would leave him, so that she and I could be together. And I couldn't understand why she kept putting it off, what was stopping her. I hated the rows; he was the obstacle to our happiness. But it went on all through the years I was growing up; and she never left him. In the end I felt betrayed by her. What I hadn't seen was that she was telling me only a part of her feelings. The other side was that she got a lot out of the relationship with him, which she took care not to tell me about. She kept him from me, she spoilt any possible relationship between him and me, she kept me all to herself and she kept him all to herself. Later on I realized all the stuff about being her little girl was all a means of keeping me from him. Eventually, I got to resent her, and we had these terrible scenes, where she collapsed in tears and told me I was cruel and ungrateful. She didn't even seem to know what she'd done.' Moira, 29, Reading.

Peter Goodman is in his late 30s. He was adopted as a baby by a family whose son had been killed on a motorbike at the age of 19. He grew up under the shadow of the boy he was intended to replace. This boy had been a paragon, everything his mother could have wished him to be – docile, malleable, compliant. He had never asserted himself, never upset his mother in any way. 'They didn't see me as myself; they just saw me in comparison with David, and of course I could never live up to the hopes they had of me. I felt everything about me was wrong; and it was. When my grandmother was nearing her end, it became pretty obvious that both she and my mother had forgotten me as being me, and they often referred to me as David. The house was full of possessions and bits and pieces that had been his. There were lots of photographs, models he had made, and his toolbox, because he had been an apprentice engineer. But I wasn't allowed to disturb any of his things. Later on, when I managed to achieve things in my own right, prizes at school, there was always this comparison between what I had done and what David would have done. It made me doubt that I even existed. I certainly found it hard to reach any sense of my own identity.'

One's childhood is never finished. Its power to illuminate our feelings and responses is one of the great consolations of growing older. It informs our adult relationships, our love for our own children, and continues as a vital force all through our lives. But even what we may think of as 'our childhood' can be modified, changed by later insight and understanding. When we talk of those years, our conversations are full of regret; and any group of adults remembering childhood will find themselves saying, 'I never realized . . .' 'It was only after my mother died that I fully understood . . .' 'I can see now that he did love me in his way'. What we had perhaps seen as indifference, we can now perceive as an inability to express feeling, their control which was oppressive was the only means they had of expressing their love, a father's authoritarianism was a desperate fear of his own weakness.

'My mother was never really well. She wasn't a hypochondriac, by any means, but she was always slightly ailing. It made me feel rather insecure, and I resented it. Now of course I realize that my father had a whole string of other women, and in her illness she was expressing her feeling that she wasn't loved enough. It was a metaphor. I wish I could have cherished her more. I never told her that I loved her.' Woman, 30s, Lancashire.

'As a kid, I was never given a word of praise. I was always

being put down. Nothing I did was right. My father's tone with me was always slightly patronizing, sneering. And my mother obviously thought he was the most wonderful thing since sliced bread. I wondered what you had to do to win recognition. If I was top of the class in maths, wasn't it a pity about my English; if I was top in English, I'd been neglecting maths. If I was good at swimming, I'd never make a footballer. If I played football, I was wasting my time when I should be studying. If I had a friend, he was leading me astray; if I stayed in and worked, it wasn't natural. Everything about me was wrong. My father's eyes were on me all the time, looking for something to find fault with. I felt discomfort and embarrassment just being in the same room with him. I left home when I was 16, went to live with a friend from school and his family. Then, when he died, I found among his things all the exam results, the little cuttings out of the local paper that said I'd won a scholarship; and all these photos of me as a child. He was proud of me; but he never did directly tell me so.' Man, 43, Northampton.

'I grew up not liking my father or my brother very much. I was my mother's inseparable companion. She confided in me when I was far too young to understand. "Never get married, Gwen." "No Mum." "Men are so brutal." "Yes Mum." "They can only think of one thing." "Yes Mum." The feeling was that men were coarse and physical, selfish . . . I grew up with all the traditional feminine characteristics, to please, to be passive, to wait for things to happen. She always diminished my father. I feel angry now, but more at him than her. I wish he had fought for me more, not allowed her to keep her power over me. I feel I never knew him. I've got to know my brother since we've grown up; but my father's dead, and there's nothing I can do about that now.' Woman, 20s, Berkhamsted.

'Our parents didn't get on. But the children never knew anything about it, at least not while we were young. I was already working when they split up, and even then I thought the end of the world had come. I couldn't forgive them. I can see now that they were so different, they never got on. We didn't think of them as ill-matched. In those days, working people never thought about that at all. Your mother was your mother and that was that. I felt I was the cause of them breaking up. I don't blame myself now, but I did for years.

'My father was earning good money, £8 a week, in a cigarette factory. Some weeks he would take a couple of days off when there was a race meeting down at Kempton Park or wherever; on such a week, he would only get £3 10s or £4. He always boasted that he gave his money direct to my mother as he received it. But I knew that he always saved up the wage packet from the week when he got only half his usual earnings; and he gave her that same wage packet every week until it was all dirty and worn out; and then, when he had another half week, he'd transfer the amount he wanted her to have to the new one. She never knew this. It went on for years. She was proud that he brought all his money to her. It made up for a lot of the discord between them. Not many other women in the street could boast as much.

'When I started work, I started with my father. I was doing a 48-hour week at the same factory, although my job was just sweeping up the dust and the waste. I got 35s a week. I gave my mother 30s and kept the 5s for pocket money. When I'd been working a couple of years, I had a rise, to 38s 6d, so I thought I was entitled to keep the 8s 6d. I didn't say anything, but went on giving my mother the 30s as before. This went on for about four weeks. Then one Friday, I got home from work, and my father was waiting for me. I knew something had happened. He showed me into the front room, which was not used much except on ceremonial occasions, weddings and funerals, sort of thing. My mother followed him in. He challenged me about how much money I was giving my mother, because he'd got to hear of this 3s 6d rise somehow, even though I'd said nothing at home. He made such a thing of it; what an underhand thing I'd done, how I ought to be ashamed. All the time I knew what he'd been doing for years. He went on and on about it, until in the end I felt so aggrieved, I blurted it out, that it wasn't fair when he was doing the same thing himself. My mother knew she'd been getting more housekeeping than many men earned, she had never dreamed he might be deceiving her . . . Well, my saying that was the beginning of the end between them. I'd sort of exposed him in her eyes, the one good thing she thought she knew about him. After that, things went from bad to worse. They separated. I thought it was my fault. I felt guilty.

'Eventually, years afterwards, my father went into an old people's home. I was the only one who visited him during the last years of his life. My mother never went, nor my brother.

When he died, he left £320. That was all he had saved after God knows how many years. I gave my mother three-fifths of it, and kept two-fifths for myself. My brother hadn't come near the old man for years; he had completely rejected him when the parents separated. I thought, "OK, fair enough." The way I'd shared the money seemed reasonable. Later on, when my mother died, my brother said she had told him I hadn't given her any of the money, that I'd kept it all. I was shocked. I made a deed of renunciation. I didn't want it. I said if I'd known she'd said that, I wouldn't have gone to her funeral. My brother said, "Go on, let it rest." But I couldn't. I had to pay back that money. It isn't the money itself; it's what it means that was so important to me, what it revealed about her.' Man, 60s, Croydon.

'Materially, my childhood was all right. My father always had work. He was a carpenter and joiner. But emotionally, it was awful. Their marriage didn't work, but they stuck together "for my sake", as they put it. I wish they hadn't. The atmosphere at home was ice-cold. There were long periods when they didn't even talk to each other. Once it lasted for six months. I dreaded every meal. I thought it was all my fault. For years, I wondered what was wrong with me, that I spread this desolation everywhere. You always think you're the centre of the world when you're a kid. It had to be me. The feeling hung there like a cloud. In the end, my mother asked my father to go. He was flabbergasted. One day, she just changed all the locks. He tried the door, found he couldn't open it and went away. She said he had another woman, which was true. He needed affection and there hadn't been any. She thought being unfaithful was the worst thing she could imagine. She couldn't see the infidelity of indifference. All through my childhood, I thought I'd caused the split between them, and it was my task to bring them together. I ought to have been a diplomat, the efforts I made to reconcile them; all wasted.' Woman, 40s, Bolton.

Most people can remember significant moments, a point when relationships suddenly appeared in a new light; an event that speaks of growing up, a new consciousness, a revelation after which things can never be the same again. These memories are often associated with a loss of innocence (or an end to ignorance): the mask of mother or father may shift and the face of woman or man become visible. These feelings mark the first insight into adult behaviour, although it often cannot be interpreted at the time. It often stays in the mind, and the illumination only occurs later, sometimes many years afterwards.

'There was an argument in our house one Boxing Day when I was ten. It began over whether my father should have sweet pickles as well as pickled onions with his dinner. It unleashed feelings I'd never suspected. He got so angry that he threw the plate down on the table, and it broke in two, and the dinner went all over the table. Then they both went into the kitchen to continue the argument on their own; and then they went upstairs, which was unusual, because they only ever talked in the front room. And we could hear what they were saying quite clearly. He said, "Ours has never been a proper marriage, ever." And that opened all sorts of possibilities. If theirs wasn't a proper marriage, were they not proper parents, were we not proper children? You felt you had seen yourself, as well as them, in a new light, and it was very frightening.' Man, 30s, Bristol.

'My parents never had rows. He always refused to argue with her. But as I grew up my mother would pick arguments with me. One day I realized that whenever this happened, it would distress my father. I found that more disturbing than the row. He would plead with us not to quarrel, to calm down. He was a very peaceful and tolerant man, but he always got agitated whenever my mother picked on me. She would attack my friends, my appearance, my manners, whatever it was; but I began to see that these things were just an excuse. Her arguments with me were really arguments with him by proxy. Arguments with him had become very insipid to her; I think her feelings had deserted him. But she knew she could get a response from me, so she poured all her emotion into me. It was the extent to which I'd taken on a sort of husband role for her that disturbed my father and upset him so much. He was obviously well aware of it, but it was one of those things that take place well below the level of spoken exchange. It can take years before you realize what is happening. That's why a lot of working-class people turn to actions, because there isn't the tradition of talking about things.' Man, 40s, Leicester.

'I tried to intervene in my parents' arguments. I thought it was up to me to restore harmony between them; after all, most of them were prompted by me. But whenever I tried to mediate, they turned on me. They were always united against me. I was about 14 before I realized that they were provoking me as a means of achieving unity between themselves. My mother would taunt me with my shortcomings, and she would goad me until I got angry with her, and then that was his cue to come in. In lots of ways, they were at their happiest when they had me to attack. It gave them a stronger sense of being together than anything else. I can actually remember the day when I saw what was really going on. It gave me a wonderful sense of strength. I recognized that what I had to do was not to respond to the taunting. That made my mother more nagging and shrill than ever, and when I still didn't respond, she became so vehement that my father actually came to my defence. I felt a real triumph over it. But I think the damage had been done to my self-esteem all the years I was the battleground between them.' Woman, 30s, Peterborough.

'I was six when the war broke out. My father was away from home a lot. He was supposed to be "fire-watching" in the Home Guard, but I came to understand this stood for something else. I found out in a very dramatic way, the night we were bombed out. We didn't have a direct hit, but the houses around us were destroyed, and all our ceilings fell down and the windows were blown out. We always went down into the shelter in the cellar, but my father never came with us. He always stayed upstairs, in his bed, as he told us, unless he was fire-watching. That night, as usual, he said he wouldn't come into the shelter, he would stay upstairs and sleep. When the all-clear went, we rushed out, and I was preparing to see my father dead in the bed. If he had been there he would certainly have been killed – there were great chunks of masonry and plaster on the bed and shattered glass everywhere. But of course he wasn't there. My mother said he was fire-watching. But I knew then he wasn't, and I could tell from the expression on her face. I was about ten.' Woman, 40s, South London.

In the memories of childhood, second only to the relationship between parents and children, is that between brothers and sisters. The same change is observable here: for older people, and those who grew up in large families, the siblings are remembered far more as an accepted part of the landscape of childhood. They represented a more or less undifferentiated companionship; of course, individuals had their preferences and sympathies, but these tended not to be elaborated. But for those who grew up with only one or two others, the change from role to relationship is more sharply defined.

'My early years to me mean the warmth of being together. There were seven of us, and I was the youngest but one. We played together, my older sisters looked after me. We fell out, but never for long. My mother used to say, "I won't make fish of one and fowl of another," she treated us all alike. You didn't stop to wonder whether you liked each other or not; you loved each other. We had a feeling of fraternity. And that spread outwards, to the other kids in the street. They weren't different from us. I slept with my two brothers in the same bed, you didn't like being the one in the middle, especially when it was hot in summer, but it never occurred to me to want to sleep on my own. I've never slept on my own in all my life, except when I was in the army. I look at my granddaughter now. She's got her own room, oh it's beautiful. She's got her own television, and all her photographs on the wall, and I say to myself, "Yes, very nice, but where are all the people in her life?"' Man, 73, Rushden, Northants.

'I could tell my sister anything. We had no secrets from each other. We shared the same pram, the same bed, we even started work in the same factory. She knew all about my life, all the years my husband was playing fast and loose. If I hadn't had her to confide in, I don't know what I should have done. My husband was always jealous of her, he was jealous of all my family . . . When Maud died, eight years ago, I was broken-hearted. I shall never get over it. She has been closer to me than anyone else in my life.' Woman, 68, Derbyshire.

'My sister died of TB when I was nine. She was 18. I've still got her diary. I can never read it without crying.' She shows me the little leather diary, with the entries through the years while the sister was in the sanatorium, feeling now a little better, now not so well, marking all her hopes and disappointments in neat handwriting: 'I love Mummy more and more'; 'I don't know who I love best out of Mummy and God'. A sad little relic of a spent young life. Woman, 50, Manchester.

'I hated my sister's guts when she was born. When I say I was jealous, that's an understatement. I was six. I was staying with my grandmother, and they phoned to say that my mother had had a baby girl. Grandma said, "Aren't you lucky?" I said, "Tell them to send it back." And she smacked my legs for it. "God gave you a baby sister." But I hated her. I tipped her out of her pram, and when we had a bath together, I gave her soap to eat. It's a wonder she survived. I can't exaggerate my feelings. I'm sure nobody had such a jealous childhood as mine. We couldn't be left in a room together for fear of what I might do to her. When she was five months old, my mother's sister, Auntie Jill, had a baby boy. We went to see the new baby, and jokingly, they said, "Shall we leave your sister for Auntie Jill and take the little boy home?" I thought they meant it. When it turned out they didn't, I screamed blue murder because we hadn't got rid of her, left her behind . . . Four years later, my other sister was born. I accepted her completely, got on well with her, and still do. But Pearl, the first one, she was like a china doll when she was born; they told me I looked like a monkey. She was pretty and she had long shining hair. I was tall and lanky and I had buck teeth, and I was bald when I was born. She was a dolly. She was everybody's perfect little girl. She looked a bit like Margaret O'Brien, lovely long plaits. People used to look at me and say, "Isn't it a shame she's so ugly", or, "It's a good job Pearl hasn't got those teeth". They used to say it in front of me, no regard for feelings, as though if you're not attractive you don't have sensitivity either. They just assumed I was a disturbed child after Pearl was born. They just accepted it. I wet the bed for years. They took me to a specialist, clinics . . . My mother went on and on about it, she used to say, "It's about time you washed the bloody sheets." She told everybody about it, and that made it worse. But it doesn't seem to have occurred to anybody that what was wrong was the most obvious thing of all.' Woman, 40s, Southampton.

'When I was 11, my brother was born. My father was delighted that it was a boy. He made it clear that boys were more welcome. I resented the new baby; and my mother never forgave me for it. At the beginning, I wanted to love him. I wanted to hold him. They said no, no. They kept me away from him. I can remember one incident. Mother and father were upstairs with the baby, and I wanted to stay with them and share their pleasure. But I had to go downstairs by myself and get on with the washing-up. I was very hurt. I stood at the sink, and I began to think "They like the baby better than me." It was obvious. I felt, not so much rejected as inferior. My father had expected certain things of me: not that I should do well at school, but that I should be polite and helpful, the female role, acquire social graces, speak nicely. The greatest consolation of my childhood was my dog. It was very important to me; especially because this dog hated my brother. She was a Corgi bitch, they're not very tolerant creatures at the best of times. She used to growl at him, even at his toys. I loved her. I wanted her to be my friend.' Woman, 30s, Blackpool.

'I was dearly loved by my parents. I always knew how much they adored me, how they gave me everything, sacrificed their own lives. But that was easily won: what I wanted as a child was a brother. The only thing they couldn't or wouldn't give me. I used to tell everyone lies. I invented a brother and I played games with him, and I went to sleep thinking about him. He became more real than any of my friends. I used to hate my parents, because there I was on my own, without a companion. The love of my parents seemed insipid beside the love I got from this mythical brother. I think my lonely childhood made it difficult for me to share things with people. I have to dominate people. I've got no way of being their equal. I can only approach them by condescending.' Man, 37, Mansfield.

'I always had this feeling that I had no place in the family. Tom was the eldest, Jim the youngest, Carol was the girl. I used to wonder who the bloody hell I was. I never fitted in. I had to try to do things to get myself noticed. That was how I became the tearaway, the troublemaker. Tom was tough, he was a champion boxer, lightweight, he could've made a career out of it. Jim was clever, he was always getting prizes at school. They said Carol was a good-looker. It seemed like all the others had got it worked out for them. I wasn't unhappy as a child, I just wondered what the hell I was doing here in the family, where I had to fight to be accepted . . . It comes out in funny ways when you're grown up. I never make out with a chick on her own; but if she's got a boyfriend, I make it my business to take her away from him. I've been in a lot of bother with married women. I think it all comes from this habit of having to fight for things. You don't know when to stop.' Man, 26, Liverpool.

'My trouble was that I could never live up to my brother. I was always asked by my parents, teachers, everybody, why I couldn't be more like him. He'd been good and clever, and everybody liked him. I felt he'd got in first, and I was a terrible disappointment. One day my mother gave me my brother's school report to show to the teacher. It was like showing them how impossible it was for me to come up to his standards. In the end I decided that if I was going to be a disappointment, I'd do it in a spectacular way. I wounded this kid at a dance. I went to Borstal. When I was doing it, I had this fantasy that this kid I was knifing was my brother.' Man, 20s, Bristol.

WORKING-CLASS CHILDHOOD:
ROLES v. RELATIONSHIPS

IF ANYONE HAD asked our grandparents what kind of a relationship they had with their children, they would probably have said, 'What do you mean? They are our children.' For most parents and children, the position was given and static. This is reflected in the words that recur as the very old recall their childhood now – discipline, obedience, 'you knew where you stood,' – expressions that suggest subordination. The relationship between child and parents was fixed; what we now, disparagingly, refer to as a role. And if you ask most working-class people what have been the greatest gains of childhood in the course of living memory, they will say quite simply, 'freedom'.

This change is reflected in all family relationships. To the old, mothers, fathers, sons and daughters were good mothers etc. according to external measures of behaviour. A good daughter was dutiful and submissive, did her share of household chores, in preparation for being a good mother in her turn; a good mother was one who managed to feed her children even when there was not enough money, who kept them warm and clean and taught them right from wrong, only calling upon father's strap cr belt to deal with major breaches of conduct. These objective standards applied even to the most intimate relationships – those between husbands and wives. A good wife was one who tended her husband's needs, who provided him with some relief from the harshness of the conditions of his work; a good husband gave her enough money for housekeeping, didn't drink too much, didn't gamble or run after other women. And if, as was frequently the case of course, people failed to live up to these standards, they could be judged – and those tight vigilant communities had long memories and could be very unforgiving – even though it was rare for people to separate. 'My mother was always moaning to anybody who would listen about my Dad; how selfish he was, how unfeeling, what a trial it was to live with him. She used to go on and on. One day a neighbour said to her, "Have you ever thought about divorcing him?" My mother was outraged. She said, "Divorce him? Never. I've often thought about murdering the bugger, but divorce him, never." ' Woman, 40s.

But in the middle of the twentieth century, those roles have become burdensome and intolerable, and we have done our best to throw them off. The whole triumph of the various liberation movements lies in the extent to which they have helped people escape oppressive roles – felt to be unreal, constricting, inauthentic – in order to explore relationships, which, by contrast, attract words like rich, deep, exciting, lasting, developing. Everything that suggests dynamism, energy, is held in the word relationship; whereas to talk about roles – the female role, role-play, implies timidity and repression, an inability to develop.

Relationships offer the promise of something not known, uncharted and unpredictable; whereas everything in a role is understood at the outset and familiar. And yet, 'relationships' in practice seem such fragile things, so susceptible to breakdown, to false starts. The courts, the lonely hearts columns, the introduction agencies, the increase in single-parent families, the loneliness – the whole of contemporary society seems to be littered with the debris of these desirable but frail associations, just as the city streets are littered with the wrappings and containers of whatever has just been consumed. It is a commonplace that marriages break down more readily than they did, that attachments are more volatile and impermanent. There are many who advance this as evidence of freedom, in contrast with the constricting straitjacket of that joyless subservience to roles that kept so many people, men and women alike, in subjection.

A network of roles implies another purpose beyond the relationships contained within it. The relationships are still there, the jealousies, the preferences, the conflicts; but they remain in embryo, controlled, and usually subordinate. In poor societies, where survival is more important than the elaboration of relationships, the kind of ferocious personal struggles that lock people together in our own more leisured society are less known.

And yet, if the opportunities in the exploration of relation-

ships for excitement, discovery and intensity are unlimited, so
perhaps is the potential for damage, disappointment and pain.
The question of what we have been liberated into is always
more disconcerting than that of the oppressions we have
emerged from. In what we like to think of as our enlightenment,
we come to regard our background as no more than that: we see
the selves we have left behind as empty husks, like chickens
looking back at the broken fragments of a shell. And when we
consider the ways in which mothers were crushed by their role
of self-sacrifice and martyrdom, how men were diminished by
their scope for dominion over the family, as well as their
obligation to be strong-willed and powerful when they felt at
their most weak and vulnerable; how children were tied by
duty, how wives effaced themselves and submitted to their
husbands' whims, we tend to say, 'Thank God all that is over;
good riddance to it.'

But then we may feel our reaction against fixed roles has been
too violent; and the destruction of them is a serious loss. Of
course it is true that roles can be crushing: the breaking of
individuals for the sake of received codes of behaviour is cruel.
But it can be no less cruel than to remove those constraints and
call it freedom. All the lonely and the separated, the poor
bruised humanity that provides so much of the raw material for
social and psychiatric work express this more than anything
else: an inability to live up to the norm that says there is no
norm. There is something pitiable about all the mothers and
children, brothers and sisters, husbands and wives locked in
struggle, trying to transcend the kinship roles, caught in a
furious fight for dominion, for recognition, for tribute, for
affirmation that they do, indeed, exist, and do have some
identity, as they seek to wrest from each other what no
individual can give – the meaning of life, a reason for living. All
the violence within families in the last decades of the twentieth
century, the beating of women and children, the rupture
between partners who thought they loved each other, the
arbitrary dissolution of relationships – these things are an
expression, not of the coercive power of the family and family
roles, but of the absence that has succeeded it.

Yet how can it be that the decay of these old constrictions
could represent anything less than a major advance, a vast
liberation of human feelings and affections? How can there be

anything damaging in being yourself, expressing yourself through your closest relationships? Many people declare that 'human relationships' are their principal reason for living. Perhaps the real question should be whether the idea of a self has meaning, if it is not anchored in social function, not defined by social role, separated from a wider purpose. Erik Erikson, in *Childhood and Society*, speaking of his experience as a psychoanalyst says, 'To condense it into a formula: the patient of today suffers most under the problem of what he should believe in and who he should – or, indeed, might – be or become; while the patient of early psychoanalysis suffered most under inhibitions which prevented him from being what and who he thought he knew he was. In this country especially (i.e. the United States), adult patients and the parents of prospective child patients often hope to find in the psychoanalytic system a refuge from the discontinuities of existence, a regression and a return to a more patriarchal one-to-one relationship.'

It is quite plain where these changes in the patterns of relationship in the working class have come from: they have filtered down through time from the example of those above them. For instance, the individuation of children is a relatively recent development among the poorest. Within living memory, a woman, being informed that her child had died at the age of six weeks, shook her head philosophically, and patted her stomach saying, 'Plenty more where that came from.' It sounds harsh and unfeeling now; but in the experience of such high infant mortality it makes more sense to be armoured against too overwhelming a grief. The controlling and distancing power of roles did provide a rampart against some of the more convulsive emotions.

And what we are pleased to look at as such clear gains appear more questionable when you think of the tendency of so many relationships to fall in upon themselves and to end in relentless obsessive warfare, where there remains no other purpose than for each to compel the other to yield to what he or she wants; when you think of the midnight phone call from those who have arbitrarily been abandoned by a partner for somebody else, the dumb misery of children who move in changing constellations of half-brothers and half-sisters and new mothers and substitute fathers, for whom, at the age of only nine or ten, the only constant feature is the inconstancy of adults; when you think of the violence, the expenditure of energy, the pain and the scarring, it makes you long for some constraint, something that will limit the expression of that raging unfettered self. Roles provided a shelter against this process of denuding individuals until they are caught in relentless struggle with each other. If the old were imprisoned in an oppressive structure of role-playing that denied self-expression, the young are liberated into a search for identity that can only be found in conflict with others – the very people to whom we are bound by love or by blood.

Most people are well aware of these changes; but because they reach into our deepest attachments to each other, go to the core of what we consider our most private emotions, it is much harder to understand how and why the changes have occurred. The search for authenticity, for self-expression and fulfilment in relationships is a result of changes which are essentially social and economic; but because these things seem remote from our personal lives, and because of the division between the personal and the social, we tend to be repelled by this idea. It is as though we believed that society, when it ceases to intervene in our lives through poverty and scarcity, ceases to exist, simply atrophies; whereas, of course, it extends its influence in more subtle but no less stringent ways than when it showed itself through the old coercive disciplines, through hunger and poverty.

Because children are at the point where a society prepares its future adults, the testimonies of childhood through time should provide a more or less clear indication of the nature of change. Certainly they will illuminate the changed function of the working class, from which so many of the modifications in the way we live are derived. It is no mystery that the control and disciplining of children at the earliest point in living memory in this book (Mr Baines, a child of the early 1890s) was a reflection of their future role as labour. The parents had to collude with the loveless disciplines of mine, mill and factory. They had no choice in the matter, even though the worst effects of these processes were mitigated by the power of their love.

And the same response is observable within the changed context of the 1980s; the same collusion is there with the external forces that shape our lives. The change for the working class has been from a complex of crippling restraints associated with the old purpose of providing labour for the capitalist machine to a state of disabling licence, as that function has, to a considerable extent, decayed. The fact that the change appears to be a complete reversal effectively conceals what remains constant through time – the lasting impotence and debilitation.

All the ambiguities, the joys and pains of love have to be expressed through these changing social pressures; with the result that many people find it difficult to disentangle them. Alterable social influences seem to fuse with unchanging human feelings. The old people who talk of their childhood and remember the stair rod, the cane, the belt, with which their parents sought to correct and control them don't think of their parents with revulsion or anger. On the contrary, the use of that considerable range of ugly chastening instruments doesn't in any way dim the memories of loving care and the utmost tenderness; so much so, that many older people say they are grateful to their parents for having freely applied the cane or the strap. Similarly today, the sometimes desperate attempt of parents to make good the deficiencies of their own upbringing by providing their children with all the material things they can, doesn't always call forth the sense of gratitude and recognition which they expect.

When this book begins, in the 1890s, the cruel conditions of work and life for the majority of working-class people created a sense of solidarity and continuity between the generations: there was no reason then to expect that the lives of the next generation would be any more free from want and poverty than the one that preceded it. The feeling of a shared project of survival worked as a powerful bond between people, and created a closeness that has subsequently decayed. Where the social conditions were damaging, they have, during the course of the later part of this century, taken on all the attributes of a healing benignity, in the form of a vast material abundance and the promises that flow from it. This has had important consequences for the sense of a shared project between parents and children. The collusion is still there, in that parents feel their primary function is to give their children access to the material riches on offer, but at the same time the defensive closeness that united them has been broken. Of course, the power of love, the inherited affinities between parents and children redeem much; but even that love has a hard passage through the materialism of the world of the young, just as it did through the exactions of poverty.

But it means that the release into relationships from the stifling roles is not the enhancement it should have been. It cannot be, because it is an expression of a change that continues to demand the subordination of human beings to the same system which formerly robbed the working class of its last ounce of effort and energy in work. The change means this: capitalism has cozened the working class out of the brave defensive response it made to poverty and work; all the sharing, the capacity for closeness and solidarity, all the human resources that were developed to humanize that poverty are being drained away. In place of all this a dependency on the market-place has been created, so that people will be goaded into trying to buy back all the things that have been taken away from them. And because a generation of children has grown up within the dependency, they seem to be strangers to those who knew they had nothing but each other.

The old look back with regret on the security the jettisoned roles gave them; and the young do not know who they are. We should not deceive ourselves, either about the imposition of fixed immobilizing responses of role, any more than we should about the liberation that really means the removal of function and purpose, and hence of identity. There can be no question of any desirability of a return to the old roles, the mute suffering and martyrdom of women and their vengeance by stealth on the children, nor to the tyranny of those men whose hearts had to be hard as the metal, steel or wood with which they worked. But neither will dignity be reached through the disabling cramping freedoms which the market-place has conferred on children. We are trapped in an oscillation between an authoritarianism and a liberation which are both inadequate, because they serve the same purpose, not serving humanity, but subordinating it to an idolatry of money and profit.

12

BETWEEN TWO CULTURES:
CHILDHOOD IN TRANSITION

BECAUSE THE CHANGES in childhood experience I have been describing are cultural rather than temporal, it isn't possible to say that they occurred at one precise moment. It is a dynamic and continuing process. I am keenly aware of how it touched me and my contemporaries in our circumstances, but it will have affected others differently, at other times, and in differing degrees.

Those of us born into the working class in the middle years of this century lived through a transition from excessive dependency on role-ascription in the family (father authoritarian, mother softer but subordinate, children absorbing appropriate sex-role responses and reproducing them in their own family) to its reverse – too great an isolation of individual families in which 'private' needs were paramount. In this altered circumstance, adult identity was something that had to be fought for and won, as though it were a prize which parents tried to withhold from their children. In theory, this process should have involved a weakening of sex-stereotyping; but because it coincided with the decay of so many traditional working-class purposes, the sex-roles became, if anything, reinforced, being one of the few tangible, given things for people to fall back on, among new uncertainties and lack of direction.

The change from a working class rigidly controlled and disciplined for the sake of its place in the productive process to a generation which has now to accept an absence of any function or purpose more significant than that of demolishing the vast output that mechanized production ensures, is, naturally enough, reflected above all in what is sometimes described as the 'revolution' in child-rearing practices. These are represented as absolutes of enlightenment and freedom, because they are set against the foil of the old repressions; and this, together with the fact that they happen to coincide with vast improvements in health and material care, masks something else that has also happened; which is that human purposes have been sacrificed, in order that capitalism might sustain itself scathelessly. Instead of the children of the working class being subjected to rigorous self-denial in preparation for a lifetime in mill or mine, they have been offered instead the promise of the easy and immediate gratification which, in the end, can sabotage human development and achievement just as effectively as the poverty and hunger of the past. The rousing of appetites instantly answered by some trifling and bought consolation – and oral dependency is its symbol – operates as a brake upon the developing capacity for a wider vision and deeper understanding, encourages the abandonment of tougher, more long-term objectives. This kind of exploitation has developed out of something that was formerly prevalent in working-class life – the indulgence of very small children. As Richard Hoggart described it in *The Uses of Literacy*, 'Babies are smothered with love and attention, not allowed to cry, stuffed till their little bellies ache and then given dubious remedies in sixpenny packets.' If we wonder at the failure of so many children of the working class to achieve, despite the increased 'opportunities', to become more wise and more alert to each other's needs, it is because the only chance many of them have to express themselves is in the closed universe, the preselected choices of the market-place. They grow without any role or function defining itself for them. The possibility now is for whole generations to grow up in good health, virtually assured of survival, but this spectacular achievement has been annexed, not to human purposes, but to a system which exists for the sake of profit; and in its interests their energies and powers have been remorselessly sacrificed, choked back, suppressed. If they grow up to an impaired sense of identity, to cynicism, violence and nihilism, indifference to others, with at the same time a vast unappeasable hunger that expends itself in worthless material things that are a deformity of human satisfactions, this simply reflects the systematic neglect of their real abilities and strengths. Of course many individuals overcome these terrible obstacles, in the same way that the spirit triumphed over poverty and squalor in earlier generations; but such obstacles are quite gratuitous in the rich societies of the West, except in so far as they serve the cold loveless objectives of capitalism.

We, perhaps more than any other generation, bestride these extremes. We are deeply aware of the childhood of our parents, denied and subordinated for the sake of the labour they were destined to become; and we have lived to see our own children delivered into a corrupting plenty, which has as its end, not the fulfilment of human needs, but that which corrodes identity, extinguishes purpose and substitutes fantasy for achievement. And both have been for the sake of profit, the one thing that remains constant and untroubled through all the changes that have convulsed people's lives. Whether human beings are formed by the earlier conditions or the more recent ones, the process is cruel and reductive; for those who live through the transition, it can be bewilderingly destructive and violent.

When we were growing up, the pain we felt in our transitional role was, we thought, a result of our unique personal circumstances. This no longer seems so. It was something of these changes, vast impersonal forces, which reached into the most secret places in our lives, invaded and broke into the most precious and deeply felt of all our relationships.

It seemed to me – and to many of those I grew up with – that our adult status had to be wrenched from our parents. We had to fight for our adulthood, as though it were a right we could easily have forfeited by default. It became the life project of our parents to resist granting it. For those of us from the working class who continued our education to university, even the attenuated rites of passage which many other adolescents went through – the first wage-packet, being called up for National Service and, later, learning to drive – passed us by. The final break with home didn't even occur as with those who got married at 19 or 20; and our childhood prolonged itself, uncertain of its limits, reluctant, in a way, to finish because, perhaps, we sensed that when it did so something irrecoverable – more than childhood itself – would be lost.

Our parents had always claimed to be looking forward to the time when we would be off their hands, the time when we would go to university, get married, find a place of our own, settle down, get a job. Ever since we could remember, they had emphatically anticipated their liberation from us. After all, we were a phenomenon virtually unknown in that working-class town: until that time, everybody, it seemed, had left school at 15, started work, got married, ensured continuity.

But as the years passed, our parents became aware that all the plans they had made for when we should have left them, the plans to pursue their own lives, were not real. Their own freedom threatened to be a vacuum. Their lives were inextricably bound up in ours, in a way that had not quite happened with earlier generations. The separation, when it came, wouldn't be the separation of simply moving into another house, probably within walking distance, and starting a family. It would be a more total and violent break.

They discovered – or, sadly, sometimes failed to discover – that they were living through us. During their lifetime, what had seemed to them the given social purpose – surviving poverty, unemployment, avoiding hunger, shame and the workhouse, had decayed. So they clung to us. We became their social purpose, their religious and political purpose too. It was this that turned our emancipation into the battle it became. It was a battle made more bitter than it had been in the generations before us, because it took place now in the decayed cultural tradition, in which the sense of continuity had been interrupted. The personal conflict was intensified; reconciliation became more difficult.

The story of our growing-up became an escape story. Far into our adult lives, we continued to exchange stories about our parents, our prolonged and painful detachment from what we saw as their impossible demands, their unreasonableness, their lack of understanding of the educational processes they had so fervently wished for us. They were merely responding with their feelings (we said), while we thought we knew of something better, which we called fulfilment, finding ourselves, self-expression. Whatever it was, it involved great emotional violence and, later, loneliness. We thought of our struggles as heroic conflicts between enlightenment and superstition. We thought of them as uniquely personal dramas; although in fact, they were almost identical in the feelings they aroused, and were far more a result of social influences and conditions than we were prepared to contemplate. Even that term itself – social conditions – had to us an archaic ring, as though it applied only to poverty, something punitive and depriving. Social conditions were what our parents had grown up in. We thought ourselves exempt from their influence.

We felt they couldn't understand us. And, as though to

support us, a whole culture was being born that seemed based on that simple proposition. What we didn't know was that our parents had never had to emancipate themselves from their parents in quite this way. There had been no need for it – in spite of the changes, there had been a general sameness of expectations over the generations, basically, that life would be determined by work and want. It wasn't that they had never known tyrannical fathers or clinging mothers, only that other things had seemed more urgent then: the fear of poverty, illness, loss, was a stronger defining edge for the personality than the attempts to resist the demands of ageing individuals seeking comfort and support in old age. The things they shared with their parents were more important to them than the things which separated them. The context in which they took place made their personal struggles more benign.

But we all quarrelled with our mothers and fathers. Their possessiveness, their custody of our youth, seemed oppressive. When they tried to perpetuate their values and beliefs, these seemed not to apply to the world we saw, and we became hostile and rejecting. They were preventing us from being ourselves. I sometimes wonder now what we thought those thwarted selves might have been, liberated from the place in which they had grown and the people who had nurtured and loved them. But we fought them all the time, and then hurried round to our friends in order to compare experience: had a mother feigned illness, had another threatened to put her head in the gas oven, had somebody's father really put all his things out on the pavement and told him to get out and never come back?

Our parents suffered doubly. Because their fight with their own parents had never taken this bitter form, it was all unfamiliar. They could see no reason why we should attack them all the time. It appeared to them horrifying and inexplicable, our endless criticism, our combative irritation, our desire to change them, to correct their attitudes, modify their values – to re-shape them, as we had been re-shaped. We were part of the assault on authority and parents, devaluing, disparaging, so that youth might acquire the power that had to be prised from them; and we broke the fingers of their grip on us as though they had been dead twigs. It all served a purpose wider than that of our personal liberation, although that was all we could see.

Well into our 20s we spent time in cruel and shameless exultation in the awfulness of our parents. We passed long evenings resolving that we would never finish up like that; being amazed at the circumscribed lives, the lack of insight, the passivity and the acceptance of things. Once the taboo was broken, there was no limit to our malice. And then, later in the evening, I would arrive home, and find my mother sipping a comforting mug of hot milk, with her hair in its thin night-time braid, and I would feel guilty at her timid approach, her anxious question as to whether I was all right or whether anything was worrying me; her shyness in front of what part of her acknowledged as superior to her.

Above all we criticized them for failing to understand the way in which we thought, mistakenly alas, the world had changed. We had to be loosed from the bonds transmitted over generations, because we were to be protean and adaptable; we had to be prepared to do anything, go anywhere. There was no knowing what might be demanded of us; we really couldn't be expected to stay tethered to a small provincial town. The social destination of our parents had always been more certain: they had been designated for the factories almost from birth. What possible relation could there be between the values required for a continuing and conservative tradition of manual labour and the sense of destiny with which we had been saturated? But they still tried, clumsily, to impose the values of their own upbringing onto us; and for us, growing-up meant above all resisting them, reacting against them. The result of this conflict would, we assumed, yield us our true identity. But it was an identity made up entirely of negation.

So when we began to fight for a kind of individualism they had never aspired to, they were deeply troubled. They had never sought to fulfil such refined needs and appetites as those we were pursuing. They might have judged their parents, declared that their mother was a saint, their father an old sod; or their mother might conceivably have been a 'wrong 'un' (though not often: saintliness was the consolation prize awarded to generations of repressed women), and their father 'a true gentleman'. But the elaborate process of emotional withdrawal that we went through was quite unknown to them, and the tearing of ourselves from them actually severed something, deep and wounding, which has never really healed. We saw our parents as obstacles to what we considered our development, and we struck against them until they yielded.

My contemporaries and I are now almost middle aged; and it is possible to assess, from the other side, what have been the gains and losses of that prolonged struggle. First of all, we are generally still in contact with each other, even those of us who had to go away to find ourselves – to Australia, the United States. But the rest of us still meet often and are still close; something of the shared experience of ancient combatants unites us. In dissolving the bonds of kinship with our families – and it was a commonplace among us that families were arbitrary groupings, and that ours meant little to us – it seems as though we unintentionally evolved a new kind of elective kinship with friends, which in effect became almost a replica of the stifling structure from which we were trying to escape. But at least, we thought, this has not been imposed upon us.

It was as though we feared the negative aspect of our new freedom – the loneliness of being without kin, cut off from individuals bound by blood to support and help each other in time of need; and accordingly, we evolved a substitute network which we could rely on until such time as we should be able to dispense with them, stand alone perhaps, find more congenial and rewarding companions.

But this primary group hasn't dissolved. It is a common thing to find in London – where most of us now live – groups of friends held together simply by having come from the same town, by having been at university together, having shared a first job. These often turn out to be attempts to reconstitute the roles that were swept away by what we, who came from Northampton, regarded as our emergence from the disabling constraints of kinship.

The early, provisional relationships persist. We still contact each other when we are in need or unhappy: tearful telephone calls in the early hours, long letters detailing the breakdown of a marriage, or the fantasies of an infatuation with someone we met at a party. When we see each other, we still talk about our parents, ageing now or dead; but the tone has changed to one of sorrowing and affectionate regret. Now that the struggles have lost their urgency, we feel ashamed of our past vehemence. We meet at their funerals, visit them during their terminal illnesses, write letters to their widows. Only the guilt remains.

And the people who seemed to free us then, fetter us now. They have become the fixed points in our lives. They remind us of our limitations, the impossibility of transcending the selves that we thought we could so easily set aside. They show us, repeatedly, the limits of human associations. They illuminate our fumbling after structures, our need for institutions and permanence after our longed-for liberation. And if, after 20 years or more, our elective kindred seem almost as unfulfilling and predictable as our parents once did, we also discover that our obligations to each other are not so binding as those which devolved on us by birth. If, as has occurred, one of us is discovered to be suffering from an irreversible degenerative disease, our lives will not be disrupted to the extent of an unlimited commitment, although we will visit the hospital, offer an invitation to come and stay for a week or two, go and help decorate a flat, keep in touch, rally round. It is at moments like these that the full extent of our gain can be measured. We know that we are not totally committed, as we would have been by birth ties, and at times of crisis; we can in all conscience withdraw, so that the surviving members of the blood-family or the statutory services can take over. We have the best of both worlds; although, somehow, it doesn't seem to amount to very much; and it is far from the fulfilment we once anticipated.

When I think now of our parents, those old people with their failing bodies and tired spirits, whom we fought as if they were our mortal enemies and not our mothers and fathers, I feel that the removal of the obstacles we thought they represented didn't yield anything like what we expected; and at such cost too. The struggle with them prolonged itself and re-emerged, elusively, in similar struggles: people we married or lived with, people we love or, more often, have loved and moved on from (and after the painful detachment of children from parents in that way, the severance of other relationships becomes all too easy); and some of them now our own children. The release from parents and kin has turned into a sterile project of fighting, fighting for dominion over others, for validation or recognition; there being no other social purpose urgent enough to absorb our energies or gain our commitment.

The fight we had with our parents was, after all, redundant and full of pain. We tried to shed traditional bonds, become ourselves, untrammelled by the restricted and place-bound vision of those who gave us birth. We created a network of relationships that was none; and we set about the pursuit of private needs, which has turned into the excavation of an immense and deepening chasm. At the bottom of it, there is nothing but our own loneliness. We have achieved a kind of community; but ironically, it is in the one thing we cannot share – our own isolation.

And the significance of the social change which we thought would bring us freedom is clear at last. We thought we were special; what was happening to us occurred only because we were unique individuals. But we were only pioneers, showing the way to the rest of the working class.

13

THE DISCOVERY OF SEX

THE DISCOVERY OF sex is perhaps the most powerful metaphor for the richness and diversity of the secret life of children. It remains traditionally submerged, unacknowledged by the adults, who want children to live in their fantasy of sexless innocence. The discrepancy between the attributed 'innocence' and the reality of direct experience is a source of much conflict and bitterness, but also of amusement when it is looked back on from adult life. Children have always been interested in sex, and the evolving sensations of their own bodies. Most adults can recall the kind of whispered half-knowledge and mythology that grew in the official adult silence that surrounded it. But perhaps a measure of the change in working-class life in recent years is the growing precision of children's knowledge of the mechanics of sex, if not of the more subtle feelings associated with it. Aries, in *Centuries of Childhood*, writes, 'One of the unwritten laws of contemporary morality, the strictest and best-respected of all, requires adults to avoid any reference, above all, any humorous reference, to sexual matters in the presence of children . . . The modern reader of the diary in which Henry IV's physician, Heroard, recorded the details of the young King Louis XIII's life is astonished by the liberties which people took with children, by the coarseness of the jokes they made, and by the indecency of gestures made in public which shocked nobody and which were regarded as perfectly natural. No other document can give us a better idea of the non-existence of the modern idea of childhood at the beginning of the 17th century.'

But the culture of the market-place, and its pervasive influence, has made children more aware of the importance of sex in the last two or three decades, because sex has become such an important vehicle for selling things to people. It is tempting to see this process as a liberating force, a return to the more open and 'natural' attitude, as described by Aries; a way of emancipating children from hypocrisy and Puritanism, traditionally repressive attitudes. And it is true that the ignor-ance and the unhappiness this caused many older working-class people (and not only working class) did distort the lives of many individuals. But the kind of liberation from that kind of repression to the salacious half-knowledge of many children is like so many of the other brave ideas given expression in the capitalist context, which instantly corrupts and spoils them, because they have to be deformed in such a way that they will not upset the existing order, or can be incorporated into it. In this way, the knowingness of children does not set them free, but helps to prepare them for the new kind of captivity which the market-place reserves for them: subordination to all the styles, fashions, artefacts, and all the manufactured attributes without which they will never be able to compete with their peers for the one commodity which everybody is known to be after, i.e. sex.

'You're a pouf.'

'What's that then?'

'It's a bloke that only fancies men.' Stephen, 8, to Shaun, 7.

'I don't have to go home from school straight away on Mondays, because my Mum has her boyfriend there, and she'll kill me if I do.' Corinne, 9.

'Your Mum and Dad don't want you to grow up, because they don't want you to get all the good things in life.'

'What are they then?'

'Money and sex.' Conversation with Mark, 11.

In the living room of a council flat in Newcastle, all the adults – mother, aunt, two big sisters – are fussing round Kim, who is trying on a sequined tutu and bra for the school play, in which she is to be a fairy. Kim is five, a grave dark-haired little girl with big brown eyes. Her aunt, a woman in her mid-20s, says, 'Who's a sexy little girl then?' They all laugh. 'No, isn't she though. Honest, anybody could fall for her. If you were to see her picture in close-up, you wouldn't know she wasn't a big star.'

Again, the testimony of people down the years speaks of the change. It isn't sudden, but emerges, uneven, according to the resistance it encounters, but relentless.

'I was married to my missis 62 years; and we never saw each other without clothes on. When I was a lad, it wasn't considered quite right to see one another's private parts. I was brought up very strict. I didn't know anything about what goes on between men and women when I got married. I don't know as it done us any harm. You soon find out.' Man, 94, Aylesbury, Buckinghamshire.

'The first thing I ever heard about sex, I'd started work. I was an apprentice. And this chap I was working with, he said to me, "What you've got between your legs, it ain't just for pissing through you know." ' Man, 80s, Coventry.

'My Mam died when I was 19. And it upset me so much, my periods stopped for a month or two. And I used to sweat a fair bit. I had these sort of turns where I went hot. I was working in the mill at the time, and the other women I was working with, when I told them how I felt, they jumped to the conclusion I was pregnant. Well, I'd never been with a lad, and I didn't know a thing about it. I said "Eh no, it can't be." They said, "Oh yes, definitely." The only thing I could remember was I'd been playing around with some friends, and this lad had grabbed me by the elbow. I thought, "Oh that must be it." So they took me to the doctor and everything, and of course, there was nothing. But I didn't know. I'd no idea.' Woman, 70s, Wigan.

'The only time my mother and father had sexual relations was when he came home from the pub drunk, Sunday dinner-times. Although they never spoke about it, it wasn't really a secret. I don't think they could have kept it from us, even if they'd wanted to. I think in those days, the rough working class – and we were rough, whatever else we might have been – they sort of mated; there was nothing very subtle about it.' Man, 70s, Birmingham.

'I remember when I was very young, I discovered the phenomenon of the erection; and I said so to my mother. She was horrified. She said, "You should never, never do that." I was five or six at the time. I found I couldn't always control it; and one day she found me at it under the kitchen table. She dragged me out and scolded me, I can see her now. She said I'd do myself damage for life. And then she started watching me. Every morning, it was like an inquisition. If I had dark lines under my eyes, it was a sign I'd been touching myself. If it had been deliberately designed to make me feel my own body was shameful and disgusting, it couldn't have been more effective.' Man, 70, Swansea.

'I used to think babies were made by the way you held your mouth when you kissed.' Woman, 60s, Blackburn.

'We grew up in shocking ignorance. When I was 18, I went for a day out to Bedford with a chap. I was never allowed to stay out after ten o'clock at night, and it was a quarter past when I got home that night. My father was there, standing on the doorstep with his strap. I said to my chap, "You'd better go home, he'll make a scene." But he said, "No, why should I? I've done nothing to be ashamed of. It'll only look as if I'm guilty." But he could see my father meant business; and he did go. My father started hitting me round the head and shoulders with this strap, and cut me all about. I was 18. My boyfriend and I couldn't have been more innocent. I knew nothing about sex when I was married. It came as a terrible shock. Fortunately, my husband was a very understanding man. He helped me.' Woman, 60s, Kettering, Northants.

'I remember how I learned the facts of life. The man next door to us was a cubmaster, and he was convicted of offences against boys. It was in the local paper. I didn't know anything about sex, until I heard my mother talking over the garden wall with this man's mother. She was never slow in picking arguments with people. I heard her say, "If ever one of my sons turned out a dirty bastard like yours, I'd throttle him. I'd put a pillow over his face." I never married until I was 26. I never had a woman before that, and I've never had any other since.' Man, 60s, Croydon.

'When I was 10 or 11, my mother came into the bathroom and told me about menstruation. Well, she didn't actually tell me about it. She said, "I suppose I shall soon be having a lot more expense with you." Well, it's not exactly crystal clear is it? The explanation made it even worse than the ignorance. Then she sent me down to the chemist to buy these things. I hadn't the faintest idea what to do with them.' Woman, 50s, Norwich.

'When I was about 11 I discovered a guilty pleasure called sex, the chief expression of which was masturbation, which was very exciting. My mother's reaction was predictable. It was a great emotional shock to be confronted with two semen-dried handkerchiefs, fished up by my mother from under the bed, with the words, "If I find that again, I'll rub your nose in it. You wait till you're married for that kind of thing." I had already learned that physical affection was wrong – I was never kissed, cuddled or fondled. That sort of thing was regarded as sloppy, or unnecessarily emotional. And now, this new aspect of life was apparently also taboo.' Man, 40s, Northampton.

'My mother was very strict. She called herself a Christian, but there was never any reference to the joys of Christianity, to compassion, only to what would happen to me if I was a bad boy. They observed the Sabbath very strictly. But even though it was wrong to do any work on a Sunday, even to sew a button on, it didn't prevent her from reading the tittle tattle scandal in the lower grade Sunday newspapers. The *News of the World* came, but before I could read it certain pieces were cut out; and of course, if you censor something like that, the natural inclination is to find out what you were prevented from reading. And when I could get a complete copy, I would find the pieces cut out referred to people's sexual or amorous exploits; things my mother would prefer I shouldn't know were going on. I think she really believed that the world was a wicked evil world, a very immoral world. Her sexual attitudes were very severe. When I was small, and my mother used to bath me, I can remember she always referred to my penis and genitals as "dirty things". When I was a bit older, I had to be circumcised, and she was excruciatingly embarrassed when she took me to the doctor. I can remember her sitting there and saying, "I've come about his . . . you know . . . his concern." The doctor said, "His what?" He didn't know what she was talking about. She could not bring herself to say it. In the end he sent her out and asked me to tell him what the trouble was.

'There was never any mention that the female might be different from the male. There was a tremendous row one day when my sister came home. My sister was many years older than me, a young woman by this time; and in fact she had already left home by the time I was born. We lived near an army camp, and my sister had boyfriends. My mother didn't approve of my sister expressing her natural urges to have the company of the opposite sex, she considered it dirty, something no decent girl would do. On that particular afternoon, my sister was getting ready to take me out. She went into the kitchen to have a wash. I suppose I was about seven. And my sister was stripped down to her bra and panties while she had a wash down. I wasn't particularly interested, she was just my sister. But my mother smacked her about the face, and literally knocked her across the room. She called her a shameless hussy and a dirty bitch and all the rest of it. She even called my grandmother round from next door, and they stood and ridiculed my sister's clothing. In spite of that, it never stopped my mother getting dressed while I was around, or my grandmother come to that. But their type of clothing was very different, very old-fashioned underwear, huge directoire knickers, bodices and vests, and of course no one was allowed to be seen nude. Mother considered it wrong for a woman to wear a bra or small panties, or anything that would enhance her figure. In later years, when I was getting married, she thought it was about time she started talking; all she said was that she regarded the sex act purely as a duty, something a woman should be ashamed of, because men, after all, were just animals.' Man, 40s, Isle of Wight.

'At 16, I was still playing with dolls. The girls at work said to me, "You can't go round looking like that." So they made me up, and gave me a suspender belt, which hung on me like a gun holster I was so skinny. I used to get called "Broom-handle". They took my hair out of its plaits, taught me to use lipstick, took my bobbysox off. The first time I went out with this suspender belt on, I got on the bus, and I found I couldn't sit down. I'd got it on back to front. I was ashamed of my body. When I was at work I used to get all hot and embarrassed if anyone talked about sanitary towels. My mother never told me anything. I didn't start menstruation until I was 16½. When I started, I didn't know what it was. I thought I'd got TB. I used to wash my pants out secretly, crying my eyes out. My mother did tell me in the end; but she seemed to think it was something dirty. I had to get married at 18. My first baby was a little boy. It was marvellous when I first saw him. I looked down at his little thing and I thought it was lovely. I'd never seen one before, because me and my husband had always made love in the dark. I'd never seen a man's thing before.' Woman, 43, North London.

'My father always had a lot of American servicemen friends. They used to come to our house during the war. They always brought cigarettes, gum, whisky, candy. My father was a driver at the base. Some of these men used to tell me I was cute. From when I was about six, one of them started to interfere with me. I knew it was wrong, but I was so scared, I didn't dare tell anybody. And since then, I've often wondered if my father knew. He used to find girls for a lot of these men. And we always had money, things in the house nobody else had. I've often wondered whether he didn't close a blind eye, because of all he was getting out of it.' Woman, 40s, Oxford.

'My mother was always vitriolic about sex. She hated it. She was always saying to me, "Keep your legs crossed." She insisted that sex was hateful. As an adolescent, I felt I had to react against this. I felt I had to be broadminded about sex. But I thought it was an intellectual issue. I lived on ideas. I stayed on at school. I must have lived in a kind of trance. I got pregnant and had a baby before I was 17. And then, when I was 19, the same thing happened again. I still think I hardly knew what was happening. It amazes me now that I did it twice. My mother was always so negative about men; but now I wonder what was the other side of her hatred of sex? Did I do what I did to prove to her that men were awful? Did she prompt it in some way to reinforce her view of the world? It was as though I was proving her own feelings, not my own. It only falls into place years later.' Woman, 30s, Manchester.

'I was never told about sex. I was just told not to indulge in it. "Don't bring trouble to this house." You more or less knew what they meant. A friend told me the facts of life when I was eight. She told me everything, quite accurately as it turned out. But at the time, I didn't believe it. It was outside my sphere of understanding. I ignored it. You can only take some things on board when you're ready for them; that's a way of protecting yourself. Knowledge doesn't hurt kids; but involving them in sex directly, I think that can be harmful.' Woman, 20s, Birmingham.

'I knew all about sex from when I was seven or eight. You can't not know. Any kid who watches television soon gets to know that something goes on between men and women that involves a lot of humping and heaving, and he puts his dong up her . . . You just know. But for me, it was squaring what I knew with my own life, with what I felt. That's the bit kids don't understand, however much they know. I used to have these feelings about kids at school. I had these fantasies, I used to dream about them, I wanted to be with them, hold them and cuddle them. Only I didn't know it had anything to do with sex. I thought the feelings I had meant there was something wrong

with me. I had my first sex when I was 13, but I didn't screw a
girl till I was 15. I thought that was it. You fancied a girl, so you
screwed her, and then that would be it. I think I was a bastard
to a lot of chicks before I realized there was something more in
life. It was getting what you felt together with what you did. It's
more complicated than you imagine.' Man, 20s, Newport.

'I was 15 when I first had sex. I didn't know what to expect,
though I knew all the physical details. I was surprised more
than anything else. After it happened, I thought, "Oh this must
be love." Took me a long time before I found out I hated the
sod. After we'd had sex, the bloke told me to go and wash
myself. So I went into the bathroom, and I washed my arms
and legs and face and feet. The only place I didn't wash was the
one that mattered.' Woman, 20s.

'I've always known about sex, I can't remember the time
when I never. My Mum was married to this bloke, he was my
stepfather, and he used to walk about in the middle of the night,
and he'd get up to go to the toilet, and just happen to wander
into my room or my sister's room. And he used to get in bed
with us, and play with us, and he'd come, all this sticky stuff all
over the bed. Then he used to pretend he was walking in his
sleep and didn't know what he was doing. We never said
anything to our Mum, because she worshipped him, she
wouldn't hear anything about him. You knew it was wrong, but
you knew you couldn't do anything about it. It made my life
bloody difficult when I got a bit older.' Girl, 17, East London.

'The trouble with my Mum is she can't make up her mind
whether she's my sister or my mother. She's always told me
everything about her life, her sex life, how she hated my old
man; and so she's more or less grown up with me. Honest, she
even dresses the same as I do. She was 18 when I was born, I
mean, she's in her 30s now, it looks a bit funny. She loves it if
we go out together and two blokes start chatting us up. It
embarrasses me. I mean, a mother is somebody who's supposed to put you on the right track . . . Trouble is, she's like a
kid herself. I feel responsible for her. She can't deal with her
boyfriends, she comes to me, "Shar, what shall I do?" I can't
say to her, "Shut up, I've got my own life to lead, I don't wanna
know." ' Girl, 17, East London.

An old man in Nottingham said to me that his wife had a
nervous breakdown on her wedding night. He said he knows he

might have been a bit clumsy, but he was frightened as well. He was 27 and she was 24 at the time. His wife never got over it, but suffered with her nerves all her life. She was completely ignorant of sex when she married. He said that a lad always knew more about his body than a girl did about hers, however much it might have been drummed into him that it was wrong or sinful. He said he had had no sex life at all. She just couldn't stand it. If he'd had any sense, he says, he would have found somebody else. He could still have stayed with his missis. All the affection he has had has come from his dog. When he was young, you felt it was the luck of the draw. You didn't think of getting out of your marriage once you were wed. 'You made your bed, you had to lay on the bugger.'

If the story of many old people is of a sad search for sexual identity doomed from the start, the story that many of the young tell is of a search for identity through sex.

14

MALCOLM VALERA

MALCOLM VALERA IS in his late 30s. Now a successful businessman, he has come a long way from his childhood, materially. He is a dark saturnine person; a preferred elder brother, all the outward appearances of his life seem to express power and self-confidence. He lives in a Regency house in a quiet part of North London; he was brought up in Ramsgate in Kent.

'I have no memory of family life in early childhood. All I have is vivid recollections of incidents with my mother, many of which had a sexual connotation. My conscious memories start at the age of about two, and from then until I was eight there are many events in my mind with a strong sexual aspect, and linked with my mother.

'I had no sense of family as such, just this overwhelming relationship with her. My father is absent from my memories. He was there, but he was excluded. In the War he was in the Fire Service. He wasn't stationed away from home, but he was a shadowy figure. We lived near Ramsgate so we were very aware of the air raids. There was just me and my mother in the world. My brother was born when I was eight. There was me, my mother and sexual experiences. I have some images of myself: at two, being washed, standing in the kitchen sink. And I can remember being stood in a tin bath in front of the fire, again, being washed, and looking down at my cock. I asked her what the little ring round it was for, like an elastic band. She told me not to be dirty.

'I learned to masturbate when I was three; and having once discovered the pleasure, I did it all the time. My mother, in horror at this, carted me off to a lady doctor; and this woman prescribed woollen gloves in bed. They were tied to my wrists so I couldn't get them off. I discovered this increased the pleasure somewhat. The only memory I have of my father at this age is of him trying to put out a chimney fire with wet sacks, and being nagged because he caused so much dust and soot.

That is characteristic of him – he was always in a slightly ridiculous posture.

'I slept with my mother. I can't remember why. I think it must have been to do with the war. I had nightmares induced by the air raids. But I used to masturbate all the time, in front of the gas fire, in my mother's bed. It was just an automatic means of comforting myself, it wasn't accompanied by any fantasies. She caught me doing it quite a bit, and she always made me feel guilty, because in some obscure way she said it was wrong. There was a girl called Shirley, a year older than I was, and we used to go into an empty house next door to hers, and play with each other's genitals. We used to go and sit in a cupboard and do things to each other; or we might go up the air raid shelter. I'd get a straw and poke it up her. I found it very exciting.

'I can remember running home one day, and my mother was at the bottom of the steps with the lady from next door. I told them that I'd kissed Shirley and was going to marry her. There were hoots of derisive laughter, and I was scolded. I was about five; in fact, less than five because I hadn't started school.

'My mother taught me to do French knitting and embroidery and ordinary knitting. I was given dolls to play with. I used to go and see an old lady who lived nearby. She was called Mrs Victoria Grey, and she loved children. She called her house the Victoria Grey School. She was very religious, and she looked after children in an unofficial way, I think because she was lonely. She used to give us clothes to dress up in. Nobody ever told the kids to stay away; she was a sad old lady really. I enjoyed it, because there were nearly all girls there. I had no friends among boys. I didn't like their play. I never liked football. There was a big shrubbery next door to our house, where a lot of boys played. I would never go and play with them.

'My mother was very punitive towards me. She had a riding whip, which she swished across the back of my legs. I have an image of her undressing in front of me. When my brother was born, I asked her where babies came from. She told me babies came from eggs. When she was undressing, I saw, or thought I saw, a scar on her stomach, and I thought that was how babies were born.

'She had ambitions for me. She sent me to elocution lessons. I talked posh. I went to drama classes in the local Wesleyan chapel. I used to recite at socials. At five, I went to a private school, unheard of. It was called Rushmere College. There were very few pupils, eight or nine. It had been a bigger school, but by the time I went there it was running down. On my first day I went with another boy into some bushes opposite the school, and we undid our trousers and got our winkles out. Then I left school, and ran into my mother who was coming to meet me. And she scolded me for running.

'I had a spell of school refusal then. There were tears and dramas. Our teacher was an ignorant woman. I can remember copying stuff off the blackboard before we could even read. She couldn't spell. My mother sent an exercise book back to her with all her spelling mistakes marked in it. Anyway, this school closed. It was hit by a shell or something; and I transferred to a primary school. My mother realized she had done me no favour in sending me to this place. By this time she was working. She was a cook at the Fire Station.

'I was always getting caught at sex. This reinforced my guilt, but it didn't at this time stop me doing what I wanted to. I was caught by my mother, the neighbours, Shirley's older sister Christine, who threatened to tell her mother.

'My mother had wanted a girl, that was clear from the start. Part of her punishment of me was for not being a girl. She wanted my brother to be a girl as well. It's funny – all the sexual things I was caught at were heterosexual.

'We used to visit my mother's parents. Her father was a railwayman in East Grinstead. They lived in an old railway cottage, with a kitchen range and an outside lavatory, with a water tap outside, gaslight, and a parlour that was never used. They used to cover the deal table with newspaper for meals. My mother always complained that when she was a girl, her mother used to give the children different food from that which she ate herself – the children would have margarine while their mother ate the best butter. My Grandma used to drink. I have a memory of her – a smelly fat lady in a rocking chair. She used to send me up the road for her pint of mild.

'My mother was one of three girls. She always said she had not had much affection from her mother. That was why she wanted a girl so desperately – I think she wanted to show her mother how a girl should be brought up; and really, that's what she did with me. "I had a dreadful mother," she would say.

Then it was, "I hope no one will ever be able to say that about me." She demanded recognition of her maternal qualities; and she never lost an opportunity to point out how much better she was than her own mother had been. It was really her own relationship she was working out on me.

'I used to stay with my grandmother occasionally. I remember being in bed in the freezing cold, with a brick that had been baked in the oven for warmth, wrapped up in a blanket. The wretched thing always came unwrapped in the middle of the night and grazed your leg and foot.

'We went to Uckfield where one of my mother's sisters lived. I liked going there. There were three boys in the family, and there were some girl cousins too. There were sexual goings-on with all these cousins. They were always playing at doctors and nurses. Cousin Julie was eight when I was seven. I was sent there when my brother was being born. I was caught with Julie by my aunt. We had taken all our clothes off, and were in the bedroom. Suddenly, there was my aunt sitting at the top of the stairs. Listening, looking at us, she was fearsome.

'My heterosexual experiences came to an end when I was nine. The heterosexual experiences had all been found out. They were wrong, I was told. Sex was always secret, but very compelling. My childhood was saturated with sex.

'I can't directly relate my interest in sex to the relationship with my mother; not consciously anyway. I can see all sorts of connections, but I don't know for sure that they are crucial, nor how they are significant. I know she wanted a girl; but I was frightened of her. She used to bully me into doing things she wanted me to do. It was always love and punishment together. The idea I have of her is of her hitting me and saying, "Love me, love me." I don't mean that literally, of course. That was the feeling. In fact, it wasn't often physical punishment. What I am aware of is the way I treat Harry – the guy I live with – is exactly the way she treated me. In my adult relationships I am my mother and he the child I was. But even that is too schematic – I'm also the child she tried to make me and the child I wanted to be. My mother doesn't influence me directly now. I feel more distant from her, more free of her than I've ever been. It took me a long time to get away from her direct influence. Of course it's still there; it's part of me, at a much deeper level.

'I can see my father in a few memories; but emotionally, he isn't significant. He kept a horse on an old tennis court, because he used to go riding. He also had an old rowing boat, but she wouldn't let him take me anywhere. I can't remember any intimation of a relationship between them. Later, she confided, "Norman was never interested in the children." But he was pushed out, he never had a chance to be. She assumed control. He did nothing. He never talked to me, he never read to me, he never told me off. He was neutral, in every sense.

'I used to go down to the beach. There were some cockle-shells and some cafés. My mother worked in one of the cafés for a time. There was an urn of tea, and there were always soldiers around. In fact, we had soldiers staying with us for a while. I have a feeling from somewhere that my mother had some sort of relationship with one of them. It was never admitted; but you know how certain things are in the air. You just absorb them. This particular soldier was killed soon after. There was a big drama when he was killed. She did talk about him; not that she said anything specific. He had written his name in candlewax on the mirror before he went away, and that was preserved for a long time.

'My lack of familiarity with boys' games led to some strange experiences. When I was at junior school, I had to play football for the first time, and I didn't know what to do. So I picked up the ball. I was ridiculed. I hated sport. The first time I did PE, I was thumped in the stomach by the PE teacher and winded. We thought this teacher was half-man, half-woman. He was the talk of all the kids round the milk crates every morning.

'Sex displaced everything else. I had more sex between the ages of two and twelve than I've had in the rest of my life. I don't know whether the sexual overtones in my relationship with my mother came from me or from her. Probably her. It was like that with a lot of things – she flooded me with feelings that belonged to her.

'When I was ten, my interests became more narrowly focused on boys. My cousin, married now, he got me interested. I was staying with our aunt. He was three years older than I was, and I slept with him. He got me interested in cocks. Whenever I stayed with them after that, I slept with him, right up to the time when I was pubescent and he was 16. Then we went to Brighton on holiday, and I was very disappointed that he didn't want to do it any more. He grew out of it. I tried to seduce him by playing strip noughts and crosses with him, but it didn't work. It was through him that my sexual needs crystallized. My mother had no idea of what was going on inside me.

'When I was ten we moved a few miles from Margate. My father had half an acre of land there. He had two horses, and he used to restore horse-drawn vehicles. At this time I made a friend at school. He was a boy who everybody knew was illegitimate. I seduced him in a den in the garden. I bullied him into having sex with me till he was 14. He didn't want to; but I was persistent and ruthless. At the same time, there was Dennis. My father wanted to start a driving and riding school, and Dennis, who was 15, was always around the place. He mucked out the horses and he showed an interest in me. I had a crush on him. It was my first emotional awakening, and it was very powerful. It was much more important to me than anything that had gone before. He often stayed at the house. My mother used to tuck us up in bed together; and the sex started. She must have known. Once, when Dennis and I were rolling around the floor – I was about 12 – she stumbled in on our activities. I was playing with his cock and shouting, "I'll make it big," and there was my mother, looking through the window, observing. I felt guilty. But nothing was done about it. It didn't stop me asking her to let us sleep in the same bed. The sexual thing was much stronger than the relationship with her. With her, there were continual arguments all the time. She would tell me to do something, and I would shout back at her. I used to get very angry. I used to show her my anger, and for most of the time this was accepted. Perhaps it was my way of asserting my denied maleness. She actually sanctioned everything I did, which of course made her power over me all the greater. I can remember once, when I was 13 or 14, there was some domestic gathering, and I got so angry and frustrated, I flew at her and tried to pull her hair out. It disrupted the gathering. I think it was somehow connected with the fact that about that time Dennis went away to do his National Service. I did love him. I felt it very intensely. I cried and cried and cuddled the pillow.

'At one point my mother showed great understanding about it. One day he was going to take me out in his car, and he didn't turn up. I kept going anxiously to the window to see if he was coming – that is something I seem to have been doing all my life, waiting for someone who may or may not turn up – and she came to comfort me. She said she knew how I felt. She had done just the same thing when my father had been courting her. I don't think she quite realized how inappropriate the sympathy was in the context. But it shows how she identified with me or, rather, how she assimilated me to herself, as though she hadn't even noticed I was of the opposite sex. When she tucked me up in bed with Dennis, she was colluding in a way that now seems very strange.

'Dennis more or less disappeared after National Service. By the time he came back, I had become too guilty about my sexuality to do anything about it. He tried. When I was 15, he tried to take up where we'd left off. He wanted me to do things I wouldn't. It was too late. Guilt had set in.

'I can remember after some Christmas gathering, when they all sat round wondering why Malcolm never seemed to have a girlfriend, Dennis told me that when he'd been away with my father once, he'd had sex with him. I wonder about that. It could be there in my father. I don't know whether Dennis said that to provoke me, or whether it was real. I don't know. I must say, I have known my father to perk up considerably whenever I've taken a pretty boy home.

'I hated school. There used to be scenes and dramas about me going to school. I hated doing PE, and I used to ask my mother for notes to excuse me, which she willingly gave me. I had a sheer physical fear of football. I remember going into the gym at secondary school, and the teacher divided us into four groups, A, B, C, D. And he said to us, "I don't like D-group boys." I was always the last one to be chosen for any team, football or anything. I was always left standing, the last lone reject. For a long time I refused to go to school. We had a friendly doctor – the one who made me wear woolly gloves. She gave my mother a note, to the effect that I'd had rheumatic fever, and that got me off the hook for two years as far as PE was concerned. But then in due course, the whole thing came up again. I persisted again. And this time my mother carted me off to a psychiatrist.

'He was a pig. I wish I could meet him again now. I was maybe 13 or 14 then. There I was, trotting off to see this psychiatrist – all it amounted to was a few sullen and inconclusive interviews – and at the same time I was going round all the public lavatories within walking distance. At 14. Before I went to see the psychiatrist I'd visit the lavatories, and then again when I came out. The psychiatrist visited the house, made a lot of notes. In the end he gave up, warning that I would come to a bad end. Before that though, in desperation, he proposed to my parents that they should send me to his house for a game of chess. He thought there might be a breakthrough, I might unbend. It never happened. I can remember fantasizing about whether we would have sex. We didn't. He had no idea of what was going on in my mind. He never got anywhere near me.

'I discovered the lavatories in Margate by accident. Even before puberty I can remember being vaguely interested, and I made a sort of mental note to return there in due course. I found it very exciting, the idea of people's cocks. But by that time I had become so guilty that I never managed to meet anyone. I was so guilt-ridden I could never let myself be picked up. All my adolescent years were filled with voyeuristic masturbatory experience. I was really fucked up by then. Guilt had cut me off from real sexual experience. And that lasted for more than ten years. I was 26 before I could actually get back to meeting real people again. I went all through National Service and the Merchant Navy before I regained the courage to meet people. I was in my mid-20s when I could openly acknowledge that I had this fixation with adolescents – that is, for boys of the age I was when guilt began to inhibit me. I think now it was very narcissistic; I was responding to myself.

'Apart from the crush on Dennis, I had other fantasy relationships. I fell in love at regular three-year intervals – at 16, 19, 22 and 25. I had a friendship with a boy who went to university, but there was no sex at all. I didn't dare do anything, I was stuck at adolescence, and it has taken me since then to overcome it. I was interested in people of my own age until I was 21, and then I started going in the opposite direction. As I grew older, I got sexually interested in young men more and more my junior.

'I continued to take boys home to my mother's house. And this wasn't discouraged. It's only the relationship I have now that she disapproves of. My father has said to me, "Get rid of

Harry," but he was only echoing her promptings. Since my relationship with Harry – which has lasted five years – I've lost interest in adolescents. I've lost that fear of my mother. I've overcome the terror of confronting her, of what she might say. Until five years ago I used to go all weak under her gaze. She could make me do anything. But it's changed; I feel I'm not possessed by her any more. And my father is the principal beneficiary – they get on better than they seem to have done for years.

'When my brother was born I resented him. I remember hitting him in his cot. And then after that I ignored him until he was about 15 or 16. I lost interest in him when it became clear that he wasn't a threat to me. He didn't displace me as the favourite son. It was obvious that his arrival was an accident. I was chosen; he wasn't even wanted. He never belonged. For me, he wasn't even there. I still feel that. He's made great efforts to develop the relationship with me all his life, but I've always rejected it. Even now, when I go to see him, I still feel, "Who's this bloke, offering me his hospitality, his family, his children?" He's like a stranger. We have nothing in common – not even our mother, because her relationship with me was nothing like her relationship with him. He feels my lack of interest in him intensely. It's important for him that I should recognize him. Ironically, when our mother gets old and fragile, he'll be the one who'll look after her. She treats his son in just the same way she treated me. He's another version of me – she brings him clothes, and my brother says, "Kevin isn't going to wear things like that, they're girls' things."

'From puberty up to the time of leaving home, I went in for torrid but isolated cottaging in Margate and the area all round. They all had wooden walls with holes in them where the knots had been pushed out, and this provided me with long hours of entertainment. It was one of the most exciting periods of my life, peering through holes in walls. If I hadn't had such terrible guilt, I would have developed more real relationships, instead of that long voyeuristic experience.

'My relationship with my mother has always been full of conflict. She always said to me, "Be a good boy and love me." I fought against it, and she fought back. She'd say, "No boy ever had a better mother." Then she'd keep on, "You do love me, don't you?" Or sometimes, "I don't think you love me at all."

She took me into her confidence about my father; how he became impotent at 38, and they had no sexual relationship at all after that; how she thought of divorcing him – all things she should never have mentioned to me. I couldn't wait to get away from it all. When I went to do National Service, I felt I'd escaped. But it wasn't so easy. My feelings were very ambiguous. She kept demanding that I should go home; and I did. I was always writing her long letters. In fact, I couldn't stay away. I was afraid of her. I think it was simply her power over me that she enjoyed. For years and years, I used to go home every other weekend. "You are coming down," she would say, and it wasn't really a question. If I took anyone with me, she'd assume that we would sleep in the same bed. I might have thought that by taking boyfriends home I was defying her; but really it was continuing proof of her power over me. I don't know what that sort of love is. It's fear, not love. She simply told me what to do for years and years, and I obeyed.

'It's finished now. I don't go there for months at a time. But what finished it was not my desire to get away, but a proper, mutual relationship. While I was pursuing what I thought I wanted, this was only a shadow extension of the relationship with her. What I have now is a relationship of equality, in which I'm seeking neither power nor humiliation, which was what all the years under her influence were about. It's taken me almost up to middle age to even begin to get over my childhood.'

In many ways, Malcolm's childhood contained much that is characteristic of contemporary childhood. This seems paradoxical – after all, it occurred some quarter of a century ago, and it was, surely, a unique, highly individual experience. It isn't the details or precise circumstances that make of this experience a kind of metaphor, but the more general pattern. For one thing, everything is sanctioned, everything permitted, and the child nevertheless remains in a state of helpless subordination. He is indulged to the limit, as long as the mother's power is not contested; and this is the social metaphor. The indulgence encompasses a profound dependency – on sex in Malcolm's case, but it could be anything – and an intense life that can only be played out in fantasy. His experience was introspective, lonely and masturbatory. It isn't

by chance that 'wanker' is written all over the walls where the
working-class young congregate.

It is the absence of any wider social purpose or commitment,
the lack of any significant function for the adults which today's
children will become, which create the need for the consolations and the indulgence which were permitted to Malcolm.
Where nothing is asked of children but to do as they please,
they fall in upon themselves in pursuit of lonely sterile fantasies.

Malcolm also spoke sadly about the frightening emotional
autism of his mother, whose life has been spent revising her own
loveless childhood, in a way so compelling that she was unable
even to take account of the sex of her son. Malcolm took me to
her house, which is full of displays of birthday cards and
Mother's Day cards from him, dating back many years, all
outsize and extravagant – the tribute she exacted from him to
her successful parenting. For many years he repeated her
behaviour, in a closed lonely response to his own needs, in
which there was no room for another human being, but only
projections of himself.

This theme – that people's search for reassurance, love,
dominion, comfort, is related to the real being of others in only
the most sketchy rudimentary way – is heard more and more in
the presence of the decay of function and purpose in the
working class. The old closeness and solidarity are loosened;
and in the space created, people discover that those they
thought closest to them are flawed, self-centred, an encum-
brance to their own development.

Increasingly we read in the actions and behaviour of those
close to us only that which has reference to ourselves.
Sometimes those readings are wrong; but whatever construct
we make of them becomes the actual state of the relationship.
Out of the formless expansion and contraction of our feelings,
we have to lay hold of something; and what comes into our
consciousness are sometimes pitiful interpretations, flimsy
constructs out of which we build our sense of self, try to protect
what we feel as our aloneness and vulnerability. We pin our
feelings to the behaviour of others simply to rescue ourselves
from our sense of chaos, even though that behaviour never
explains the feelings; and our knowledge of ourselves always
limps helplessly behind what we feel.

15

JANE FELLOWES, 38

JANE LIVES WITH her two children, Simon, nine, and Gillian, seven, in a redbrick terraced house near the centre of Bedford. She is articulate and vivacious; perhaps a little melancholy at the thought that her present knowledge of herself was acquired at such cost – the ending of her marriage, and the loneliness of all children in a one-parent family, whatever efforts she may make to compensate for it. She herself is the product of that breakdown and scattering of the old working-class family. One of the results of the greater emotional mobility of recent years has been to create, with the large numbers of second and even third marriages, many half-brothers and -sisters, new mothers, second fathers; we have produced for many children those same feelings that premature death brought about at an earlier stage of working-class experience – all the accounts of stepmothers and replacements, false brothers and sisters. It is an irony that our new freedoms evoke many of the same negative feelings in children that our old unfreedoms created.

'I was adopted, and I never knew my real mother and father; but all through childhood there were these half-whispered conversations which I could never quite get to the bottom of. When I was about six a neighbour's child in the street told me I was adopted, as they usually do. It was awful. I confronted my mother with it. She could see how upset I was, so she denied it very vehemently. She continued to deny it, and she never would admit it was true. I still can't talk about it to my father to this day. In fact, I only discovered I had brothers and sisters a few months ago.

'I discovered that I was in fact born in Oxford. From somewhere I have the idea that my parents were not married when I was born. As I was born in 1946, I must have been conceived at the end of the war – perhaps during Victory celebrations. I was probably the outcome of some wayside lay. My father was French Canadian. But all the time, somewhere in my head, there was an idea . . . You can't always put it into words, the kind of knowledge you glean.

'My mother had kept me for some time after I was born, and then I must have spent some time in a home in London, because that was where I was first adopted from. My mother was a bad 'un, and I learnt that in adolescence, when I went off the rails. There were all these comments in the family, "What's bred in the bone . . ." "Well you know what her roots are," "You know what she comes from." I had a terrible crisis of identity in adolescence.

'My mother – that is my adoptive mother – died when I was 11 just starting Grammar School; although the full effect of that didn't hit me till three years later, when I was 14. Then I became uncontrollable. It messed up my life for a hell of a time.

'I always wanted to know what my origins were. I know that my mother was devastated when I asked her. I could sense the panic in her when I confronted her with it. And I desperately wanted to accept what she told me. Perhaps she denied it a bit too vehemently. But it was always there, something about me, hidden from me. I tried to tap others in the family, but wherever I turned, it was the same reticence. Like a conspiracy. It's still a taboo subject. Over the years things emerge. Apparently my real mother tried to claim me back. Before the adoption was finalized, she came to the house. And my auntie told me, "Your sister came with her." I never knew I had a sister. So even though my adoptive mother has been dead over 20 years, her relatives will not talk about it. I think this is because she was the eldest in the family, and they all looked up to her. They feel it would be a betrayal to talk about things she wanted to stay a secret.

'I don't have such a burning urge to discover things now. I think my identity has grown through other people. It no longer seems so vital to me to find out. I only discovered what my real name was when my marriage was breaking down. It's funny: it became of burning importance to me, not when my adoptive mother died, but when my relationship was breaking down. It was as if I'd lived a false persona. The trauma of my mother dying was re-awakened when I lost my husband, like when things began to go hopelessly wrong between us. The two things were interrelated, obviously. I had the feeling that I lost them both because I didn't know who I was.

'My childhood has left me with a sense of continually expecting things to go wrong; a feeling of not belonging anywhere or to anybody. In the main, I end up with rather superficial relationships. When I got married, I knew from the start that it was a mistake. The man I married was the opposite of all the things I admired and wanted. It may have been my own weak sense of who I was that made him seem strong by contrast, and therefore what I needed. Perhaps I thought he would help me to define myself; which he did, but not quite as I'd expected.

'He seemed a challenge to me. I'd just come out of college, I was mixing with semi-intellectual people, which I felt wasn't me, because of my working-class background. He was very working class, rather brutal in a way. I'd been very influenced by reading D. H. Lawrence at the time. He seemed dark and brooding. I was partly in love with an image – an image of physicality that stood out in contrast against the academic world. However humanizing literature might be, it's a mistake to go and find your own identity through it. He turned out to be violent, and I don't get any pleasure from that at all. I was terrified of him in the end; I still am, a bit. He had no logic, no words. He couldn't argue or abstract from his own situation. He was very anti-intellectual. He works as a gardener in a new town now.

'I grew up to be very dependent on my parents. When they adopted me my father was 40 and my mother 36. They couldn't have children, I don't know why. They were over the moon when they first adopted me. I was showered with love and gifts. I had only to mention that somebody I knew had something, or that I needed something, for them to do their best to get it for me. My father was always down in the cellar, sawing wood, making things – toys, stilts, a go-kart. I had everything. But the thing was, I didn't want any of it. I wanted what all the other children in the street had, which was brothers and sisters. Being an only child, I stuck out like a sore thumb. My mother was a dressmaker. I had dresses of white lace, of taffeta, of organza. I had long hair, which I could sit on, and it was carefully plaited and tied with white bows. But I was always very thin. I remember at school we had to line up and be fed with a spoonful of malt and a capsule of cod liver oil. But the problem of who I was began with not belonging, being different from all the other children, and this has stayed with me all my life.

'I was a bit of a victim of other children's cruelty. In street games, I was always the one on the end of the tag-line, which meant I always had to run the fastest and fall over the hardest. I was always being hurt, both verbally and physically. I was always being teased about my thinness. We had some neighbours, the man worked in the docks, the wife was a rather tarty busty woman, and she thought we had ideas above our station because my father was keen on education, and my mother used to dress me in these frills and lacy dresses. My father taught me to read before I started school. I had piano lessons, and I was encouraged to give little concerts when relatives visited. I had every opportunity to shine.

'I was lonely as a child. I didn't fantasize about companions, but my toys became real for me. I always used to create nests to hide in in various corners of the house. In bed, I always used to churn the sheets and blankets into a nest, a sort of womb for myself.

'I suffered at school. I was above average. There was a lot of pressure from home to succeed. Everything sort of worked up to the 11-plus in those days. I was sensitive, always hated the noise of school, the echoing classrooms, the shouting of other kids. And I was always terrified of getting into trouble. I used to put my fingers in my ears to block out the noise; the London School Board buildings, so cavernous and echoing. I hated the roughness of it. We had one teacher who had tufts of whiskers on her chin and a massive bosom, and she towered above me with her glinting National Health glasses. But I discovered she had a heart of gold, and she protected me as far as she could. There was also a withered prune of a woman, who once made us all assemble in the hall, while she caned a boy for doing something he shouldn't. That upset me terribly. I went home and wept my eyes out over it.

'My mother and father were united in their love of me. I was aware of no friction in their relationship; although later I realized that my mother was not a very sociable person, and my father was. He must have led his own life – he went to the pub with his friends, while she was immersed in the life at home and me. Their roles were defined very clearly, and they were both content to stay within that definition.

'I think when I got married, part of what was at work inside me was a need to sabotage myself, that came directly from childhood. At the time, everything was going well for me. I was teaching in a village school, and renting a lovely stone cottage. But somehow I always have to feel I've done something to deserve bad treatment. It's the feeling, "Oh she's turned out just like her mother"; as though my mother was bad and has to go on being punished; and because I was the cause of her being bad, I have to be punished as well. And then, when my adoptive mother died, that confirmed how awful I was. I'd kind of killed off two mothers, something like that makes you feel terrible.

'After having been a model pupil at school, I began to truant. I became destructive. When I was about 14 I used to stay away from school and then forge notes, with all sorts of impossible excuses, like saying I'd got polio. In the end my father had to take me forcibly to school. I was turned out of practically every class. The thing was, they kept on being so understanding. They knew I'd lost my mother, so they kept on and on giving me another chance. And I delighted to rub my heel in their faces until they couldn't go on being magnanimous and keep face at the same time.

'I was in with a group of girls who used to go up the West End, and I soon started not coming home at nights. Later, I got heavily into drugs. When I was 15 or 16 I got picked up by a Frenchman in a club, and that was my first sexual experience. Actually, he was terribly naïve, as naïve as I was. And then I started going out with a bloke who was hooked on purple hearts. We used to get stoned regularly. A lot of us used pills, just at the weekend, to get high, and then go to school or work quite normally for the rest of the week. But I was taking them all the time. One night, I got stoned out of my head with pills and drink, and I was picked up by a bloke who took me somewhere in North London, I'd no idea where I was or how I got there. I can remember being with him and some woman in this filthy house, and we were drinking and smoking grass. Somehow I'd lost my shoes and I was wearing my mother's wedding ring. It was the only memento of her I had. This man said he wanted to meet me again, and he removed this ring from my finger, because, he said, that way he'd be sure I would turn up when we arranged to meet. Needless to say I never saw him again. I left this house at five or six in the morning, no shoes. I walked right through London; I saw these two policemen coming towards me. I remember thinking, "I must walk straight," and I walked between them. They didn't even stop me. I must have often come close to danger. I was very promiscuous. I felt I could find my identity through sex. You don't – in the end you lose what sense of self you have. You look for affirmation, but it's only one part of you that is involved. So I started stealing other people's husbands or boyfriends; a way of proving that I was more desirable than the partner the bloke had. But that is just as unrewarding. I could only prove myself by coming between people. It came home to me sharply with one bloke I liked a lot. He refused to sleep with me. He said, "It isn't that I don't want to; I don't want to be just another notch in your belt." And that made me realize what I'd been doing.

'Unfortunately my husband tended to reinforce this rather unloving attitude in sex. By the time I met him I was ready to give up promiscuity. But he always wanted me to be more and more wild, to act out fantasies of being a prostitute. In the end I didn't like the separation of feeling and sex, and it revolted me. I found I couldn't operate sexually under those conditions. He accused me of being frigid; me. Actually it turned me off so much I did become frigid in the end.

'I suffered a terrible guilt when my mother died. I didn't even know she was ill. I think she suffered in silence for a long time. Then one day, she was suddenly in bed, and my grandmother was there. It was in the school holidays. I'd planned to go to the Horniman Museum with a friend; and I couldn't go because my mother was ill. We were waiting at home for the ambulance to come. And this friend said something like, "Oh damn"; and I said, "Yes it is a bloody nuisance." Anyway, the ambulance came, and they took my mother to hospital. And I never saw her again . . . This feeling has stayed with me all my life; the guilt at being so insensitive that I didn't realize it was the last time I'd ever see her. Objectively, I don't think it could have been helped, they didn't know she was that ill. But I was programmed for guilt anyway. She died of colitis. She had been very ill for a long time; it was hidden and she was stoical, like those working-class women always were. They operated on her, and I kept asking, "When can I go and see Mummy?" And in fact, they did arrange for me to go and see her in the hospital.

But she died the night before. She did write me one letter, in a faint scrawl. They told me she died with my picture in her hand. It must have been hard for her as well as for me, the fact that we'd been so much to each other and were never to see each other again.

'My uncle and aunt were living with us in the upper part of the house. The day she died, there was this heavy oppressive atmosphere. I could sense it the minute I got out of bed. Everybody was trying to be normal. I knew, before anybody said a word. I had breakfast that morning in my aunt's kitchen. I even remember what I had for breakfast – cornflakes with banana. And then, when I'd eaten it, they told me to go down to my father. I had this dread of seeing him. He sat there, and he pulled me towards him, and then, as he started to say the words, I couldn't listen. I put my hands over my ears and I ran down the hall. It wasn't a very big hall, but I seemed to run and run, and it appeared to go on for ever. I started banging, banging at the front door . . .

'After that terrible panic, a coldness came over me. It went inside, and I couldn't cry. It was too much of a grief, it was beyond tears. But years afterwards, they said of me, "She never even cried when her mother died." They thought it was a sign of hardness; whereas the truth was, I couldn't grieve. It was too awful, there would have been no limit to it if I'd let myself go; it would have been fathomless.

'But then later, when I went back to school, I even grew rather proud of it, the fact that I didn't have a mother. "I haven't got a mother" – that gave me some sort of identity, however pitiful. I knew who I was for a while, I was the little girl who had lost her mother. They thought I was hard and cold, they assumed it meant I had no feelings. I can show feelings now, but at that time, it all had to be crushed back. I couldn't accept that my mother had died. I couldn't take it in, that was what they didn't see. For years after, I had this recurring dream, that my mother hadn't died at all. She would come into the school where I was, make her way into the dining-room, take me by the hand, and I'd go home with her. All my life I've carried that loss, and that dream has come back to me again and again. The first time I fell in love, when I was 18, I had the same dream about the bloke when he left me. He rejected me because I asked too much of him. But I used to dream that he came back, just as I'd dreamed that my mother had come back.

'When she died, there was some talk that I should go and live with my auntie. But I was against it. I wanted to stay with my father. But when she had gone, my father was at a loss. They'd had these distinct roles, and, apart from his interest in my education, my father's function had been outside the house. He had no idea of how to care for a child in the practical, physical sense. He found it difficult to cuddle me or touch me. He has always been like that. Even now . . . I saw him last Saturday. He's had a slight stroke, and he was in bed and had lost his speech; but last Saturday he was up again, and his speech was returning. I was so happy to see him beginning to get better that I held his hand. He seemed pleased, but he still retrieved it as soon as he felt he could without hurting me. He's uncomfortable holding, touching.

'I stayed with my father from the age of 11 until 14. All that time I was shared round with grandmother and all the members of the family. They were very close-knit. They all lived within a square mile of Peckham. I used to have some of my meals at my grandmother's. I was shared between the women of the family. But whenever I was at home, I was aware that these women were also trying to arrange a new marriage for my father. They sort of encouraged him into female company, to go out and meet people. He was out a lot, and I was often on my own. I was terrified of the house once my mother was dead. This terror was intensified one day when my grandmother went upstairs to make the bed, and she came down and said she had seen my mother lying in the bed. I was afraid even to go upstairs. When my mother died, I couldn't bear to go and see her. I was frightened of what I might see. I didn't go to the funeral either. There was always this rather morbid attitude towards death in the family, a kind of melancholy.

'I was 14 before all the repressed feeling caught up with me. I went off the rails. I don't know whether the process started with my stepmother, or whether it had already begun when she appeared on the scene. To a certain extent, it was there before she arrived. Anyway, one day my father said to me suddenly that Mary was coming to visit us. At the time I was pleased and excited. I tidied up the house, got out the nice china, cut some sandwiches. I must have been between 13 and 14. Anyway, she came, we had tea, she seemed pleasant. I don't think I quite understood what was happening. I thought it was a good idea. I thought she would be a mother replacement for me rather than a wife for my father.

'It was a disaster. They got married. Everything started off wrong. We had this house in Peckham, there were 3 or 4 bedrooms. We'd always had people staying in it – newly-wed relatives, aged aunts, there had always been some peripheral member of the family lodging or staying with us. Mary had a two-bedroomed flat in Crystal Palace. I was informed that we were going to give up our house and go and live there with her. That was a mistake. Apart from the flat being so small, I lost contact with my roots in Peckham and the street. The family had been very supportive since my mother died, and that created an additional sense of loss when we went away from there. When you're a child, you pinpoint small things, apparently trivial, but they have a meaning for you. For instance, I had two budgies, and I was told I'd have to get rid of them before we moved. And then, when we got to Crystal Palace, it turned out that Mary's daughter Sally had a budgie. She was one year older than I was, and she was everything I was not. Sally and I were worlds apart. I'd spent all the years of my childhood longing for a brother or sister; but when I sort of got one, it was all wrong. Sally was cool and calculating. She had had the same boyfriend from the age of 12, and later she married him. She was neat, tidy, successful. She looked after her clothes. She was materialistic and self-possessed. I'd always had a casual attitude to clothes; so if I borrowed a jumper of hers from the wardrobe, she would get into a fury over it. There was tremendous friction in the flat, because it was so small. We gave up everything. We even got rid of the photograph album with all the family history, even the photographs of my mother – he burnt them all. It was a symbolic rejection of all those years. It was heartbreaking.

'My father regretted the marriage. There were always tensions. There were always sexual tensions. She said once that he couldn't climax, there was some difficulty there. But she was a shallow trivial woman. To me she wasn't kind at all. I know I must have been a difficult little bitch, I don't want to exaggerate her part in it. But she wasn't outgoing; she was small-minded, gossiping, with no depth. She had suffered. Her husband had died of cancer of the bowel, and she had nursed him through it. In fact, she used to delight in telling everybody the details of how she always used to change the bag he had to wear . . .

'My father was frantic over me. He desperately tried to protect my image in front of her. But he was fighting a losing battle. One night, I remember, he locked the door on me and went upstairs. I ran out of the block of flats, out of the glass swing doors and into the street. The chap who'd driven me home was still there, so I got back into the car. Then my father appeared, and chased us in this car round the green. He was in his pyjamas. It sounds comic now, but at the time he was at his wits' end about me. Everything more or less seemed to confirm publicly that I was no good.

'The crunch came one day when I'd been in the West End on a binge. I was with a chap heavily into drugs, and the binge had lasted all the weekend. We'd got stoned on pills and drink, and we were somewhere in North London, I don't remember where. I never actually knew. I remember going with him into a shop early on Sunday morning, and we just picked up all the things we wanted and walked out with them. Nobody stopped us. We got on a bus. I'd got sixpence or a shilling or whatever the fare was in my pocket. And after that, I remember nothing until I woke up in hospital in North London. They had the stomach pump on me. I'd been out for some days. I'd been almost in a coma. Then when I came round, I had such a lecture from the consultant. My father came to collect me. He was so hurt, worried, anxious. But he didn't say anything to me. He was just glad that I was alive. Do you know how he'd found out where I was? He'd read about me in the *Evening News*. I'd no identification on me. No identity – it was like the whole root of the problem was there. There had been a photograph in the paper, saying that this unidentified girl was in hospital. That was me. An unidentified girl. I think it shook Mary. There were no recriminations after it. My father just said, "What on earth made you do that?"

'But afterwards, Mary started being cruel, using my father against me. I used to say to her, "Well at least my father cares"; and she'd say, 'Well, he's not your real father." I can laugh at some of it now, but at the time it was so painful. I remember one night; I had a shortie nightdress, and I came down into the kitchen, to get a drink or something, and then I went into the sitting room to say goodnight to my father. And Mary was outraged. She said, "Fancy kissing your father goodnight in those things. I suppose you'll be wanting to sleep with him next." I took up a knife and tried to stab her with it. As a matter of fact, I had slept with my father for a time when mother died; we had shared the same bed for comfort. So what she said, she was attacking something that had been very soothing and very loving to me.

'I left home as soon as I could, at 16. My father was trapped. He had got married again, chiefly to provide me with a home and a mother. It was sad. I got a flat. I got my first job. With my first wage packet I moved into a flat with a friend of mine off Goose Green, not far from where I'd lived as a child. I went home and told my father. He was up a ladder, changing a light bulb. And he said, "You walk out this door, and you'll never walk in it again." He must have felt so hurt. And I continued to hurt him.

'It really cracked him up, when my marriage broke. He'd've killed my husband if he could have got his hands on him. I felt I had to protect my father from knowing what was happening in my marriage. I said nothing to him for years. It wasn't until all pretence at civility had broken down in front of him that he asked me, "What is going on, Janie?"

'But in the end I did go to college. I did become a teacher. And to my father, that vindicated so much that he had wanted for me. He was ecstatic when I went to college. His pride in me was a wonderful sustaining thing. I feel this is my way of repaying his concern. It is partly my attempt to obliterate all the pain I brought him when I was younger.

'I've two children. I sometimes wonder if I'm over-anxious, especially about the little boy; but then I'm afraid I'm being neglectful at the same time. There are so few certainties about being a parent, and such scope for anxiety because of it.

'I sometimes think the years I spent with my husband were wasted. Eight wasted years. But when I think of the day Emma was born, when I first saw her, the unbelievable sense of achievement, of creation, of fulfilment, everything, it was the most wonderful moment of my life. The trouble was, I'd no experience of knowing what to do as a mother. There was nobody I could ask. I had a book propped open all the time when they were young.

'But I'm left with strong feelings that my whole life blossomed out of my childhood, directly. There's no gap in it for me. I'm very aware of my childhood and its bearing on my life. I still have access to all the feelings that were there. They still are.

'I'm lucky that in adolescence I didn't get addicted or destroyed in my search for who I am. I realize how close I came to falling apart completely. It was luck that saved me; but once I'd survived, it was the love of my father, and my mother, even though she was dead, which cradled me through the years of restoration and development.'

16

STEPHEN WILLIAMS, SOUTH WALES

IF THE WIDER extended working-class family helped to mitigate some of the worst effects of loss, illness and premature
death that were associated with poverty, the model of the
nuclear family, held up everywhere as the norm within our
richer society, only makes worse the sense of uncertainty and
lack of definition for those children who suffer under its
increasing strain and breakdown. The shifting alliances between adults, the arbitrary disappearance of fathers and arrival
of stepmothers, the changing constellations of brothers and
sisters, offer to children few of the freedoms which the adults
claim for themselves. What children learn about adult life is its
inconstancy, its unreliability, the fragile and not the enduring
quality of human attachments. This cruel and bitter lesson is
no doubt not without its uses in the kind of society in which they
are growing up. To learn that people are not to be trusted and
not to be depended on only ensures that that other dependency
will grow instead – children will fall back on the material
consolations which nobody ever calls into question. In this
way, people can pursue their lonely trajectory through time;
even in the same family, each individual pursues his or her own
dreams, fantasies, relationships, while the children learn that
the best of everything can be measured in material terms. Of
course the love of parents for their children creates a resistance
to the worst ravages of these processes; but where it is weak or
non-existent, the children are exposed to their most damaging
effects. If we want to understand some of the disturbance and
violence in the working-class young, we have to understand the
nature of those influences that find such an easy passage
through the vacuum left by the collapse of those old networks of
strong and protective relationships, and how this is connected
with the decayed function and the sense of identity that was
connected with it.

Stephen Williams is 27. His parents were both from the

Rhondda in South Wales. His father worked in the Rio Tinto works, smelting lead. He says that his mother and father came together out of desperation more than anything else, out of inexperience and the force of circumstances.

'My mother was the youngest of three girls, my father the youngest of four boys. They got involved too soon. Of course, marriage was the only way into sex at that time, and a lot of people made terrible mistakes. My father came out of the army, and was working on the buses. They were both 21 but had no experience of life.

'They went to live with my paternal grandmother. She is by far the most significant character in my childhood. She had brought up these four boys. She had rheumatoid arthritis, which crippled her. She was a big woman, with a large round face, and she sat in her armchair, from where she controlled and directed the lives of the whole family. She had a very powerful presence, which sort of pervaded everything. I can picture her, very vividly, in this chair, with all the moquette worn away where her hands had clutched the arms because of her arthritis. She was very badly affected by it. She had to take cortisone, which was a new drug at that time. You can tell how tough-minded she was, because her abiding passion was whist, and this was the only thing she left the house for. She would take a week's dose of the cortisone to enable her to get to the whist drive.

'She was very determined. She imposed herself on everybody around her. Nobody ever challenged her. She herself came from Cwm, a steel town, which was the furthest east she'd ever been in her life. She had never been out of Wales. My parents had two rooms in her house. But my mother was a very timid person, and this grandmother – her mother-in-law, of course – was always very belittling to her, always crushing her with scorn. That was my grandmother's way of making a relationship with people. She dominated all her sons, all their families, and in due course, all the grandchildren. She had them all by the balls.

'She had a miserable existence because of her disablement. She was determined to have company in it, and she made everybody she knew miserable as well. Everybody close to her suffered. She was wilful: the doctors knew nothing. No one could help her. Nobody knew how she'd suffered or could understand what she went through. She died only three years ago, and she was over 80.

'My mother's parents moved out of their house to a council flat when all the three daughters had left home; and we moved into the house they'd left. I was born 12 months after my mother was married. But I was essentially brought up by my grandmother. I can still hear her voice chiding me down the years, "Don't speak till you're spoken to, stop biting your nails, don't take the last cake off the plate." My mother's mother was a kind, warm person.

'At the beginning I was very much my mother's child, and in my early years I was closer to her mother than my father's mother. My earliest memories are of their house which we moved into. It was opposite a rail depot, and they used to move cattle in the night. I can hear the sound of trains and cattle lowing all night in these trucks. The house was very small, one up, one down with a glass lean-to kitchen, an outside toilet. We all had to sleep in the same room.

'My father never hit me. I don't think he had the guts. He was a bugger for a gamble, he used to put his money on the horses. I think the marriage very quickly started to go downhill. By the time he was 26 or 27, he knew he'd made a terrible mistake. He took to drinking quite a lot, and he gambled even more. All his money was blued on beer and horses, and there wasn't enough left for my mother to manage on. My father knew a chap, he'd met him in the pub, a sort of drinking companion really; and he used to bring this chap home. He was a local builder, and they would come home from the pub and carry on drinking there. This bloke, Fred was his name, would stay over sometimes; spend the night, or the weekend there. My mother would say to my father, "Oh, make us a cup of tea, Will," and he'd say "Oh, Fred'll do it." He was almost inviting him to take his place. And before we knew where we were, Fred was screwing my mother. Father saw it as a way of getting out of the marriage. I think my mother considered she had failed; she saw it as her fault. There were terrible rows. I can remember my mother going for my Dad with a poker.

'So my father used to take me off up to my grandmother's. It was partly her suggestion that made him want to leave his wife. She would plant ideas in his head that he wasn't being properly cared for, that she wasn't a good wife. She might say, "That collar's not very clean." "Well, I've only had it on two days." "Well, it doesn't look very clean." Implying of course that my mother wasn't carrying out her duties properly – there were lots of things like that. My grandmother was a wrecker. She sort of suggested to him what he should feel, she prompted him, she fed him her ideas.

'Well, Fred stayed on. He was there for maybe nine months or a year. And in the end there was a terrible argument. One night my father picked me up and said, "Right, we're going." We went to live with my grandmother. When we got there, she wasn't upset or surprised. It was just, "I told you so." She shouldn't have been surprised – she'd been working on it long enough.

'Eventually my mother and father were divorced. But before that happened, a strange time began for me. During the time they were waiting for the divorce, I wasn't allowed to go out alone, in case my mother tried to get me back. I was brainwashed – told my mother was bad, dirty, a nasty woman. I was told above all I must not speak to her, not go with her if I saw her. I was five at this time; and I was bombarded every day with what a terrible person she was. At that age of course you believe it – you've got to, you have no choice. So I grew up feeling my mother was downright bad.

'Then I had a long spell in hospital. I was in for nine weeks with osteomyelitis, that's a disease of the bone marrow. My father and grandmother told them at the hospital that under no circumstances should my mother be allowed to see me. I did see my mother in the ward one day: she was just standing there, but they wouldn't let her come in. I felt I didn't want to see her either, and I started to cry. They asked me if I wanted to see her. I said, "No." In a way I did want to see her, but I was full of what I'd been told, I didn't dare say so.

'My father came to see me every day. He gained a special concession that he could come in after he'd finished work. This made me feel special, because I was allowed a visitor when all the others had gone. Coming out of hospital was one of my big disappointments. For some reason I expected that the house would have changed. I was excited at going home, but because I'd suffered I thought everything would be different. I felt I deserved something. I expected to see balloons when I got home, I don't know why. But my sense of disappointment somehow focused on this lack of balloons. I expected all sorts of people to be there, where in fact not even my father was at home. And all the toys I'd had in hospital, I had to leave them there. My father said I had to leave them because they had been in contact with disease. Not long afterwards there was another disappointment. We had an Irish terrier. One day we went to the pictures, and when we got home, this dog had ripped the three-piece to shreds. Absolutely destroyed it. The dog had to be got rid of. I expect they had him put down. My father told me he'd been given to a blind boy in Carmarthen.

'By this time, we were living in a council house, and my mother was living not a mile away with her new husband. She'd married Fred, the man my father had brought home. He had left his wife and taken his six kids with him, so now my mother had a ready-made family, with six kids. By this time, she was about 27, Fred must have been in his late 30s.

'These kids, we shopped in the same place, played in the same park. We couldn't miss each other. They used to harass me. They'd come up to me and say, "You're our brother", and I used to run away because I didn't want them. I attributed all my mother's badness to them. I used to have nightmares about them. They chased me; I think they were being friendly, they were only playing, but I was terrified. I got so scared, I was afraid even to go to the shops.

'My grandmother always sent me to Sunday School. She always took what she saw as my moral training very seriously. She insisted on good manners. I hated Sunday School. On Sundays, I had to be in at twelve for my dinner, so that I could be off by one to Sunday School. What I detested most was that I never had a pair of long trousers until ages after everybody else. My grandmother didn't believe in it. Long trousers were a symbol of growing up. I used to say, "When can I have long trousers?" "When you've worn out all your short ones." That was really depressing, because I'd got pairs and pairs of them in the drawer upstairs. This must have been when I was about eight or nine. She was obviously thinking back to the time when my father was a boy, when they did wear short trousers till they were much older.

'When I was eight, I was taken to court for the divorce proceedings between my parents. My grandmother was with me. My grandmother showed me the courtroom, and I was

lifted up so that I could see what was going on. I saw my mother
and father shouting at each other in the court. I can see my
mother's face. She was pointing and shouting something. I
believe they all ganged up on her. She didn't stand a chance
right from the start. She was overpowered by my grandmother's personality. The thing was, my grandmother knew
that as long as she had me, she still had my father. That was the
key to it all. I was the centre of it, but it wasn't really on my own
account that I was so important and so much fuss was made of
me. My mother said to me much later, "Of course your
grandmother didn't really want you; only she desperately
didn't want me to have you." And that is right. That would
have defeated my grandmother. And my mother wasn't strong
enough to break through all her manipulating and scheming.

'Custody was given to my father. But one of the conditions
was that my mother should have access to me once a week.
Every Saturday she was supposed to see me, between noon and
eight o'clock in the evening. When the first Saturday came,
waiting for twelve was a nightmare. "Now Stephen, do you
want to go with your mother today?" "No Nan." "Are you
sure? Because you can if you want to." "No Nan." But what
made me say, "No", was the thought of going back and facing
grandmother afterwards. I could never have dared to go back if
I'd said, "Yes." But I had to go of my own accord to tell my
mother that I didn't want to see her, that I wasn't going with
her. My mother would say, "Are you coming today, Stephen?
I've got some sweets, we're going to the fair, we might go to the
Gower to the seaside for the day." I'd say, "I'm not coming."
My mother would try to stop herself from crying. "Are they
stopping you from coming?" "No." My mother would be all
dressed up nicely, ready to take me out, and every week I said,
"No." That was repeated perhaps eight or nine times. Then
when I got back to the house, there would always be a shilling
for sweets, and they would be specially nice to me, grandmother in particular. In the end, my mother gave up. She was
pregnant with her husband's child; and then she had a second
one later.

'But part of me did want to be with my mother. To be with
my grandmother was agony. I never saw enough of my father. I
always wanted him to come between my grandmother and me.
I used to stand behind her and make V-signs and faces at her. I

knew she couldn't turn round suddenly because of her arthritis. I was her whipping boy. I was always doing errands and being criticized for it. My grandmother talked about absolutely everybody behind their backs, whoever it was – whether it was the eldest son, the insurance man, the neighbours. She complained about everybody to everybody else, quite indiscriminately. She was a very bitter woman.

'My father's eldest brother Len was the most intelligent member of the family. He had a son called Keith and I was always made to feel inferior and subservient to this boy. Because Uncle Len was bright, Keith had to be bright as well. They came up every Sunday, regular as clockwork, for a bit of tea. It was all predictable, the cakes were baked, you knew what time to expect them and what time they'd go. It gave you a sense of security, this timetabling of life; but sometimes it was overpowering.

'After the divorce proceedings, my father wanted to join the army to get away from it. His mother stopped him. "No," she said, "you've got a son to look after." She used me as his responsibility to stop him from doing what he wanted. And this was the pattern of his life. He never really broke free of her, and I was the pawn in this game of keeping him tied to his mother.

'I recently discovered that my Uncle Len had wanted to adopt me. They were quite well off. If my father had gone into the army, and they had adopted me, well, you can't help wondering what life would have been like. I would have known a good and stable background, with discipline. My cousin Keith was always held up as a model to me.

'I never saw much of my father. He used to come home from work, wash and change, then off on the piss, not come home till bedtime. He was a good-looking bloke, I think he had a few women from time to time.

'I passed the 11-plus and went to Grammar School. I was still in short trousers. On my first day at school, I started off with everything I needed, briefcase, metal box of maths instruments, setsquare, compass, coloured pencils. Within a month, everything had been nicked. My grandmother said, "Oh well, we can't afford to replace it." That influenced me more than anything else in the way I got disaffected from school. I had to carry my books in my hand, and keep a biro in my inside pocket, and I felt they weren't trying, so why should

I? It was spoilt from the start. I wanted to play rugby, but the boots I had were really archaic, they were leather, very old-fashioned, and they'd belonged to my uncle. It made me feel conspicuous, and had a very demoralizing effect.

'I was bullied, terribly, at Grammar School. My grand-mother never understood it, and I could never catch my father at home long enough to talk to him. I had to grin and bear it. I started to smoke, and I started nicking things in shops in the town centre. I never got caught. I felt I was in a void, but I didn't know what caused it. There was a vacuum at the centre of my life.

'My grandmother never let me go to parties. I was never allowed to have the light on in bed, so I couldn't read. Beds were for sleeping in. I was in bed every night by nine. I used to sleep with my father. I had to be in by seven-thirty every night, ready for bed at nine. I sometimes used to sit in my pyjamas, watching telly, trying to be very still so they shouldn't notice me, so I could stay up a bit longer. I wasn't getting enough conversation or stimulus. Everything in the environment was control. I didn't understand it; it was power, not love, that was at the root of my childhood. When I was there, if my grandmother was talking to people, she used to spell out the words she thought I ought not to understand – d-i-v-o-r-c-e. Of course I could spell, I knew perfectly well what she was saying. I used to read the *News of the World* whenever I could get hold of it. It was pure hypocrisy. How they imagine a child can't see through it and grow up to resent it I don't know. She used to tell me not to eat with my mouth open, while she used to chew like a cow.

'At one time, my father went away to work in Caerphilly. They were building a conveyor belt, and he was working as a steel erector. Work for him was an escape. He came back one weekend and he and my grandmother had words. She told him, "You should see more of that child." She'd just had an operation for ulcerated legs, and she wasn't herself. The result was that he took me to Caerphilly with him. Those few weeks I had a fantastic time. It was heaven. What an escape! We stayed in digs. My father drank at the local pub there, and the landlord had two daughters who took me about everywhere. One of these daughters and her husband came to stay with us in the lodgings at Caerphilly. One morning, this chap, the husband, was downstairs eating breakfast, while his wife was upstairs, dressing. I went upstairs, and I saw my father and this bloke's wife kissing. I couldn't understand what was going on. I was about nine or ten. I felt my father was being unfair in some way. Anyway, my grandmother found out somehow or other what was going on, and she wrote to this woman's parents in Caerphilly and told them, and blew the whole thing. But my father seemed to accept it. She could do as she liked. Her word was law.

'Then, when I was 11 or 12, my father came home and woke me up one night and told me he'd met a woman he was going to marry. I couldn't take it. It made me very unhappy. My father didn't understand. His love was measured in pounds, shillings and pence. He didn't realize that I didn't want to share his love – there wasn't so much that it could be spread any more thin than it was already.

'I met her. She seemed all right. She had a daughter one year older than me, and a son who was four years younger. I was 12. I'd done one year at Grammar School. They got married, and I went to the wedding. There was a piss-up in the pub. The woman had three brothers; the family seemed quite nice. My grandmother couldn't quite cope with it of course. This was going against everything she had worked for. She wouldn't give up yet though. She didn't regard the fact that my father was getting married as being the end of him. She hadn't done the first time, why should she now? I went to live with them in my new mother's house.

'For the first three months everything was idyllic. Things were perfect. Those were the happiest days of my life. I had everything I wanted. My sister got 30 shillings a week spending money, I got a pound, and Graham got 12s 6d. It was great. But then, after about six months, things started to get a bit familiar. There were little rows. Graham, who was eight, would want to go out to play at nine o'clock in the evening. My father would say, "No". He was pushing for some respect; he'd been treated without it for most of his life. Then Graham would go and ask his Mum, and she'd say, "Yes, you can go out for half an hour." And that's how conflict between them would start. My father was about 34 at this time. We'd been living with grandmother for about seven years; it was a bit late for him to start asserting himself. He'd say, "Who's boss here?" She would say, "That doesn't matter, he's my son." By this time I was getting a bit worldly wise. I'd begun to see a bit further than face values. Their relationship was getting all twisted up. I could see it wasn't going to work.

'When we moved in with them, we went to get my long trousers. We went down to town. Lois, my stepsister, said, "When am I going to have a new dress?" "Oh, we can't afford it this week." Then she started crying, because I'd got something new and she hadn't. And that was the last time Lois didn't get her way. Her mother relied on Lois. She looked on her as an adult, a mature person, and she was more of a companion to her than a daughter. I realized that Lois was the king-pin of the household. I very much took a back seat. Graham was getting a lot of attention, I was getting F-all. It all seemed again to come back to power and not love. The marriage was soon in difficulties. So they had a child, a little boy. They had a child as a bit of a diversion from all that was going wrong, to hold the marriage together, I don't know. Anyway, soon after he was born, the marriage went dramatically downhill.

'My first sexual awakening was with my stepsister. I didn't screw her, but I saw her body, and went through the touching bit. All quite healthy. Masturbation started. But school at this time was terrible. I had been bullied there. I found out I wasn't an academic, so I wanted to be one of the heavies. But I was the weakest one in the group of heavies, which isn't a very rewarding position to have. I was with them, but I was always being shoved around by them. I liked sport; that was the one consolation at school, even though I never had the proper gear. I always wanted my father to watch me play. He never did.

'I called my stepmother, "Mam". My grandmother always referred to my real mother as "that bitch". I never got to know my real mother. She isn't a forceful personality. My grandmother easily supplanted her, and took her place in my father's life. I was always an extension of my grandmother. I thought and talked like her. There was no fighting her. I often thought of running away. But I realized there was nowhere to go. I think I realized I was unhappy, but there was nothing to do about it. If I ever tried to say anything to my father, he would say, "Don't be silly, here's 2s 6d, go and get some sweets." I had good toys, I wanted for nothing material. But we never went out together, we never sat round the table for a meal. We always ate on our laps in the front room. My grandmother sat in her chair, and she could see out of the bay window, and there was a mirror over the fireplace, so she could see anything she wanted to twice if she missed a detail first time. She was a great monument of a woman, statuesque. She was the most informed woman in the street, even though she never went out. They all came in to see her. Everybody who wanted a natter or a moan knew she was always there. And so, according to her, everybody in the street was terrible.

'I stuck with my father and stepmother for four years. I didn't want to stay there. It was a dilemma for me – I could have left, but the only place I could've gone was to my grandmother's. Then one day, my father was ill. He got pneumonia. And my stepmother went to Bingo rather than stay with him. For him, that was it. His son Jimmy was three. He left him with his wife, and went back to grandmother. In fact, as far as that kid was concerned, that was it. He's never been back to see him since. My father as a parent is a bit of a dead loss. He knows no more of being a parent than I do and I've had no kids. When he left, I stayed with my stepmother for a few weeks, and then I went back to my grandmother as well. I was 16.

'I'd left school in fact when I was 14, just before my fifteenth birthday. I started work just before I was 15. And within six weeks of leaving school, I was wishing myself back there again. I thought starting work meant freedom. I went to work as a sheet-metal worker, earning £3 17s 6d a week as a labourer. Later, I got bitter about having to leave school. My cousin Keith failed his "O" levels, and then he had to re-sit his "A" levels the following year because he failed them as well. I felt I had the ability to do well but no pushing, where he'd had all the pushing and no ability. That made me resentful. I quite enjoyed working in the factory. Somehow, I always thought I was something special. The way I looked at it was, I thought it was impossible that I could have such a hard time and not be something special. When I started work, I was giving my stepmother £2 a week, and keeping £1 17s 6d to spend. That seemed a hell of a lot at the time.

'I'd been working a year when I went back to my grandmother's. I got a job repairing car radiators. I left that, because they'd said I could go to Tech. and be an apprentice, but it turned out that it just meant doing a panel-beating course. One day, when I was pissed off, I went back to school, and the careers teacher said he would get me an apprenticeship at a sheet-metal works. I was lucky. They took me on, although I'd no qualifications. They gave me block release, and I spent a year at college. But within eight months I'd blown it. I worked there for a year, and I signed my indentures. That was great. But then I went and threw it all away.

'Two years before this, my mother's husband, Fred, had died of cancer. Their life together hadn't been very happy. He'd beaten her about a bit, there'd been trouble with the police. Anyway, one day my father came home and said, "You'll never guess who I saw the other night." "No, who?" "I met your mother." "Oh." He said, "We're going to give it another try." I didn't cry; I was 16. I said, "Dad, you can't." My grandmother was disgusted. My grandfather – oh hell, isn't that funny, I haven't even mentioned my grandfather, even though he was there all the time. Oh, isn't that odd . . . Because I loved my grandfather dearly. It's just that she sort of eclipsed everybody else. Me and my grandfather were allies. Together, we could just cope, whereas on our own, she could always defeat us. He liked a pint, did his garden, kept chickens. I feel that my grandfather died before I had a chance to talk to him. I felt I owed him so much. What he did for her was above and beyond the call of duty. He was loyal to her, although she crushed everybody around her all the years of her life. He just lived in her shadow. I went to see him when he was very ill in hospital. I came down from London to see him, and I said, "Come on, Gramps, how do you expect to get out of here if you don't eat?" And he looked at me, and he said, "Oh no, Steve, I'm not coming out of here now." His life had been and was such a misery that to die was the only way out of it.

'My father said that he and my mother were going to live together. He got digs near my mother's council house. He didn't move in with her, because he didn't want people to talk. My father said, "Come and live with me." I said, "No." My father said, "I'll never ask you to do anything for me again." I was 17; and for the first time in my life I had stood up for myself. I said I'd move in with my mother. I hadn't spoken to her for 11 years. I hadn't even seen her for six of them.

'It was a touching reunion, the first time we all met together. My father sat there and said the reason why they had separated

was all his fault. He admitted it. It hadn't been my mother's
fault at all. She was completely absolved from any of the blame.
I thought, "Fuck it, they've told me lies for 11 years." My
father plummeted in my estimation. And since then I've not
been able to look on him as a father. He's a friend now, but he
isn't a father.

'At this time I got involved with a rock group. I got into
drugs, smoking and dropping LSD. It didn't do me any harm,
but I got some terrific highs. The group played a lot of Jimi
Hendrix numbers. One night my mother tried to stop me from
going to play with the group. My mother and father had an
argument. I packed my bags and left. I got a flat. I was still
doing my apprenticeship – this was just as I started my year at
Tech. But after eight months of life with the group and drugs, I
got so that I just couldn't get up in the mornings. I stopped
going. I had nothing.

'I bummed around, did some rubbish jobs. I played the
drums. It was a good group, and we made a few bob.
Everybody thought I'd gone off the rails. At 18 I couldn't give a
fuck. I was rebelling – doing what I should have done years
earlier. I moved to London. The first year I was there, my
father wrote and asked me to go and spend Christmas with him
and my grandmother. It had been a couple of years since I'd
seen them. I felt I'd needed to put a distance between me and
them, they'd crapped on me all those years. So I thought,
"Well, maybe it's time I went back." A bit of a reconciliation.
When I got there my grandmother had gone to stay with my
uncle for Christmas, my grandfather had died. I had been in
the middle of a ten-week tour of Holland when I received a
telegram saying that grandfather was dead, and asking me to
come home for the funeral. I couldn't because it would have
meant leaving the group in the lurch. That was another reason
why I'd decided to go home for Christmas. Not only had my
grandmother gone away, but my father had gone to stay with
the piece he was knocking off at that moment. He'd even taken
the television with him. So there I was, sitting in a house with
no food, no TV. Christmas Eve. I'd been told, "Your
grandmother would love to see you." So I phoned my mother.
Her attempt at reconciliation with my father had sunk long
ago. She had married for the third time, and was living in the
pub she kept with her new husband. I went up there, and we

had a great time. We had a good talk. I began to see things as they really were, and not through the filter of my grandmother.

'After that, I started going home twice a year, every Christmas and once during the summer. But I couldn't let either my mother or my father know that I was seeing the other. In fact, it started to get to me. I'd been shunted round all those years and survived. But now I became obsessed that I'd got to keep these two parts of myself separate, just like I had as a kid. It started to crack me up. I could feel there was something I couldn't quite get hold of. It got harder and harder to go there. In the end, I went to them all in turn and told them. My father was living with a woman by this time; he always needed a companion. I went and told him, "Look, Dad, I'm seeing mother, and you can say what you like." And then I went and told her. And when I'd done that, all the problems seemed to melt away. I wasn't scared any more. I told them all I'd see them equally. I couldn't stand the deception any longer. I found I couldn't lie – I'd been fed lies all my life.

'My grandmother died a couple of years ago. At that time, I was seen by all the family as a bit of a yob. I'd been in a group, I'd had long hair and all that. On the day of the funeral, I wore a three-piece black suit, I was immaculate. All the relatives looked at me and said, "Who's that?" I was the only one in a black suit. Inside, I felt good. I looked round and I said to them, "You know what? I've never seen so many smiling people at a funeral."

'Considering what a time I'd had, I think I've not done too badly. I've never brought the police to my house, I never brought shame on the family. I got over it, overcame all the insecurities and the conflict that had confused me. Drugs helped me, cannabis helped. I found that I could make friendships, relationships with other people. Once I got away from home, I could take responsibility for my own life; I could get stoned, have a laugh. The group was my salvation. I played the drums. I always had the feeling that I was something special; and when you saw all those crowds of people who'd paid to see you play, they'd paid money to see you, it sort of confirmed the feeling that perhaps I had got something. But when I hit those drums, I did it with such a lot of pent-up feeling, such aggravation! I used to hit the bollocks off those drums. I vented all my rage, all my feelings, all the controls I'd been under on those drums. I gave it all I'd got. I'd come off stage drained, every time. Those drums stood for a hell of a lot of things, I beat all my childhood out of me.

'I'd always been disparaged by my grandmother. I learned the violin; she said, "You'll never be able to play that." She said I'd never learn to play the piano properly. She always sat there, with a blanket round her legs, always so right, always dominating, controlling. I could never let go at her. By the age of 17, 18, you can't, she's too old. I used to get it out of my system by going on the piss and then having a punch-up with somebody afterwards. She was a powerful woman though. My father went back to her in the end. My childhood seems a million miles away now, but it's still there. Some things she gave me: I'm stubborn like her, a certain strength. But I'm not getting married yet. I'm living with a girl. I don't want to rush into a situation that repeats what I was brought up to.'

17

THE STRUCTURE OF CHILDHOOD

THE OLD DEFENSIVE culture of poverty gave working-class children (apart from the poorest) a sense of security which is denied the present generation. There was something in the very texture of social life itself that was cradling and comforting. The price that was paid for this advantage was high: the stifling conformity, the feeling of oppression it left in many individuals. The more mobile and open experience of recent years provides possibilities formerly undreamed of; but the price exacted is again high – the sense of disturbance in many children, the violence and absence of direction – are at the root of a different kind of damage. The question remains – who says that the sense of socially secure identity is incompatible with the wider individual freedoms? It is the false either/or, the artificial alternative, the sham antithesis which has hurt, and continues to hurt children and the adults we have all become. If we believe that the kind of suffering associated with the older experience, and the sort of damage we permit to be inflicted on our children today are somehow inevitable, a kind of necessary human sacrifice, it is because we have lost the ability to imagine real alternatives, real choices in which human tributes to economic processes might not be necessary.

As recently as 30 years ago that older experience was still relatively intact in the working-class streets throughout the country.

Time was heavily structured. Partly, this reflected the discipline of the industrial timetable, but partly it resulted from living close together. The whole street seemed to acquiesce in order and ritual, which were a kind of substitute for privacy.

The weekdays were not the same; each was associated with a different consciousness that stained them all a different colour. There was a reluctant sense of renewal about Monday mornings, that gave even the boots on the pavement at half past seven a determination, a ring of the victory of will over inclination; a regimented tread of iron economic necessity. In the houses, the domestic wash exhaled the smell of sour grey suds, an affirmation of cleanliness won with difficulty from the once universal dirt and infestation; woollen socks were rubbed together until they foamed, coarse yellowish vests with buttons at the throat – underwear that chafed the skin like a penance; the grime at the collar and cuffs of shirts, the smell of sweat mingled with water and soap. On Mondays meals were always subordinated to the need to keep clean. The sheets, heavy with water, left a trail like blood as they were carried over the dull red kitchen tiles, and rotted the coconut matting that stood in front of the sink. The dried peas for Monday dinner had been put in soak on Sunday night in a chipped enamel dish, and they were allowed to boil away until they had almost disintegrated into an olive-coloured soup; the potatoes were eroded by the water they were boiled in, the thin slices of reddish-veined cold lamb frilled by a border of white fat were bland and savourless.

Monday evenings were always quiet. The pub on the corner of the street was empty. In winter, the washing would be steaming on the plain wooden frame of a clothes-horse, held by canvas hinges. Women would iron the sheets into immaculate rectangles, taking care to avoid creases that would warn of a death when the diamond-shaped fold appeared as it was thrown over the bed the following week. The iron was heated over the gas-stove, and before they used it, they spat on the shiny black triangle, and silver balls of saliva danced down the surface. There was a silence and weariness about Monday night; saturated with the inevitability of the week to come; a reassertion of discipline after the relaxation of the weekend. The glimpse of leisure had been shut off, and the only perspective was an endless future of work. On Mondays the fire was allowed to die down early; the rasp of clocks being wound, the raking of embers through the grate, the hot water falling into the stone bottle. Conversation was spare and functional, punctuated by yawns and sighs. On Monday, the whole street would be in bed by half past ten. Anybody out after that time was said to be thieving or whore-hopping.

By Tuesday morning everything had been re-established, the weekend forgotten. There was a more automatic rising, a more even tread of boots on the pathways and back alleys. Tuesday meant the first renewal of provisions in the week – fresh bread and vegetables. More women went into the town

centre to buy food on the few market stalls; these were
completely absent on Mondays. It was a day of minor
household chores, only a shadow of the major scouring that
would occur later in the week. If the weather was good, the
airing would be on the line, held aloft by a prop that had once
been the branch of an old tree, the shirts inhabited by the wind,
the noisy music of the sheets, ghost-white in the fugitive
sunlight, flapping in the women's faces as they walked down the
yard to feel the dampness, and unpegging the washing from the
gipsies' pegs which they held in their mouths like disfiguring
wooden canines. Perhaps on Tuesday afternoon a relative
would visit; stay for a cup of tea, but be out of the way by the
time the man of the house got home. He would be a little less
taciturn on Tuesday night; but would still step out of his
overalls, undo the laces of his boots that were left for cleaning,
drop his canvas bag in the passage. Tuesday evenings were
slightly more animated. The radio played in the background;
the children lay on their bellies on the floor, colouring, or
reading a comic. Mother would sit, darning, showing her
husband the 'potato' she had found in his sock, breaking the
thread with her teeth from time to time, offering any information she had gained about anybody else's life during the day;
and he would acknowledge her intermittent monologue with a
syllable that neither confirmed nor challenged what she said.
Bed-time would be a little later; but the boiled milk seethed up
in the saucepan, there was the same, almost obsessive check on
the gas-taps; the last reassuring look round, to make sure that
nothing had been neglected, might even take place as late as
11.15.

By the middle of the week, the rhythm was so securely
established, it might never had been otherwise. But there was
greater liveliness and mobility in the whole town. For one
thing, it was market day; and some ancient memory of
excitement stirred through the women. They walked between
the primitive booths, rough struts and bare planks, but
obscured by the piles of home-grown tomatoes, reddening skins
still sparkling with September rain, the blanched roughness of
cauliflower heads, pressing the hearts of the lettuce, the ridged
dewy cucumbers, so covered with bloom that the marks of
fingerprints could be seen where they had been touched. The
women came home with a leather shopping bag full of fresh

stuff, 'local' grown, which gave it a familiar and homely quality. When the men came home for dinner – which most of them still did, propping their black-painted bicycles against the windowsill – there would be spam and tomato with boiled potatoes. If they were in a bad mood, they might turn over the lettuce and say, 'Call this a proper bloody meal.'

Wednesday evening marked the passing of the half week, and the first moment of real levity. Perhaps the men would splash and sing in the kitchen, filling the enamel bowl with hot water from the kettle; a shave, a lick and a promise before going out for an hour – not to drink heavily, because money was getting low, but for a game of cribbage or darts or skittles, and a comment on the news. Perhaps the women played with the children, rummy or I-spy; or they repeated nonsense-rhymes from their own childhood; until the children started to cheat or to quarrel; and then she would say, 'Come on, the sandman's been,' and then she would fetch the bowl and wash them all in the same water, perhaps crossing it with a forefinger before she did so, and singing

Wash me in the water that you washed your dirty daughter,
And I'll be whiter than the milky coconut.

The children would be allowed to sit up a bit later; and then, when they were in bed, she would do some chores, a saucepan and a pile of runner beans, pared round the edge so that a pile of green strings grew on a piece of newspaper, and the beans themselves were cut obliquely into neat lozenges; or she would shell the peas, popping the pods with a minute explosion by pressure of her thumb; she would make tea, and sit and read the evening paper, to see who had been pinched, who had died, who had had a baby.

Thursday already promised the wage packet and the weekend. But the money was low by now, and the meals correspondingly austere – offal or scrag-end with pot herbs, and just bread and jam for tea – the jam a reminder of blackberries gathered in blue sugar-bags over the fields late last summer. It seemed to be a day for visiting relatives. When the children got home from school in the afternoon, there was grandmother, some aunts, perhaps a neighbour, drinking tea and talking about who'd got thick with whose wife, who'd been found with her head in the gas-oven. Perhaps to compensate for the dwindling material resources, they needed the security of being together. Even the shop halfway down the street was closed on Thursday afternoons, blue holland blind fading in the sunlight, cat resting serenely among the humbugs and toffee. On this day, when the men came home, the women didn't automatically get up and get ready to leave saying, 'Ah well, this won't get the baby a new frock.' Even if the men said, 'Stop chopsing and let's have a bit of tea,' it was said without acrimony. If they were feeling cheerful, there was a half-amused indulgence of the women and their trivial intercourse.

By Thursday evening the week's tiredness had caught up with them – the mornings always up before seven without ever needing the alarm clock. The women always boasted that they could wake up at any hour they willed; and they would cut sandwiches, wrapping them in greaseproof paper, chunky doorsteps with a cold sausage, or some cheese and slice of raw onion. The men always expected, and always found, their clothes, not where they had left them, but where they needed to step into them in the morning.

Friday was the busiest day of the week. It was the day for cleaning the house. Scrubbing, blackleading, dusting, Brasso-ing, scouring the doorstep, cleaning the windows – standing on a box or leaning outside from the upstairs sill, clutching the raised sash and stretching to reach the top panes, and waiting for the sun to catch the glass to see whether it had been smudged. Mats were hung on the line and beaten, while the clouds of dust particles dispersed in the air. The galvanized zinc bucket was fetched out, and the green grit-covered soap which smeared the bristles of the scrubbing brush before it was passed in soiled arcs over the kitchen floor. The shopping was done on the strength of the expected wage packet, and when the works buses or the bicycles brought the men home for dinner, there would be meat pudding or liver-and-onion roll.

Friday evening was the time of greatest relaxation; although many men had to work on Saturday morning, it wasn't a full day, and with luck there was always a way to finish early. Friday tea was perhaps the most joyful meal of the week – herrings or sardines, egg and bacon or pork pie. If the moment of relaxation and levity was broken by the men who had to get ready to go out – they would put on a suit and smooth their hair with Brylcreem, while their wives had a pang of anxiety that they might be going to meet other women (in spite of the fact that there were virtually no other women to meet), there was still enough of the gaiety left when they had gone for the children to be allowed to sit up late, and for the women to receive the neighbours or relatives. The kettle was placed on the fire instead of the gas-stove, so that it boiled continuously for fresh cups of tea. It stood, black and permanently unsteady on the burning coals, frothing and spitting onto the blackleaded bars of the grate. They talked, always of the same things – their past poverty, orange boxes draped with lace for furniture, boiling water poured on toast crumbs to simulate tea, earth closets, migrations from the countryside, harvests and pig-killing, and their memories of long-dead parents and grandparents. The children played or listened, made themselves small so that they wouldn't be noticed and sent to bed.

Saturday was busy, spent preparing for the weekend. Saturday dinner was always a makeshift – fish and chips from the shop; and it was timeless, perhaps as late as three o'clock, whereas on most days meals were decidedly fixed feasts, functional and silent events, often despatched within 10 or 15 minutes. After dinner the men who didn't go to the football turned on the radio, and, under the pretext of listening to gabbled and breathless commentaries that issued from behind the dusty orange dial, slept; and the only thing that roused them to angry protest was any attempt to turn down the radio or to hold even the most subdued conversation in the room.

On Saturday night the men and women often went out together, although they might well sit apart in the pub. In summer the children could be left to play in the pub yard, with its green-slatted garden chairs; in winter they would be left in the care of an older daughter, who had strict instructions to come and find her parents if the little ones were naughty and refused to do as they were told. Saturday night often involved clumsy sex or quarrels, or both, while scared children crouched, looking through the banisters at adults, who always imagined their own relationship to be out of reach of the understanding of their young, even when stridently conducted in front of them. Saturday night in the street was noisy: laughter, prolonged goodbyes, breaking glass, ribaldry. The lights were on in many front rooms until one o'clock, while people played cards, told stories, knitted, patched and darned as they talked.

Sunday morning left a silence brooding and total as death over the streets. Bottles of milk could remain late on the doorsteps without exciting comment, an indulgence not extended to weekdays. Church bells were an intrusion for most people, a signal for putting your head under the pillow, or for getting the first cup of tea and the paper. Sometimes Sunday morning tea was the only concession the men made to tenderness. The women would sit up in bed, sip the dark liquid, bite their lip and not say, 'too strong' or 'not enough sugar'.

Sunday morning meant the Yorkshire pudding, yellow liquid in a yellow pudding basin, brussels sprouts in their enamel colander, potatoes in bone-handled saucepans. The men came home late and unappreciative, sometimes critical of the sameness of Sunday dinner. The washing-up was always done as soon as the meal was finished, the swirl of greasy water rushing down the drain, the sound of the bowl scraping against the sink and chipping the enamel. Then silence again and sleep. The children who didn't go to Sunday School played in the street, but their play was muted by the universal hush. Only an occasional voice raised in domestic argument interrupted the peace. Relatives came to tea on Sundays, and tea would be a later and more substantial meal. There would be tinned fruit and fish. But nobody had much to say on Sunday evenings. The relatives would go by eight-thirty. And then Sunday evening was always invaded by melancholy, a stillness that could never be kept at bay. It was perhaps the time of the week when people got closest to each other: unity in face of the time when the ritual would finally finish; a contemplation of mortality, afterlife. Something of the decayed religious tradition lingered and somehow penetrated the dense mesh of secularized ritual. There was silence; the rustle of newspaper, coals burning low in the grate, embers fanned into a glow from a draught under the door. Then an early night; everything prepared for the men in the morning, the dustbin put out for collection, 'the pavements taken in', as they used to say in our street.

Time was so densely structured that it seemed closed to all innovation or change. Not only were the times of ceremonial highly ritualized, but the weeks, the days of the week called forth an appropriate response.

It was very much into this kind of world that Ken and Jean

Lovell were born 40 years ago. Both were brought up poor in adjacent streets in Bolton. Jean's mother was widowed, and worked in a shop. Ken's mother had been a textile worker; his father was asthmatic, a bit of a boozer, an unskilled labourer who worked only intermittently. They knew each other as children in primary school, in the Methodist Chapel, at secondary school. They were teenagers in the 1950s; both felt the sense of relief and excitement that swept through what they saw then as the meanness and narrowness of working-class life at that time. Ken had an apprenticeship in an engineering firm, and became a shop steward and trade union official. Jean worked in the mill for a time, but now works in an old people's home. Their two children are Sandy, 18, and Paul, 16.

JEAN: 'As a kid, they were very narrow-minded where we lived. One woman in our street, she used to have a bloke round while her husband was working. The women of the street all got together, and they came round to my mother's house to decide what they should do about this woman's carrying on. They had a proper council of war. It was like a bloody parliament, our front room. In the end, they elected a deputation to go round and talk to this woman. They made all their plans; they would give her a chance. They told her she had to give it up, and then they'd be magnanimous and not tell her husband. She told them to mind their own sodding business. So they had another day-long debate. They decided it was their duty to tell the husband. So they went and buttonholed him coming out of work. And he more or less said the same thing to them. I believe he was carrying on with somebody himself. The last thing he wanted was them disturbing his arrangement with his missis. I think it was more or less the dying embers of all that, but it was very narrow.'

KEN: 'Not only that, but they were such hypocrites. My Dad, he was pathetic outside the home, always buying all the drinks in the pub, but inside the home he was a proper tyrant. If he didn't like his dinner, he'd just get the plate and throw it at the wall..Mam wouldn't say anything, she'd just go down on her hands and knees and clear it up. Not a word of protest. I mean, he was only a little shrimp, she could have belted him, but the role thing was so powerful, they just did what was expected of them. He was a dirty bugger. He used to blow his nose onto the grate, and if it missed and went on the floor, she just got a piece of newspaper and wiped it up. He was idle, he was so lazy the tails of his shirts were always covered with shit, and he just stepped out of his clothes, and she had to run round after him. Once he swiped her, and he must have hit her a bit too hard, she fell off the chair and lay on the floor without moving. He thought he'd done her in, he started to panic. That was the only time he ever showed any feeling, and I think that was because he was scared he was going to find himself on a murder rap. He went to get her some water, and then just sat there crying, "I've killed your mother, I've killed your mother." He sits there, tears running down his cheeks, "What shall I do? What shall I do?" I was eight, and my sister six. I said to him, "Don't sit there bawling, go and get help." He bloody went and all. He was like a kid himself. But do you know, that was enough for her. For the rest of her life she quoted that at me if I ever criticized him. It proved he loved her! "I should want better bloody proof than that", says Jean and laughs. It was as if she forgot he was the one who laid her out cold in the first place. She said, "He went and got me some water," as if it was an act of pure human charity. She said to me, "Oh you are hard, Ken." Talk about living on crumbs. My mother never had new clothes, she never went out. All her social life was either in the back garden hanging out the clothes and talking to the neighbours, or going up the shops. I got really angry with her, "Why do you put up with it?" When I was about 15, 16, I really despised my old man. Mind you, he'd been one of eight, brought up by a stepmother who had never really liked him. My mother used to say, "He'll know one day, when he hasn't got me." But he didn't. He took care to die first. He was always a bit of an invalid, he had a bloody suitcase full of embrocation and patent medicines. He had this mystery illness that finally killed him, but it took four years. It was the longest death-bed scene in history.

'She only got her own back on him once. He used to do a lot of fishing; that was the only thing I ever remember doing with him that I enjoyed. And one night she left all his maggots in the hearth. In the morning, the whole house was swarming with bloody blow-flies, they all hatched overnight. She was the one who had to clear them out though.'

JEAN: 'We wouldn't want a childhood for our kids like we had. We wanted something better for them. I was a little drudge. My Mum loved us, especially when Dad died. I mean, you could rely on her, she was a tough old girl. But she controlled us, my two brothers were terrified of her. Complete silence on sex. When I was nine, she said to me, quite seriously, "Jean love, I've got something to tell you." "Yes Mam." "Never, you must never let any boy come anywhere near you not till you're married." That was all she said. I thought she meant it literally. It meant they mustn't touch you, even brush past you. For two years I used to avoid all contact with boys. If we were playing tag, anything, if one of them even grazed past me I'd worry rotten for days that it was wrong and something terrible would happen to me. I got into this habit, literally of not letting any boy near me. I can laugh about it now, but it was a nightmare for well over two years.'

KEN: 'You think when you're young anything must be better. I mean, I loved being a teenager, we went through rock 'n' roll, Elvis, it was another world. It made you feel superior to the older people, you felt it was something that didn't come from Bolton, it had to be good. The trouble was it didn't do us any favours. I left school at 15. They wanted me to stay on, which I should've done. My Mam was willing, my Dad didn't have any ideas on it one way or the other. But I thought, "No, that's where real life is, juke box, down the caff, dancing, the Hit Parade, the *New Musical Express*, Cliff, Tommy Steele. You think that is what your life is all going to be about. It isn't till you grow up that you realize you've lost your chances. I was lucky. I had an apprenticeship, and I've found a lot of satisfaction in my union work.'

JEAN: 'We've made a life for ourselves, I enjoy what I do, I get a lot of satisfaction out of working with old people. But what it does, you make up your mind your own kids are going to do better. You want to re-write your own childhood through them. And that isn't easy, either on the personal level, nor in what you want for them, from the point of view of achievement. People always react against what went before. We were so poor, it was such a struggle when Ken and I were kids, you think "Oh whatever happens, it's got to be better than that." But you're so busy reacting to your own childhood, you don't see all the bad things that affect your own kids. You concentrate on heaping material things on them, but that isn't their problem, that's yours. It takes a hell of a lot to see through that. And then, where your parents used to control you – my Mam was a Tartar, even though she was on her own – that isn't the issue for your kids. You don't have those unreasonable attitudes. I remember the first pair of jeans I wanted, you'd've thought it was asking to be put to apprentice to a whore. She'd been brought up very chapel, and all this religious stuff came out, which I'd never had actually rammed down my throat, but which my Mam always fell back on when the power of her own personality failed. One pair of jeans was like Armageddon to her.'

Sandy is about to do her 'A' levels, French, German and English. Ken and Jean are proud of her, and pleased that she has made it through the Comprehensive School, even though the pressures on her to give up have been considerable. For her, it has meant detaching herself from the group of her own age-mates; and this has been painful and difficult. Paul can't wait to leave school. He wants to be a motor mechanic.

KEN: 'Where with us it was parents, with them it's their mates. The biggest influence. It's through the pressure of their mates that they've got to have everything the same. You feel if you don't go and buy them whatever bit of rubbish they all have, you're failing them. You wouldn't believe it, some of the kids who've trooped through here over the years, they own everything, but nobody cares about them. They buy their kids off. I think Sandy and Paul understand it. It's the easiest thing in the world to give in and buy peace and quiet by giving kids everything they ask for. And a lot of people who were brought up poor think that's the right thing to do.

JEAN: 'A lot of parents, you can't blame them, they're fighting the battles they had as kids, and it's very hard to see that that isn't the kids' problem. The problem for the kids is something else – it's finding something to hold on to, values, balance. We thought we were fighting against superstition and ignorance and religion. And it's not till everything's been torn down that you realize you haven't left anything for the next generation. When all that's gone, there's nothing but money and what you can buy.'

KEN: 'Kids see only what is in front of them: they've got to have exactly the same as everybody else. Dress the same as everybody else, put on the uniform. Paul comes in one day in the summer, hair cropped, like a bloody convict. Then it's an ear-stud, then Dr Martens. And it's all money. Everything they want to do, it all costs. It makes you feel ashamed, because we were the ones who thought we were the pioneers, and it's the biggest bloody con in history. I mean, we could fight the control our parents had over us. We knew what it was. But now, you can't defeat it; you can only hope that your kids grow up realizing that the important things aren't in all that.'

JEAN: 'What you can give them is love and security. It's a struggle. So when you say, "No you can't go to Manchester for an all-night party when you're 14," they don't think you're being a spoilsport. But to fight it makes you look a bit cranky, a bit as if you're trying to be better than everybody else. If I say, "No, I don't want my kids chanting TV commercials as soon as they can speak," people say, "Why not, what's wrong with it?" It looks petty. But you know it isn't that, it isn't about singing commercials, it's what they tell you about the values of the society, about buying everything.'

KEN: 'Well I was talking to a young bloke at work, and he was saying him and his wife couldn't afford another child. As though you bought them at the supermarket.'

JEAN: 'I read somewhere recently how many thousand pounds they reckon it costs to bring up a child. It's terrible. I never thought the day would ever come when I'd quote my own childhood at my kids. "We never did this, we used to do that." But then you start to realize, all the things that were good about your childhood you took for granted. It's true that we had good times without a ton of money. We had a shilling to go to the pictures and money for toffees. But their friends, digital watches at the age of ten, bikes, electronic toys, what sort of an influence is that going to have on them? It means they can't do anything for themselves, they need such a lot to keep them entertained and occupied; and still they're bored. But to make sense of it, it's like hacking your way through a jungle.'

Sandy and Paul listen to their parents with good-natured tolerance. They have heard it all so many times. They argue back. Sandy says her mother should have been a social worker; that she's all right, that she wants to lead other people's lives for them. Jean reflects on this and wonders if that doesn't make her like her mother – precisely what she is trying to resist with her own children. But the feeling between the parents and their children seems to offer the surest guarantee that they will grow into reasonably sensitive and loving adults – the most powerful source of resistance to adverse social conditions, whatever their nature; but however powerful, it isn't inexhaustible, and certainly no argument for not fighting all the things that unnecessarily harm the growth and development of children.

18

MAISIE GREEN, 30: A DAMAGED CHILD

MAISIE IS A vigorous and unself-conscious woman who looks older than she is. Her adult life gives the lie to the generalization that an unhappy childhood must inevitably impair adult relationships.

She lives in a 1930s block of London County Council dwellings, once a showplace of working-class housing, but now a squalid and run-down wasteland of asphalt, and littered with broken glass and rubbish and waste paper. The metal plaque commemorating the civic opening of the flats is covered with verdigris and graffiti. Some of the poorest and most demoralized people in London live in these flats. Maisie works with the Tenants' Association; energetic, passionate and committed; but she insists that she would have been nothing like this but for the relationship with her husband, who has helped her heal the wounds of her childhood. Her flat is warm and untidy. She doesn't go out to work, but is happy to stay with her children, five and three, and listen sympathetically to the people who come to her flat every day with their problems – money, marriage, children. People recognize in her a mothering power which certainly didn't come from her direct experience of being a child.

'My mother was cruel to me, God forgive her. I can say it now she's dead, nothing can make it any worse for her where she is now. I hope there's no such place as hell, because if there is, she's bloody in it. I thought I was in hell, the way I was dragged through life as a kid. My God, I've searched my memory to find something nice to say of her. I can't find a whisper of anything that makes me feel any warmth. She was not a bad-looking woman. There you are; but that's no bloody virtue is it?

'My Dad left her when I was less than a year old. She felt if it hadn't been for me, he would have stayed with her. I don't think that had anything to do with it, that was her way of justifying her hatred for me. It was her delight to torment me.

When I was ever so little she used to hide, after telling me she was going away and never coming back. She'd strap me into the pram, say goodbye, then go into the next room to enjoy my screams. And then, she'd appear suddenly out of nowhere to scare me, shouting. Her face'd come round the pram or the door, with a stocking over her head, and she'd shout, "Here comes the bogeyman." If I was naughty she'd lock me in a cupboard. I can remember what it was like in there, smell of old newspaper, mouse turds on the floorboards. I was naughty; as far as she was concerned I was never anything else. Being with her was enough. She wasn't an adult herself really, she acted like a kid. Her own mother had been a bit ramshackle, dumping her on anybody who'd have her. She'd once been sold to a woman who couldn't have children. I don't know how it came about, some tatty deal with somebody her mother had met in a pub. She was left with all sorts of strangers at one time or another. She wasn't loved.

'We lived in rooms up Clapton. The hours she left me on my own! She used to go out, and before she went, she threatened me that if I made a squeak, she'd leather the daylights out of me. I can remember her going out, and she left me in this cold bare room, tied by my reins to the leg of the settee, and there'd be just a cup of water left for me. I didn't dare make a sound, because I really thought she would be able to hear me. I never knew if she was still there, hiding.

'This particular day, I watched it get dark, and she never came. I saw the light from the street in the room, and I sat on this cold lino with this cracked cup of water. I knocked it over, and I was scared I'd get hit. I don't know exactly how long she stayed away that time; but I know it got light, I saw the window go all blue. I got thirsty, and I tried to lick the water up off the lino. It tasted of dust. The lino was yellow and blue. I must have been on my own for 24 hours. I remember listening for her steps. You'd listen, and hear people outside, and hope the steps would come upstairs, but they didn't. They always went past. I was about three I think. I was more scared of her than I was of the dark; and I was bloody terrified of that.

'She was sadistic, you realize that later. When I was very small I was neglected, because I was just a nuisance to her. She only started being really unkind when she knew she could get some reaction from me. When I got a bit older, but still young,

she wasn't particular about using me to get the blokes she
couldn't get for herself. There's always a kind of bloke who goes
for little girls; though what she wanted that sort for, God
knows. God knows where she fished them all up from. They
have an instinct. I was always being left outside pub doors, in
pub yards. From the age of about 12, she started dressing me up
and taking me to the pubs with her. She was thick with the
landlord at one place, and she encouraged me to sit on the bar
and sing; bloody hell, I was a proper little performer. The men
used to pet me, I'd feel their mitts all over me, I can still feel it.
She used me as bait. Christ knows, I was a skinny thing and a
thank you, but there you are. There was one bloke she went
with for a little while. He was little and he had hairy hands. I
used to be left alone with him, and he'd touch me up, these
bleeding fingers like caterpillars crawling towards me. I hated
it. I don't know what the deal had been, if she'd been paid or
what. I never complained, because there was nobody I could
complain to. You accept it, whatever is there, as a kid. It's
normal, because you don't know anything else. You know
where the power is, and you give in to it. But all the time, I
never lost the feeling that something terrible was being done to
me; and I knew it was wrong.

'In any case, it wasn't all heartbreak. When I grew up a bit, I
enjoyed myself. I could get other girls at school to do things, I
was a bit of a leader. A ringleader, they called me. You know
parents are always saying that their kids are easily led? Well I
was the villain that done the leading. I never knew what it was
to be afraid. I guess if you've been tormented by your own
mother, anything else is a bunch of roses. I used to climb over
the balconies in the flats, four storeys up, from one ledge to the
next, open a bathroom window. I was only little and like a
bleeding monkey the way I could climb. There's me, chucking
things out of windows to my mates, and then dancing round on
the roofs. They talk about kids now, believe me – I started it all.
I've been creeping about inside people's houses, while they've
been sitting there, watching television – they've been gawping
at some programme about cops and crooks, and there's me,
going through the bedrooms, getting me thieving maulers on
anything that's movable. I've even been there while they've
been having it off in the bedrooms. I've snatched handbags
from old women. We used to take money from kids all the time;

wait round the shops for kids running errands, getting the money from them was like taking candy from a baby. You hear about muggers, we were muggers all right, 15 years before anybody had heard the word.

'My school was a farce. I only used to go when there was nothing better to do, or if it was too cold to be outside. There was not one adult I ever cared a toss for. Some of the teachers were nice. I can see that now. They used to try and talk to you, and they'd be very kind. You could see they really wanted to get to you. They'd have you in after school, and their voice would be very cajoling. I would never give any clue that I understood. I used to say, "Dunno what you're on about." But I think a part of me would have liked to let go, be cuddled, break down. But I said to myself, "No, girl; not yet; not here." I never did. I never cried after I was very little, not till I met Marvyn. I've never shed a tear for anyone else. I can see a film on the telly, and bawl my eyes out at what's on the screen, but for another person, not a drop. I'm a hard cow. She knocked it out of me. I'd done all my crying by the time I was five. I'd done so bloody much it was enough to last me a lifetime.

'After my old woman, I could never put up with people aggravating me. I've got no patience. I used to hate myself. For years I thought she done that because I wasn't worth loving. I've got scars all over my breast where I dived through a window one day when some bloke was getting on my nerves. If I feel bad, I'll burn myself over the gas or with a lighter – look, I've got scars all up my arms. Marvyn hits me sometimes. I don't mind that; it keeps me under control. No, it makes me feel I exist, I'm still there. I can't explain it to you, but when he shows me his temper, I know he's there, and I know I'm there.

'My mother came down from Glasgow just after the War. I don't know what she was running away from, but she never stopped. She died of drink. It was drink all the time. She liked drink better than me, that's why I think I'm useless, I had to play second fiddle to a bleeding bottle. When I was little I did long for her not to drink; because sometimes she made promises about what we'd do together – we'd go to the country, to the seaside. Some hopes. I suppose I might have believed her once. But I soon realized that was only another one of her torments. She was like two people; and the bad one took over more and more.

'She was smoking in bed one night, she wasn't very old, in her 50s, and she set fire to the bed and herself. She died not long after. She was like a great kid herself. She couldn't keep a man close to her more than five minutes; the drink and the lies.

'What chance did I have? I think I'm horrible. It was no wonder I had a kid by the age of 16, only it was taken away, put into care. I couldn't have looked after him. When I was 16, finding myself with a baby, what could I do – go and ask my mother? What a joke.

'It was a funny thing. Because I'd never had any love, I went looking for it among all the blokes I could find; talk about a needle in a haystack. Then you get caught in the sex trap: you don't know what love is, so any sign of affection, you grab it, and you don't know the difference between somebody screwing you and loving you. Then you get a kid, somebody else who needs affection before you've got any yourself. That's a disaster. You can't give a kid love unless you've got a store of it yourself, inside you.

'With Marvyn I've had Kim and Rosetta. I was 27 when Kim was born. Since then, I've done more things like a child with Kim than I ever did when I was little. Playing with her, running round, sitting in the swings. Eating ice-cream, there's me and her sitting in the bleeding sandpit, I swear I don't know who enjoys it most.

'I didn't grow up till I met Marvyn. He's from St Lucia, he's had a rough time. A woman walked out on him, he worked on the railways, get treated like he's subhuman . . . When I met him, I was ready to let myself go . . . I sort of broke down, a lot of crying and tantrums. He helped me through it all, and he was still there when it was all over. He's a lovely bloke. He's strong, he accepts me. He's saved my life. The other part of it, it's like it all happened to somebody else. That's why I can talk about it now. Ten years ago, if anybody had mentioned my childhood, I'd probably have sloshed them round the face.

'I mean, it doesn't stop you feeling how horrible you are. I'm not very pretty am I? I'm covered in scars. They used to know me at the hospital; I put my fist through a window, I jumped down a flight of stairs, broke both ankles . . . I still get the moods come on me sometimes if Marvyn's working late or something. But I'm better than I've ever been. And I can help a lot of other people now.

'When you've not had love, it isn't true that you don't know what it is. You're a bleeding expert. The only thing is, you don't know how to get it. You're scared maybe. You're so used to thinking of yourself as rubbish, unlovable, you daren't let yourself go.

'I might be a stupid cow, but one thing I do know is, if you haven't got love, you don't exist. Well you exist, but that's about all you do. I was like the blob from outer space.

'I don't know if I can forgive my mother. I've been lucky. If I hadn't met Marvyn I would still have been screwing my way through half the men in London and wondering where love was. But it's him I owe it to, not her. She was an ignorant woman. She suffered. If you'd seen the way she was living when she was on her own – the dirt, all these bottles. Nobody in their right mind would choose to live like that. So I suppose I do forgive her, yes. One thing she has left me, I can't stand people being shoved around, poor people, people who aren't very sharp, women on their own, blacks, kids. I'll do battle for anybody. I can see myself in people who suffer – the little kid sniffing in the dark and wondering who on God's earth was ever going to help me.'

19

THE SEARCH FOR IDENTITY

A WORKING-CLASS town, built on mining and engineering. Many older men knew they were destined for the pits from the first glimmer of awareness. The girls were brought up to service and marriage, and the transition from one to the other was sometimes not very clear. Many parents felt they would do anything to prevent their own children from following this hard predetermined path; and their hopes for their children coincided with a significant decline in the numbers working in the pits. A majority of the young have been freed from oppressive and dangerous employment; but at the same time, they have also been liberated from the sense of function and identity which the coalfield conferred on all those who worked there. And there has been no equivalent purpose for many of them, they are not expected to define themselves by what they do, only by what they can buy. And they pick their way through styles, fashions, the alternatives offered through the market-place, looking for meaning in the very thing that has robbed their lives.

Colin is 20. He is a big man, with heavy shoulders, a powerful frame, thick arms, warm brown eyes. His arms are covered with tattoos, all carried out by his brother, and which have that slightly smudged look of unprofessional tattoos: a swastika, a cross, a skull with feathers. His sideburns have grown almost to his chin. He wears a leather jacket and a T-shirt. The medallion round his neck is marked SOMMERSCHLACHT IM OSTEN. He has LOVE and HATE tattooed on the knuckles of his hands.

'I was born and dragged up here. I like this town. I've never really wanted to live anywhere else, although I have lived in plenty of other places, especially when I was on the run. I was spoilt as a kid. I was told I could have everything I wanted. I was allowed to do what I liked. Then, when you come into contact with the outside world, you realize life isn't like that. You can't have what you want. That's how I got into trouble.

'My father was ex-army, he'd been a sergeant in the Commandos; and that was something he never forgot. He was the biggest influence on me. He brought me into the world, he cut the cord, washed me; he always had more feeling for me, and me for him. My mother, well, she was always there; eating bacon butties and reading a book – that's the picture I have of her, and still do have. She never got in the way. My father was boss, there was never any question about that. And my father wanted to make me better than the rest. I had to be better, smarter, cleverer than anybody else. He taught me to play chess when I was four; and by the age of 12 I could beat him. He was always drumming things into me, what I had to do, how I should behave. I think that's where I got my resentment of authority from. Although he spoilt me, he was hard at the same time, I couldn't get away with anything. But it was my brother – he's older than me – who got the most stick from my Dad. It was always his fault: even if I did wrong, he got the blame. I was the favoured one. I lived with my Gran from the age of four till six, because she lived near the school, and my Mum and Dad both went to work. I went to them just at weekends. My Gran was all right, but she used to turn funny if I wouldn't eat cabbage, things like that. Then she died, and I went back to my parents, my brother and sister. I was lonely. I never really got on with other kids. I've always been a bit of a loner. I never really had close mates. I preferred being on my own. I don't like having to live up to other people's expectations of me; I didn't want to be what my father wanted me to be. I could have done, I could have gone along with it, but it wasn't me.

'I got sent down even before I left school. I went to a community home – that's an approved school under another name. I absconded from there. I was already a bike lad, an Angel type. I was in West Bromwich at the time, and the kids there took a dislike to me, because there's not many Angels in that town. In fact, when I got to the home, I got out the car, and I ran back down the drive because I didn't fancy it, and as soon as I got out I was jumped by a load of kids. So that night I went out through the window, and it took them three months to catch me.

'I was in care, and I kept running away with my girl-friend. That was what I was done for the first time, USI, unlawful sexual intercourse. We both got done, because she was 14 and I was 15. We kept running away together, they couldn't stop us. Her parents didn't like me, and my parents didn't like her. We kept going off together, and I absconded from wherever I was. We were always on the run; the longest time was six months. I was committing offences all the time I was out. You had to, to survive. I was nicking milk and food. We'd sleep in old houses, thumb lifts. People used to let you stay in their flat for a few days. You get through, spend a bit of time with a mate here, somebody you know there. We were living only a few miles down the road from where our parents were; and still they didn't find us for six months. They don't expect that you're there under their nose all the time. After that I went to a remand home for three weeks for social reports. That was when I was put in care of the Local Authority, and so was my girl. All that meant was that the social worker used to come and visit you every so often. So we ran away again, and were on the move for another spell.

'It was the first time I'd ever been really stopped from doing something I wanted to do. I didn't like it. If you're told you can do anything you want except one thing, that one thing is what you'll want more than anything else. I thought, "Why should they stop me?" I was in the Scrubs at 16. You went from the court to Winson Green, then to the Scrubs, and then you were sent to Borstal from there. I was in Glen Parva. One day, my girl was coming to see me with my best mate. They were on his bike, and they were coming round a curve in the road, and they went into a car, head-on. They were both killed. I thought I loved her when I was 15, but by that time it was over. I'd told her not to come and see me, but she wanted to come. I was more concerned about my mate really than I was about her. He was a really good bloke. He wouldn't hurt anybody, he'd always help you out. The bike crashed head on, just outside Leicester. I felt guilty after it, I felt terrible: they'd both died coming to see me. They had wanted to make me happy. I was 17. I came out of the Borstal; I met a girl three weeks later, we were engaged and married three weeks after that. I've still been in and out of trouble since then; at least I was, up till about 18 months ago. In the last year, things have got a bit quieter.

'I'm getting a divorce from my wife. We're splitting up, but it's friendly like. She'd already got a little boy from her first marriage, and we had a baby 18 months ago. We get on all right. We get on better now that we're breaking up than we did all the time we were together. When we got married we didn't know each other.

'I've always been a Hell's Angel, always been interested in bikes. Right from when I was a kid. I'm not a Hell's Angel now; we're in a breakaway group. The Filthy Few is the name of our club; we're Outlaws. The Hell's Angels back the National Front, and the Outlaws don't. We've got one or two coloured guys in the Outlaws. We're known as the Onepercenters. Outcasts from normal society, the one per cent who won't conform. We sleep out on the hills, in cabins, caravans; this is our life, this is the way we want to live. We're happy to let everybody else alone as long as they don't insult us or do us any harm. We want to live for our beliefs; that's what is important to us. We wear denims, T-shirts, leather for the bikes of course, with the colours, "patches" we call them, emblems like. Different clubs will come and try to take your patches, and if they do, you have to go and take theirs. We're not so violent as Hell's Angels. The colours, patches, you can call them what you like, might be a death's head, or a skull with 13 feathers like I've got tattooed on my wrist, a bike or a skeleton . . . A loner is someone who has our beliefs but doesn't belong to any particular club. He might have a hand in an "Up yours" sign on his back. There's a lot of bikers in this town. In West Bromwich, they're mostly smoothies and skinheads. The chapel I'm with grew up in this area, because it's near Coventry, where a lot of bikes were made.

'A lot of people think Hell's Angels started in America; but it originated in Germany. After the war there was a group of young men, ex-army, who used to go round on BMW combinations with submachine guns, and they used to make lightning raids on the bases of the British or other occupying powers. They refused to accept that the war was lost, and they defied the allied victory. They were desperadoes, a lot of them knew they had no chance, they wouldn't survive, but they were so dedicated to their beliefs. That was how it started. It took root in America, and they're more violent there, there's a lot of shootings.

'I got into it by chance really. I've always been into motorbikes, and I've always had this don't-care-about-anything attitude, and I just found I fitted into the beliefs. My brother is the same as me, he's an Outlaw as well. So when I came to be a bike boy, my father had already been through it all with my brother. He kept telling my brother he was useless, no good, an outcast. The first offence I ever committed was taking and driving away my sister's bike.

'I never knew anything about sex until I met my girl, when I was 15. She'd already been with a bloke, and she led me on. Once I got into it, well, I liked it, I didn't want to stop. It was the first thing my mother and father ever tried to stop me doing. That made me more determined than ever. My mother stood up in court and said she didn't want to know me, she was finished with me. I turned round and let her have a mouthful, which didn't do me much good.

'My father thought if he let me do what I wanted, I'd turn out a little angel; not a Hell's Angel. My sister's the good one of the family. She's married to someone who's well off. I mean, I understand now I'm a father, I can appreciate what my parents must have gone through. They want their children to achieve things, it's only natural. My father still bails me out, even now. We're friends, in spite of everything. At the time when my wife was pregnant, she lost the babby, and the police were after me for not having paid a fine of £70, and my father went to them and put it down just like that. My mother spoils my kids now; she has more interest in them than I think she had in me. I'm soft with the kids. If there's any discipline to be done, I leave it to my wife. I've got a lot of my father in me. He took me back home when I came out of the nick. I was baffled. After all I'd done to them . . . In the end, I stopped going back home. I felt I couldn't. I had to go my own way.

'I feel I could have done and been what my father wanted. But I didn't want to be the best at everything. I just wanted to be myself, do what I wanted to do. That's why I won't live up to somebody's idea of what I should be.

'Up to the time I was 14, I was very obedient. I'd never been denied anything. So I did try to do what my father wanted, I tried to be the best. I did well at school. When I went to the children's home in West Bromwich, all the stuff they were teaching us, I'd already done it all a year before. They wanted me to go in for GCEs, but I decided I'd leave school. I left while I'd still got four months to do. In my last year at school I went

to work on a coal lorry, and that was the job I did full-time
when I did leave. Then I was driver's mate on a mail order van.
I work sometimes. I don't claim the dole, I don't believe in it. I
worked on an oil-rig near Dunkirk, but I was only washing
dishes; 12 hours on, 12 off, but it was worth 200 quid for ten
days.

'I like to live in peace, but I've got a temper if it's roused. If
someone threatens my wife and children . . . The bloke she's
going with now, he threatened her with a glass in the pub. Well,
I went outside with him and beat him up. He still goes with her.
I don't bear him any grudge, we're good friends.

'I keep thinking, "How've I got here, to this position I'm in
now?" When I was first separated from my girl, they put her in
care in Warwick and me in West Bromwich. They tried all sorts
to keep us apart, but they couldn't. They tried places for us
where we were a week in, a week out at a time, and they made it
alternate weeks so we should never be able to meet. But we
always defeated them. In the end, they were the ones who gave
up. They said, "Well if you want to meet each other that much,
do it properly." And they tried to arrange meetings so that each
other's parents were there.

'I belong to a special group within the Outlaws. We're called
the Exilons. I've got it tattooed there, on my arm: people who
are in exile. A lot of us have been in prisons or homes or
Borstals. At one time, we decided to become self-sufficient, we
went round and screwed all these garages and shops. There
were 14 of us, all living in one house. I was on bail at the time for
the attempted theft of a hundredweight of coal. And the police
raided the house, arrested all 14 of us. One of them grassed us
all up; and the funny thing was, the grass was sent down for 18
months.

'My wife used to be a Hell's Angel as well. She was one of the
Cossacks from Cheltenham when I met her, but she's turning
smoothie now. You want to stay with your own kind. We go and
nick patches from other chapters. That means you go out on a
raiding party, you beat them up and cut the patches out of their
jackets. Then they come and take their revenge. If you've been
attacked, you have to take the double of the patches they took
from you. If they took two of ours, we'd have to go and take
four. Then they'd have to come and take eight; we'd take 16,
and so on, until one club recognizes the other. Once you

recognize each other, you join together, and then you're all in the brotherhood.

'I know there's no future in it really. You might carry on till you're 33 or 34, then you might settle down. You might keep the same beliefs, but you sort of stay in your families, you cut off relations with each other after that age. We've all got names: you get a name according to things you might have done. I'm Butch, because I had a dog that went everywhere with me, he was called Butch, and he was an outlaw himself. I've a lad living with us now, he's called Kid Scum, because he dresses scruffy; there's another bloke called Scum, and this kid is his shadow, sort of thing. There's one called Chicken Shack, because he used to live in chicken sheds. There's Speed, because he's always taking speed and rushing round all over the place, Rabbi, because he's interested in black magic, Custer, because he has a beard like Custer. We believe in justice, an eye for an eye, a tooth for a tooth sort of thing; but only if we're attacked, only if we're not allowed to live in peace. We don't jump people for no reason, only if they start getting personal with us. There's a lot of pubs in this town that won't let us in, they judge you by your appearance. We don't look for trouble, only what we believe is like our politics and our religion. We worship the colours, the patches.

'Eventually I want to own an artic lorry, the biggest thing on the road. It costs £34,000, the one I want. It's a Volvo, with a sleeping cab – you could live in it. Driving across the continents, that's what I want to do. But I shall always care for my home town, the things you've done in a place when you're young, you never forget.

'I've had a lot of experience. That's one thing your parents can never understand. They've been brought up to stay in one place, do the same job. They don't see that life is different now. I shall be 21 next week.'

Paul is 22. He is tall and thin, with dark curly hair, and several days' growth of beard. He has a narrow sensitive face, with dark intense eyes. He wears a 'Legalise Cannabis' badge on his T-shirt, jeans, a check lumber jacket. He is a rather shy, introspective person. He works as a polisher in the paint shop of Jaguar Cars in Coventry. He would prefer to work in the open air, with the Forestry Commission or in the countryside. To get the works bus into the city he has to get up in the early morning, and he enjoys walking across the fields, picking early mushrooms, watching the sun rise. He says he wishes he knew the names of some of the plants and flowers; but you need someone to teach you, you can't really learn them from drawings in books.

Paul is distrustful of feelings. He was with a girl for over a year, but felt unable to commit himself. She wanted to get married, and she talked enthusiastically about the house they would live in and the children they would have; and he felt he had to withdraw. He still sees her, although she has somebody else now. She tells him that she still cares for him more than anyone she has met since. Paul says he cannot let himself go. The risk always seems too great. This anxiety he attributes directly to his relationship with his mother.

'I was always closer to my sister than to my father or mother. My sister is seven years older than I am. She has four children now, married to a miner. But I always looked to her for comfort and reassurance. I can remember on Saturday nights when my mother and father went out, she would cook a supper for the two of us. That was a good memory.

'From the age of about eight, there was always this man around the house, who I knew as Uncle. He was my mother's lover. I didn't understand this until I was 13 or 15. And by that time, I'd realized there wasn't just one, but quite a few of them. I think it was this that turned me away from her during my childhood. Perhaps I felt there wasn't enough love for me there. It wasn't till I was 15 that I actually mentioned it to my Dad. He seemed upset. He said he didn't know what to believe. Either he really didn't know, or he shut his eyes to what was going on. Perhaps what I told him really was news to him, or perhaps he always knew, but couldn't face it.

'I left home as soon as I finished school, at 15, and stayed away for a year. Even after that I had no contact with them for two years. I see them now sometimes. I don't mind a few hours with them, but I start to get uncomfortable, irritable, if I spend too long with them. I'm still closest to my sister. If I have anything go wrong, it's her I turn to. She was more of a mother to me than my mother was.

'I think, when I was very small, I was quite happy with my mother. You don't notice things then. It's when you come to think about what is going on that everything changes. Even what has seemed good up to then starts to suffer from the knowledge that comes to you later. The more I thought, the more I disliked her. It messed me up for quite a while.

'When I was younger I was good at school. But from about 13 I just lost interest in everything. I played truant a lot, I didn't think of learning. The only thing I was interested in was having a laugh with the lads. I always used to go around in a group, because that way, you didn't have to think about things. If you're on your own, you're inclined to dwell on it. I suppose I was shy. I've never been bothered with girls. I mean, if one comes up to me and asks me to go to bed with her, I'll say yes and enjoy it. But that's how it has to be; and that tends not to happen very often. Sex, I can take it or leave it.

'I feel empty towards my mother. I go and see her, I'll go and have tea with them and we'll talk. She'll be there, talking away, but never about things that mean anything. There's no feeling in what is said. I did go back home to live when I had nowhere else to go. It lasted six months. I used to come home from work, and I felt like a lodger. There was no communication. I used to work with my father. I got on all right with him. So I went to live with my sister, although she was having her first baby at that time. But if I feel down now, I can always go to her.

'For a time I despised my father. I felt, well, he's been married to my mother for so many years that I suppose his love for her must be stronger than his love for me. I felt she ought to be kicked out, and I ought to be able to stay with my father. But that couldn't happen. And perhaps I despised him for not preferring me, for not sticking up for me.

'My father is a machine-tool setter. My mother pushed him. When I was 11, we moved house, for my mother's sake. My father got interested in politics, the Labour Party. I think it was her pushing him. I felt he wasn't really into it, but she wanted him to get on that way, socially. She saw it as a way of improving things. She was always the stronger character, and she encouraged him.

'When I think back, I do have memories of being taken out by this Uncle all the time. And when I got a bit older, I'd go home when I was hopping off school, and I'd see the familiar car always there. He was a nice bloke. He has re-married since then. I liked him, and I still do. I always felt it was my mother's fault. Later on, when I got a bit older, she did try to make it up to me. She made some attempt to be friendly, but by then I had rejected her. I pushed her away. She'd always carried on regardless of me until she was suddenly aware that I was growing up, and then she felt she had to show a bit of concern, a bit of interest. But by then it was too late.

'When I realized what was really going on at home, it didn't occur to me in a blinding flash. It dawned on me slowly. I remember thinking, telling myself, "No, it can't be." I'd try to forget, not think about it. But it stared me in the face; there was no way of getting away from it.

'My sister left home. She was married at 18, and soon started her family. She understood my feelings, but she'd always got on all right with the parents. She hadn't realized what was going on till she was practically grown up. It didn't affect her in the way it affected me. It seems that if you don't feel there's anything wrong, that's good enough, then there is nothing wrong. But if you're aware of it, there's nothing you can do.

'After the second year at school, I gave up. I enjoyed sports, but as far as learning was concerned . . . I was always being sent out of class and told to go home. It wasn't till the last year in school that I started having trouble with the police. It was my own fault. Me and a few other lads, we all got together and went a bit wild. There were about five of us who were close, and then a lot of others were on the fringe, sort of hangers-on. We used to go home at dinner-time and not go back to school. We played some rough games. I knocked a guy out when we were playing fly-back. I had a lock knife and we used to play stretch – you have to throw the knife between the legs of your opponent, and then he has to put his foot where the knife went, so his legs get closer together; an older kid tried to take this knife from me. I put it to his throat and told him to fuck off. And the Headmaster called the police, and they fetched my old man up to the school. He was supposed to have a word with me, make sure I understood the seriousness of what I'd done and all that; but I didn't take any notice of him.

'Then one night we climbed onto a factory roof, and somebody said we'd broken in. They kept us in the police station that night. Then next time, I think it was being drunk and disorderly. The trouble was, getting caught didn't deter you. You thought, "Fair enough"; if you get caught, you're being punished for a crime. But eight times out of ten you got away with it. And the times you got away with it more than made up for what happened when you were caught. You think, "Well, they can't do much to you." And there's the sense of a dare, the excitement, it gets the adrenalin going. If you go and nick something, it isn't what you get that matters, it's the high you get from doing it. It makes you feel different, it sets you apart from all the other kids; makes you feel you matter. I carried on, more and more, and gradually, the punishments got harder. I got a suspended sentence, detention centre, fines, community service. The detention centre was three months. It's like the army; you have to dress properly, fold your clothes, go on marches. After a few days, you think, "I'm here for three months, I've got to do it, I might as well accept it." It didn't hurt me in any way. That was for assaulting the police, that is, resisting arrest. I'd stolen a car. It was Christmas Eve and it was two o'clock in the morning. We'd been to a club and a party, and the best way home was to travel by car. When you're high, you feel that nothing can stop you doing what you want to. If you want something, you just take it. But the reason why the punishment is no good, it only relates to what you do, nicking or fighting; it doesn't do anything to what you feel inside, what is really upsetting you. So you just carry on as before.

'My father tried to talk to me. He'd been in trouble when he was my age, he understood. "Make sure it's the last time you get into trouble." It doesn't reach you. You listen, you think, "Yes, that's right," but it doesn't really get to you. You don't feel it where it matters, inside. I got sacked from the first job I had for telling the foreman what to do. Then I went back for my cards, and he told me he didn't have them. So I went away, and then I realized he was just running me around, so I went back a second time. He said, "I ain't gonna give you your cards," so I just hit him a few times. I got a fine for that. That was the first time I got done for assault. My father said he understood, he could see how the guy had annoyed me, he'd deserved it. He was trying to excuse me. But that wasn't what I was looking for.

'I'm living with a friend of mine who's married with a family. I used to be by myself, but this is better. They have two children, and I enjoy playing with them. The guy is about 30. I feel like one of the family. Quite often in the evening we sit and have a smoke, talk. I feel very strongly about getting married. If you get married, you shouldn't carry on the way my mother did, not if there's children. I feel I won't get married for a long time. When I was going with my girl, I went along with all she said about getting married, but I didn't feel I could be sure of myself; or of her, I don't know. I felt I didn't care too much. I've always found it hard to show my feelings, a bit slow to find them. I shared a flat with a guy for a year. There were several people living in the house, and one night, they sort of confronted me. This guy said he'd lived with me for a year and still felt as if he didn't know me. I couldn't face it. I just left.

'As a child, I lived in good surroundings. I had a lot of freedom, I could play where I liked, go with whoever I wanted. I had a lot of toys, sweets, I wasn't deprived of anything in a material sense. I always had close mates, there was a kid next door, I was friends with him from the age of 11 to 26. But I'm restless. I'm working at the minute, but I'm not bothered about it. I go fruit picking in Kent sometimes in the summer, get some money and then be off. I don't know how long I'll stay at Jaguar. I want to travel around. I'd like to leave the country for a year. I find it hard to stick at jobs. I've had a lot, some of them only lasted a couple of days. One job I went to, I was only there from seven-thirty in the morning until half past eleven. I couldn't stand the noise and the stink. The blokes took no notice of you. I just took my sandwiches and went home. The longest job I had was bathing attendant at Atherstone Baths, that lasted over a year. I wouldn't say I was happy. I'm not miserable. But I could be more contented. I think I won't get into trouble with the law again, unless it's for smoking cannabis.'

The experience of Colin and Paul is not unusual, even though the detail of their lives remains uniquely their own. The feelings they express are common enough. They were brought up in one of the most solidly working-class communities in the country. Yet for them, work has no importance. In that sense, economic changes that are anticipated, whereby work will become more subordinate, will pose no problem. The trouble is that as the sense of work has diminished, the importance of money has grown in proportion, and separated from any feeling of reward. The end of the work ethic is painless enough; the pain only begins with the vacuum in which they find themselves, where, whatever 'free choices' they make, these will all be contained within the market-place. Traditional social determinants have decayed – social function, value; and the young talk of journeys, of finding a self not defined by society. In doing so, they are reduced and denuded to the most basic needs and instincts, which they are invited to express only through what can be bought. It involves a paring away, not only of traditional work skills and abilities – it's hard to say how great a loss this is – but also of all the resource and humanity with which people confronted adversity in these recently poor towns and cities. All that is left is a bare bundle of appetites and instincts, delivered to the market-place. Of course, people resist and overcome these obstacles, just as their parents and grandparents overcame some of the worst visitations of poverty; but that isn't an argument in favour of inflicting them. For many young people, the only way back to wholeness, completeness, is seen to be through the power of money, which, because it has locked up so much human potential, is seen as a healing force, although this is the cause of the violence done to them in the first place. Even the love of parents for their children – all those people haunted by memories of insufficiency and poverty – has been annexed to the culture of buying and selling in such a way as to make them believe they must pay if they want to show that love. And the parents learn that if they acquiesce in the surrender of their children to these processes, there are consolations for them too: they are free to pursue their own wants and dreams. And while this may produce great guilt in them, there is no one to break the collusive silence about the way we live; and the feeling that their children have been given over to forces beyond their control, as a generation of foundlings might be handed over to the care of an impersonal institution, remains unexpressed; even though it is their life-blood that is being tapped by stealth and sold back to them at an appalling price. And all our cherished totems – the value of family life, the caring society, our devotion to children – only conceal a deeper dynamic, which is a continuing expropria- tion of our humanity and its continuing subservience to those who have learnt the most terrible of all secrets – how to turn the greatest powers of man, his capacity for altruism and disinteres- ted concern and love into the cold insentience of material wealth.

20

MIGRANTS AND CHILDHOOD

IN THE CULTURE of North America, and increasingly in Western Europe, a key figure is the successful migrant, the millionaire who arrived destitute, often as a refugee or a labourer. This fact should not surprise us: the success of the individual only serves to conceal the experience of the majority, the pain and dislocation.

We don't like to think it possible that in moving from a poor society to a rich one, the losses could at least equal, if not exceed, the gains; any more than we care to dwell on the thought that the terms on which life has been made better for the indigenous working class might have involved considerable forfeits. But so it is for many people; and one of the greatest losses is the ability of the working class and of migrants alike to perceive that their experience is the same. What they have gone through is part of a continuing process; but instead of being able to illuminate each other's suffering and loss, we see only threat and incomprehension.

With the act of migrating, all the human resources so laboriously developed and garnered to confront subsistence poverty become redundant. They are immediately surrendered for a promise of material riches, which, for the most part, fail to materialize. The hope of migrants is the most touching and dramatic example of the way people will sacrifice everything for their children; and they illustrate how cruelly that sacrifice can be exploited, and how hope can be poisoned. The children grow up to be dependent on a way of life that can only fulfil itself through money; and there is never enough money to compensate for all the things they have forgotten, all that has fallen into abeyance through the simple change of environment. Even the modest achievement of their parents who knew how to deal with the glaring absences of their primary poverty lapses in the new surroundings. What happens between the generations of migrants is a metaphor, if a heightened one, of what has happened to a whole generation. And in that sense, all children are migrants, through time if not space.

Phyllis and Conroy Martineau came to South London from Jamaica and St Lucia respectively at the end of the 1950s. They live in a poor rundown council estate in Lambeth, built in the 1930s. Their flat is full of memories of the West Indies, faded photographs of parents, grandmothers, siblings. Both left home before they were 20. Neither has been back. Their childhood has taken on something of a lost paradise. There is a painting of a grandfather's house, built of wood, with a verandah, and surrounded by fruit trees. There is the Lord's Prayer, painted white on a black background; but the lettering gets smaller towards the end of the frame so it can be all contained. On the opposite wall there is a modern painting of a Garden of Eden, with Eve up to her navel in water, and an Adam like Mr Universe. Conroy has been out of work for nearly three years. He worked, first of all in a hotel, then in a plastics factory. Since he lost his job, nothing new has been bought for the house; and all the things that only three years ago looked new have become dingy and worn out. The rexene three-piece is split and the foam escaping in places; the oval punch-bowl with its cups on hooks hanging from the rim looks tarnished. The deep-freeze has broken. When they talk of the West Indies they evoke a landscape vividly remembered, tears come to their eyes.

PHYLLIS: 'Parents in the West Indies are very strict; church and school as well, because you have to get up on Sunday and go to church. You stay for service, then come home for dinner, and then go back again four o'clock; and then a prayer meeting as well. My children don't go to Sunday School. But some of the people in the West Indies are not religious anyway, some of them is just like Satan . . . My childhood was happy. I had four brothers and one sister. We live in the country, St Catherine . . . We had some family in town, but my father wouldn't let us go and live there. Say he don't like the idea because it a bit rough. He say the town people ungodly . . . My father work on he own piece of land. He had cane, banana, plantain, coffee . . . and breadfruit, oranges. When they passing and ax for oranges to sell, he sell to the truck, or banana. In one part of the land he plant yam and potato. All the children help. I do anything. One thing, my father can't climb, and my mother can't climb, but I could . . . I help get all the fruit from the top of the tree.

'My father was strict, but my mother stricter. If I ax my

mother for something, and she say no, I go and ax my father, and he have to hide and give it to me . . . We couldn't quarrel as children. If we fight, they beating all of us. We couldn't make a noise, we had to whisper. He beat us with a belt, leather, real leather . . . When they kill the cow, they take a strip of leather off him to dry. Then they put it to cure and they make shoes . . . our father build shoes for us.

'One of my brother now in this country, one at home, he is a mechanic. The other brother in Kingston. My sister in New York. We all scatter. Everybody sad when I leave. My father didn't want me to come up in this country . . . I miss everything from childhood. Where I was living, we have a big orange tree there, you could just walk by and pick an orange off the tree . . . But even though I not see them for 20 years, they still talking to me. When my grandfather died, I knew. I dream-see him in the night. He tell me, "Look how long I gone", and he is going; so I say, "Where you going?" He say, "I have to go away somewhere." And then I see him sitting under the plantain tree, and I see him just pull he hat over he face; the way I see him sit, he look so sad, I know he gone . . . There a lot of spirits and ghost where we live, but they don't worry me. We get up early in the morning to work the land, but they don't bother me. You see like a figure coming down, you don't know if it a man or a woman, and when they get in front of you, they just disappear . . . One time one coming up and I saw him, he going down, down, and I turn round and I see him spring up tall, tall. And I tell my father and he say to me I shouldn't do that. It could turn my head if I look behind me at them, it could turn and never come back to the front again. That would show everybody you passed a spirit. My daughter, she can see them too. The first time I did frighten, it a shock, but after that I didn't. The first time I see a spirit, it was my Granny. I ax me mother who she is, she ax me how she dressed, and my mother tell me it my grandmother.

'My grandmother came from India and my father from Barbados. Some of my brothers are Indian, some very Negro. If all of them went out, if someone come up and say, "Is that your brother?" he could say, "No . . ." But they never disown one another. My grandmother family come there at the time of slavery. That's what our father tell us anyway . . . Some have Indian hair, some have Negro hair; some of them is pretty, some ugly you know . . . One of the sisters a twin, one is Indian and one Negro. And they always quarrel . . . It all comes back to me. I can see where we did live . . . And I remember having baptism at church. You fill the pool on Saturday, and Sunday you get up and bring these people in that water, and you dip them in it . . . When they have service in the morning, they look so sweet and pretty . . .'

CONROY: 'I was born in Grenada, but brought up in St Lucia. My mother had 11 children. I was second to last. Eight of us were alive, four boys and four girls. When my mother die I was quite young, and I went to St Lucia to my older sister. She was very strict, and my brother-in-law was very strict. I have to work before I go to school, and I have to stop behind to get me work all done before I could go to school. Where we live, when the weather fair and the time calm, I stand and watch the sea. When I first go to my sister, she like a mother. But when I start to grow up, it bring a grudge, because as I got a bit older, I had more and more work to do. Two of her boys have to full up a drum of water, and I find I have to full up two; and then go and get molasses for them pigs . . . get grass and all that kind of thing. So I always used to be late for school, late to church. When I study the past, my brother-in-law, he used to make me a lot of promise, and tell me when the pig have young, he will give me one; you know a young pig worth quite a lot of money, when it three weeks old or six weeks, they sell it. And then the time come to sell it, he tell me, "Well next time, next time." It always next time.

'My mother die when I was very small. I sorry my mother die in one way, and I glad she die in one way . . . Because my mother helping me and guiding me quite a lot. Especially when my father die as well, I feel she give me a lot of signs . . . Many a time I sleeping, and I see my mother as clear as I watching you, talking to me and showing me all different things, she tell me which path to follow . . . Probably through the sake of that, that why I cry a lot of tears, because I have a lot of sickness . . . Every time I sick and go to the hospital, I can picture my mother face, and she give me the strength.

'My brother, the one who send for me to come up in this country, he go back and buy a set of land in the West Indies, and he buy a big house in St Lucia . . . But I missing the West Indies . . . When banana time come, they cut the banana and sell it to the banana truck, they cook the yam, you know, dry it and bag it up and sell it by the bag . . . nutmeg by the basket . . .'

PHYLLIS: 'My mother not sell the cocoa, she put it to dry and she make chocolate and she sell it so . . . Three piece of land we have, it is all cultivate – cassava, nutmeg . . . You keep a portion to use for the house, and the balance you sell . . .'

CONROY: 'My sister house was lovely. The first house she have was built of blocks, a bungalow. Then we had a bad time was passing, a hurricane, and we had was to leave. I was with my uncle, and the message meet us and tell us that the house sink, go right down to the ground. We rush down there, and my brother-in-law taxi go down through the ground because the road split, and the onliest thing we could have see when we reach down there was the top of the house, no bricks, nothing. My sister start to cry. She lose everything . . . They get a set of money from the Government. They dig up foundation and build a bigger house; galvanized roof bungalow, made with blocks, and you have a nice porch, a veranda you could walk right round, and a big yard. There was a big pen where you can raise a set of pig . . .

'My sister and brother-in-law have two boys and two girls. I didn't stop in school up to the age I should . . . Growing up in that family, their two boys always get the best part of everything, I always behind.

'If you have your own place in the West Indies, the family, you work for them when you leave school, you working for yourself . . . When the weekend come, you get a few dollars to put in your pocket, a certain amount of money, what they can afford to give you . . . Because you help them with everything. Certain times you have to do the planting, banana, cocoa, you do the pruning and all them kind of thing . . . When the time reach to cut cane, you help them do that.

'My sister had a shop. She put me in the shop sometimes. But people used to come in there during the day and say Well, they wanted two pound of rice or some ice and a drink, but they don't have the money. So I used to give them free . . . So when they put me in the shop, what they used to do was check the money in the till. Then when they got back, they count up and say so and so, and how much missing. And I say, "They didn't have the money to pay," and they say I giving everything away free. I was only a kid.

'One day my brother-in-law wake me up at six o'clock, and tell me I have to go and cut grass for the pig, we call them swiper, razor grass, they cut you bad. So I didn't decide was to go. The other two boys was in bed; so I didn't go and do it. I lay there in bed. And all the day I stay in the house and I help my sister draw water and wash and everything; and the night when he come, he say he go beat me. He take a piece of tyre that he cut out from an old car wheel, and he hit me two lash across me back.

'I wouldn't say he was unkind to me, but he made me so much of promise he never keep. He have so much of hog, and I was looking out every time the one he go give me . . . One hog have seven pig, and six he sell, he will get 25 dollars for it, and he tell me I get one. Then when he selling it he don't give me nothing out of it . . . And I keep on looking, looking for it . . . And I taking the most care of them, because while he kids at school, I helping at home.

'I think my childhood happier than my kids. Plenty.'

PHYLLIS: 'Yes, because if you get up in the West Indies, when you go to school, you could have guavas when you going, or June plum or blackberry – you just burst it and suck the juice out of it, you have golden apple and mangoes, all different kinds of mangoes . . .'

CONROY: 'Them kids more demanding than I was in my childhood. In this country, you have to give them everything they want . . . You have to give them money whenever they go out . . . when they go to school. Here you have to buy everything . . . In the morning, if I going to school, I go slipping in by my sister and get a cup of milk . . . You didn't want sweets in the West Indies, you have a June plum and that's it . . . And if you got plenty and your friends poorer than you, you hand it out . . .

'I didn't have a rough childhood; some of it sad, but plenty good as well. I was 22 when I leave St Lucia. I go back to Grenada before I leave, to see my father. He start to cry and he tell me he wouldn't see me again. I tell him he mustn't cry; and I make him a promise, and tell him I coming to find him in five years, I will be back. I believe that is the mistake all West Indians make, all who leave to come up in this country, they say they going for five years . . . And he tell me he wouldn't live to see me . . . He say he would cook a meal for the last time. And he cook me two finger of banana and a piece of yam and two greenjacks . . . And then we sit down and talk, and then when he look at the time, he tell me it time for me to go, and me pick up me suitcase . . . I had the food still eating in a cup. He come with me; and we had was to pass a little stream, and when I reach the stream I finishing the food; and before he take the cup, he tell me I must put it on the stone; and when I put it on the stone, he pick it up and sit down to eat, and he tell me that is the last time he would see me.'

As time passed Conroy's marriage broke up; he felt his children were becoming estranged; he lost contact with his brother who was also living in England. Conroy became ill; Phyllis found someone else, and this produced in Conroy all the feelings he had had as a child, excluded from his sister's family, the sense of being an outsider in his own home.

Conroy and Phyllis have three children, a boy and two girls. The conversation of their parents was always full of a sense of loss which the children couldn't understand. But because of the advantages gained through migration – the improved health care, the shelter of their council flat, and the invalidity benefit Conroy received when he fell ill with a rare blood disease – the forfeits were not perceived as such until it was too late, because they were not material ones. The children grew up to feel superior to their parents and their country ways. They feel they have access to greater truths, although these turn out principally to be a heightened awareness of the importance of money and what it can buy. The children are alert and intelligent; but they have not been successful in applying that intelligence very effectively to the idea of achievement as defined by the educational system. They have been deeply disturbed and stimulated by the images of the pop world, fashion, the getting of things. Gloria gave up Spanish at school 'because it was too hard'. Paul couldn't be bothered; everything was 'boring'. All the resources, and the accumulated knowledge of their parents, won through struggle and work, could not be transmitted to the children, who have been formed by a quite different culture. In fact, it is they who, despite all the advantages the parents have tried to provide for them, will pay the forfeit of migration. Their parents have a wisdom and a depth of experience that cannot be taken away, however archaic these things may appear in the changed context of their lives. Gloria and Paul are both out of work. Paul wanted an engineering apprenticeship, Gloria wanted to work with children. They feel obscurely cheated; but because they don't quite know what they have been cheated of, they do not know how to claim redress. They are profoundly aware of how they are discriminated against, and they assume that all their troubles come from being black in a white society. Paul and Gloria were excited by the riots in the summer of 1981; and hovered on the edge, watching but not taking part. They have a sense that the processes that have left them feeling functionless and without resource, hungry for some kind of purpose and validation, have affected all their generation, black and white alike, to a greater or lesser extent. The inequality comes from the fact that the change from the West Indies to Lambeth makes them even less resistant to the pressures that have tended to rob their white counterparts of so many of their traditions and values too.

21

TIM: A CHILDHOOD REDEEMED BY LOVE

TIM IS JUST 21; very tall, with fair hair and a pleasant, gentle face, he is shy and taciturn, intelligent and easily upset. Until August 1981, when he was 'rescued' by strangers, he had been living rough in a tent on some waste ground in the middle of a Lancashire town. He had been there for several years, and had regressed so far that he was unable to use a knife and fork or to hold a cup without spilling it. He trembled uncontrollably if anyone approached him.

Rose and Peter, who 'found' him, took him into their house – a two-bedroomed terraced house overlooking the site of a disused pit, which they share with Rose's mother. In the past few months they have offered him the care and patience that have transformed him, in Rose's words, 'from a frightened animal into a human being'. She is appalled that the welfare state failed, not only to prevent him from falling into such a condition, but also to provide help for him when they sought it. It has been left to concerned individuals to help restore some of his damaged sense of self; even though, as Rose acknowledges, the harm and hurt of 20 years cannot be reversed within a few months.

Tim is the youngest of three boys. His father was a miner. When Tim was four, his father had a brain haemorrhage down the pit. He was in hospital for some months. During that time, Tim's mother left the family for another man. The children went to live with their grandmother, and stayed there for four years. Tim's father married again when Tim was eight, a woman 14 years older than himself.

The stepmother tolerated the older boys, but she conceived a violent resentment of Tim, the full meaning of which has become clear to him only since he has been talking to Rose and Peter about his experience. From when Tim was a small child, his father had abused him sexually. 'One day, she came into the room when he was mauling me about. She never said anything, but just walked out again.' But from that time her hatred of

Tim began; it was rooted in sexual jealousy. But she also had a hold over his father, and he began to beat and punish the boy as well. Tim had no sense that his father's behaviour was unusual. He says simply, 'I thought that's what all fathers did', even though he would clamp his hand over the boy's mouth when he was assaulting him, to prevent him from crying out.

He was never given enough to eat. 'She used to mark the jam jar, so she'd know if I'd been at it while she was out. She counted the slices of bread in the packet. I used to hide under the bed; I can remember clinging to the springs of the mattress while they tried to drag me out. They used to lock me out of the house. I'd have to sit on the wall waiting for them to come home, even if it was one or two o'clock in the morning.' Tim began to steal. He took things belonging to his stepmother and sold them to the junk shop. His father, coming home from work, would see the familiar objects on sale, and that would earn him another beating. He never went to school regularly. He was kept at home to do errands and chores, and then when he did attend, he was punished for his absences. In the end, he simply stayed away all the time. When he was 16, his stepmother took possession of his dole money and allowed him 50p a week.

Rose's mother says: 'I had a bad childhood, God knows. Poverty and hunger and cold. But never anything like that. If anybody had behaved to a child like his stepmother did in our street, they'd've dragged her out of the house and given her a damn good hiding.'

One day, when Tim had been locked out, he broke a window, and stole £4. His stepmother went to the police. He was arrested, taken to court and fined £25. That was when he left home.

At first, he went into a disused air-raid shelter. It was wet and full of rats. A lad he knew gave him a tent. He pitched it on some waste ground just outside town. In the tent he had a sleeping bag and some old newspapers to put his head on. Having no fixed address, he had to collect his dole money every day – at that time about £1.50 a day. He soon became a familiar figure in the neighbourhood. Everybody knew him. Occasionally, one of the lads from school would let him into his house when his parents had gone to work, give him a meal of egg and bacon, let him have a bath. But for most of the time, he was in the open air. He would go for days without food; and then, when he had money, he might go to the chip shop six or seven times in the evening. He spent his days sitting on the wall at the edge of the waste ground. If it was raining, he would stand. On Sundays he would buy a Mars bar and a can of Coke. In the launderette there was a tea and coffee machine. He spent hours there, getting warm or drying off. His only other refuge was the betting shop. The girl who worked there would make him a hot drink, and he stayed there until it closed, not betting, but simply sitting there without talking to anyone. It was this girl who saw him deteriorating badly in the summer of 1981, and she told Rose and Peter.

He was picked up by the police for non-payment of his fine. It was a Bank Holiday weekend, and he was kept in the cells until the Tuesday. When he came into court, the magistrate asked him how much money he had. He had ½p. He was given a pound to buy food, and put on probation for six months. The probation officer offered him accommodation in a hostel. He agreed, but when the time came to go to Manchester, he changed his mind. By that time he had become afraid of living with other people.

Tim began to lose track of time in his tent. 'I thought, "That's it, I'm finished." I just thought about getting from one day to the next. I never thought of anything. I just let my mind go blank.' He began to drink, mainly cider. He spent most of his money on cider, eating less and less. He would start drinking at about five o'clock in the afternoon. Then he would go to the pub. In the end, he was banned from the pubs in the neighbourhood. He looked too scruffy, he frightened the customers. He found that if he got drunk every night he could at least sleep and forget the cold and the weather. But he is very proud of the fact that he never took cider inside the tent; some vestiges of self-respect remained, even though by this time his thoughts had become confused and disordered. He couldn't remember how old he was. He would wash his face and head in the canal. His only lavatory was in the open air.

He started a work experience course at Technical College, in the building trade. He was too weak to work and had no money for food or bus fares. The boots he wore were too small and his feet had begun to bleed. His work experience lasted one day. He wanted to die. Some friends obligingly brought him a bottle of tablets. He took a few. He was drinking five or six bottles of cider a day. He became something of a curiosity in the neighbourhood. Sometimes, when he woke up in the morning, he had an audience. People used to tiptoe past him as he slept. One night, some kids jumped on him and held him down while they shaved all his hair off. When he saw his reflection in the window of the launderette, it gave him a scare. After that he wouldn't go out in daylight again until his hair had grown.

His tent was stolen. Somebody found him another, and this time he pitched it under some trees, in a position where it was less conspicuous. He had to crawl through the undergrowth to get to it. A rat used to visit him regularly. He fed it crumbs. It came every day. One morning, the tent fell in on him. It had snowed in the night, and the tent had collapsed under the weight of the snow. He says that was the worst day of all. He was numb with cold, and it took him over an hour to crawl from the tent to the launderette. All this time, the whole neighbourhood knew and recognized him. He received many small acts of kindness, but nobody did anything. Tim said he had no hope or expectation of any kind.

'When we found him,' says Rose, 'he was wearing a little black coat, the sleeves nearly up to the elbow. He had three shirts on, but there was a gap between where they finished and the top of his trousers. His boots had fallen apart, and his feet were bleeding. The boots were two sizes too small. His feet still bleed if he walks any distance, he's still going to the chiropodist. He had long hair and a beard: his hair and face were clean, but he looked dirty and neglected. He weighed $8\frac{1}{2}$ stone. When we went to fetch him, he thought we'd come to lock him up. He was trembling all over and for a long time afterwards he started to shake if anyone he didn't know approached him. At first, he could only eat small meals, and it was four months before he could eat in company. We had our first meal together on Christmas Day.'

Rose and Peter took him home, intending to give him a meal and a bath before they found somewhere for him to live. 'He was that long in the bath, we were afraid he'd drowned in it. I kept going out into the yard to listen for sounds of splashing. Silence. It really frightened us. But when he did come down, he looked a different person.' They took him to the Housing Department. 'They sat him in a corner on a chair, miles away from anybody. They thought he was tarpy (full of fleas). He wasn't actually. They said they couldn't do anything to help him. We sat there for hours in the Housing. They said they had no obligation to house him because he didn't come into the "vulnerable" category – if he'd been a pregnant girl under 18 or a widow over 60 they might have been able to do something. You only had to look at him to see if he was vulnerable or not. They said there's 20 kids sleep rough every night in this town.

'They offered to put him on the waiting list. We had to fill in these forms. When it came to the bit that said ADDRESS, we wrote, "A tent near the old pit workings." They tore it up, said it wasn't a proper address. We filled it in six or seven times. They tore it up again. Apparently, in order to be homeless you have to have an address to be homeless from. Nobody wanted to know. We rang the three Labour councillors for the ward. They couldn't do anything. We went back to the Housing and filled in the forms again. They were asking him these daft questions from the form – was where he was living detached or semi-detached, had it got a bathroom? We went mad at them. I said, "If he was a dog, the RSPCA would take him in." And do you know what they answered? "Yes, and you know what they do with dogs after seven days." Tim says, "To them I wasn't a person, I was just a beast."'

In the end, Tim stayed with Rose and Peter. He has to sleep on a sofa downstairs, but for the first time in his life he has begun to feel secure. In the past eight months he has improved spectacularly under their care. He has put on $4\frac{1}{2}$ stone. He doesn't leave the room if anyone calls. Above all, he has been able to cry, and release some of the frozen numbness of feeling with which he lived for so many years. He sees his father occasionally, and no longer shakes when he comes close. His feelings are ambiguous: he feels betrayed by his father's failure to defend him when he was a child, but he is magnanimous towards him, and says that he understands that his behaviour was partly a result of the brain haemorrhage. Now that he is so much improved, his stepmother is even more jealous of him. 'If she sees him,' says Rose, 'she looks straight through him, ignores him completely. If he goes to see his Dad, she'll leave him standing at the door. "Your Tim's here." It places his Dad in a funny position. I mean, she had this hold over him, knowing what was going on.'

Tim goes down to the club with Peter in the evenings for a

game of snooker. He hasn't touched alcohol since last August. He has just begun to go out on his own, even though he won't stay away for very long. He is easily hurt. Only once Rose spoke sharply to him, and he was quite overwhelmed by what was a gentle rebuke. He has learned to cook, and helped look after Rose and her mother while they were ill during the winter.

As it has turned out, the failure of any of the caring agencies to do anything for him was to his advantage. It is certain that no professional social worker would have been able to give him the healing and restorative sense of himself that he has received from Rose and Peter. 'But that's not good enough,' says Rose. 'You can't guarantee there'll always be someone there for all the other kids who are suffering like he has.' She says scornfully, 'What caring society? Societies can't care. Only people can.'

AFTERWORD

ONE OF THE consequences of the long collusion between capital and labour during the years of continuous growth was that the continuing expropriation of working people and the damage to their lives became for a while obscured. But the area of political debate shrank and contracted, until people came to believe that the very cause of the sufferings of the poor – the power of money – could somehow be made to cure those sufferings. In this way, all that prosperity promised, which should have meant release from the ancient experience of exploitative and ill-rewarded work, became instead the source of a new kind of pain. The end of primary poverty and those disciplines that went with it should have put an end to that injury of body and spirit. But for that freedom, the determining power of the market-place has been substituted, a dependency on it so complete, that the social identity of a whole generation has been formed by it. In this way, one of the most significant aspects of human development – the social part – has been subordinated to and determined by the selling of things. That the reaction of the victims to this imposition is unhappy, often violent and destructive, should not really surprise us. It is a change which, while producing a great chasm between the generations in working-class families, has nevertheless ensured continuity in the process that continues to subject people to influences that deform and distort our human growth. The freedom of children (and hence of the adults we become) has meant the passage from one kind of oppression into another. Apart from that, nothing has changed.

Some Working-Class Autobiographies and Autobiographical Novels

I am indebted to Ken Worpole, and his work at Centerprise, which has encouraged so many working people to give expression to their experience. (See *The Republic of Letters*, Working-class Writing and Local Publishing, ed. Dave Morley and Ken Worpole, publ. Comedia Publishing Group, 1982.)

1930s

These Poor Hands	B. L. Coombes	Gollancz 1939 (reissued 1974)
Love on the Dole	Walter Greenwood	Cape 1966
Grey Children	James Hanley	Methuen 1937
Unfinished Journey	Jack Jones	O.U.P. 1937
Cwmardy	Lewis Jones	Lawrence & Wishart 1937
The Second City	Montagu Slater	Lawrence & Wishart 1931
Heaven Lies Round About Us	Howard Spring	Collins 1939

1940s

I Was One of the Unemployed	Max Cohen	Gollancz 1945
Dance of the Apprentices	Edward Gaitens	McLellen 1948
The Rolling of Thunder	W. Gallacher	Lawrence & Wishart 1947
East End My Cradle	W. Goldman	Art & Educational Publishers 1940
A Man's Life	Jack Lawson	Hodder 1944
Our Flag Stays Red	Phil Piratin	Thames Publications 1948
All Things Betray Me	Gwyn Thomas	Michael Joseph 1949

1950s

Kiddar's Luck	Jack Common	Turnstile Press 1951
A Miner's Son	Len Doherty	Lawrence & Wishart 1955

The Furys	James Hanley	Lythway Press 1974 (reissue)
Once a Miner	Norman Harrison	O.U.P. 1954
The Weaver's Knot	William Holt	Harrap 1956
Cider with Rosie	Laurie Lee	Hogarth 1959
Down Donkey Row	Len Ortzen	Phoenix House

1960s

All in a Lifetime	Walter Allen	Longmans 1969
London Morning	Valerie Avery	Kimber 1964
Men of the Tideway	Dick Fagan	Robert Hale 1966
Sum Total	Ray Gosling	Faber 1960
A Hoxton Child-hood	A. S. Jasper	Barrie and Jenkins 1969
The Only Child	James Kirkup	Pergamon 1970
An Irish Navvy	Donall McAmh-laigh	Routledge 1964
Heat the Furnace Seven More Times	Patrick McGeown	Hutchinson 1967
Hard Way Up	Hannah Mitchell	Faber 1968
The Big Load	Ted Murphy	Foulis 1964
This Time Next Week	Leslie Thomas	Constable 1964

1970s

Coronation Cups and Jam Jars	Ron Barnes	Centerprise 1977
The Smell of Sunday Dinner	Sid Chaplin	Graham 1971
The Right Place, The Right Time	W. H. Davies	C. Davies 1972, Triskel Books 1975
My Part of the River	Grace Foakes	Futura 1976
A Bolton Childhood	Alice Foley	University of Manchester Extra-Mural Dept/ WEA 1973
A Child of the Forest	Winifred Foley	BBC 1974
Growing Up Poor in East London	Louis Heren	Hamish Hamilton 1973

A Cage of Shadows	Archie Hill	Hutchinson 1973
Born to Struggle	May Hobbs	Quartet 1973
The Great Apple Raid	Arthur Hopcraft	Heinemann 1970
The Town that Died!	R. L. Lee	R. L. Lee 1975
One Small Boy	Bill Naughton	Longman 1971
Poverty, Hardship but Happiness	Albert Paul	Queenspark, Brighton 1975
The Classic Slum	Robert Roberts	Manchester University Press 1976
A Ragged Schooling	Robert Roberts	Manchester University Press 1976
Mother Knew Best	Dolly Scannell	Pan Books in association with Macmillan 1975

These are, of course, only a representative selection of the memoirs, novels, anthologies produced by working-class people in recent years.